STEVENS AND

THE INTERPERSONAL

STEVENS AND
THE INTERPERSONAL

MARK HALLIDAY

PRINCETON UNIVERSITY PRESS

PRINCETON, NEW JERSEY

Library of Congress Cataloging-in-Publication Data

Halliday, Mark, 1949–
Stevens and the interpersonal / Mark Halliday
p.   cm.
Includes bibliographical references and index.
ISBN 0-691-06548-9 (cl.)
1.   Stevens, Wallace, 1879–1955—Criticism and interpretation.
2.   Interpersonal relations in literature.   I.   Title.

PS3537.T4753Z655   1991
811'.52—dc20

This book has been composed in Linotron Baskerville

Princeton University Press books are
printed on acid-free paper and meet the guidelines
for permanence and durability of the Committee
on Production Guidelines for Book Longevity
of the Council on Library Resources

Printed in the United States of America

10 9 8 7 6 5 4 3 2 1

CONTENTS

ACKNOWLEDGMENTS

FRIENDLY but tough criticism from four persons helped me to improve parts of this book; I am grateful to Allen Grossman, Robert Pinsky, Christopher Ricks, and Joan Rutter.

Also I thank Janice Hughes and Al Hughes of The Write Type of Philadelphia for expert technical assistance in preparing the final manuscript; and Victoria Wilson-Schwartz for her insightful copy-editing.

An earlier version of chapter 2 appeared as "Stevens and Heterosexual Love" in *Essays in Literature* (Western Illinois University), vol. 13, no. 1, Spring 1986; and an earlier version of chapter 3 appeared as "Stevens and Solitude" in *Essays in Literature*, vol. 16, no. 1, Spring 1989. I am grateful to the editors for permission to reprint this material.

Excerpts from the writings of Wallace Stevens are reprinted by permission of Alfred A. Knopf Inc., publishers of *The Collected Poems of Wallace Stevens*; *Opus Posthumous*, ed. Samuel French Morse; *The Necessary Angel*; *The Letters of Wallace Stevens*, ed. Holly Stevens; and *Souvenirs and Prophecies: The Young Wallace Stevens*, ed. Holly Stevens.

Excerpts from the poetry of John Ashbery are reprinted by permission of Viking Penguin Inc., publishers of *A Wave*, copyright 1984 by John Ashbery, *Selected Poems*, copyright 1985 by John Ashbery, and *April Galleons*, copyright 1987 by John Ashbery.

Some excerpts from the poetry of Emily Dickinson are reprinted by permission of Harvard University Press and the Trustees of Amherst College, from *The Poems of Emily Dickinson*, ed. Thomas H. Johnson (Cambridge, Mass.: The Belknap Press of Harvard University Press), copyright 1951, 1955, 1979, 1983 by the President and Fellows of Harvard College. Other excerpts are reprinted by permission of Little, Brown and Company, from *The Complete Poems of Emily Dickinson*, ed. Thomas H. Johnson, copyright 1929, 1935 by Martha Dickinson Bianchi; copyright renewed 1957, 1963 by Mary L. Hampson.

An excerpt from "East Coker" by T. S. Eliot is reprinted by permission of Harcourt Brace Jovanovich Inc., publishers of *Four Quartets*, copyright 1943 by T. S. Eliot and renewed 1971 by Esme Valerie Eliot; and also by permission of Faber and Faber Ltd.

Excerpts from the poetry of Robert Frost are reprinted by permission of Henry Holt and Company Inc., publishers of *The Poetry of Robert Frost*, ed. Edward Connery Lathem, copyright 1916, 1928, 1942, 1947, 1969 by Holt, Rinehart and Winston; copyright 1936, 1942,

1944, 1956 by Robert Frost; copyright 1964, 1970, 1975 by Lesley Frost Ballantine. Permission to reprint this material was granted also by Jonathan Cape Ltd.

Excerpts from the poetry of Thomas Hardy are reprinted by permission of Macmillan Publishing Company, publishers of *The Complete Poems of Thomas Hardy*, ed. James Gibson, copyright 1925 by Macmillan Publishing Company, renewed 1953 by Lloyds Bank Ltd.

STEVENS AND

THE INTERPERSONAL

INTRODUCTION

> Life is an affair of people not of places.
> But for me life is an affair of places and that is the trouble.
> ("Adagia")

IN THIS STUDY I approach the poetry of Wallace Stevens from a perspective he would not endorse, asking questions which most of his critics would consider inappropriate. Today nearly everyone seems to agree that Stevens is a great poet, and I assume that my reader agrees or at least considers Stevens very important. But I believe there are omissions and distortions in his account of human life more drastic and pervasive than the omissions that can be cited in the work of other great poets, and that these omissions and distortions deserve attention they have not yet received. They are acknowledged in passing by most critics of Stevens, but in this way I think the critics let Stevens off the hook, bowing to his severely constricted claims about what matters in life.

Stevens' poetry largely tries to ignore or deny all aspects of life that center on or are inseparable from interpersonal relations. I doubt that this can be said of any great poet before Stevens. Certainly some poets have implied that the interpersonal is not the realm of ultimate value, but this is not the same as trying to ignore or deny interpersonal life altogether. The references to "friends" and "the town" in the following stanzas from Herbert's "Affliction (I)" locate even this thoroughly devotional poet in a peopled landscape:

> When I got health, thou took'st away my life,
>   And more; for my friends die:
> My mirth and edge was lost: a blunted knife
>   Was of more use than I.
> Thus thinne and lean without a fence or friend,
> I was blown through with ev'ry storm and wind.
> Whereas my birth and spirit rather took
>   The way that takes the town;
> Thou didst betray me to a lingring book,
>   And wrap me in a gown.
> I was entangled in the world of strife,
> Before I had the power to change my life.[1]

Herbert's discovery of a life higher than social life has not required him to obliterate social life from his account of what has mattered to him. Similarly, the explicit interpersonal concern in Hopkins' "Felix Randal" and "Brothers" may be unusual in his oeuvre, but not anomalous. We do not sense that the interest in the effects of one person upon another in those poems is at odds with Hopkins' religious themes; his religious vision acknowledges and encompasses interpersonal experience.

My reader may now think of Shelley, Keats, Dickinson—but for each of these three poets the nature and possibility of romantic love and of friendship between souls, and the rights and obligations of citizens in relation to one another, were subjects of passionate concern. That this is true for the author of "Ode to Liberty," "Julian and Maddalo," and "Letter to Maria Gisborne" seems clear enough. In the case of Keats, admittedly, our sense of his interest in social relations, other than erotic ones, depends on his letters and his light verse, as well as on the Moneta scene in "The Fall of Hyperion"; Keats saw fit to exclude from his poetry some kinds of experience that he cared intensely about, but he hoped to broaden his poetry's scope, and might have done so had he lived longer.[2]

In Dickinson, social concern is extraordinarily oblique, but I would argue that her oeuvre gives a sense of someone who talks with people, listens to them, and thinks about their mysteriously separate existence as a crucial influence upon her own experience, whereas Stevens' oeuvre adopts various strategies to make these activities seem unnecessary or fruitless or worse. When Dickinson writes about ostracism, she enters a subject area that Stevens cannot enter because he is unwilling to contemplate such vividly consequential separateness between people.

> Much Madness is divinest Sense—
> To a discerning Eye—
> Much Sense—the starkest Madness—
> 'Tis the Majority
> In this, as All, prevail—
> Assent—and you are sane—
> Demur—you're straightway dangerous—
> And handled with a Chain[3]—

The sense in Dickinson that one can be isolated with no one on one's side depends on her awareness of other sides populated by persons ranged against the solitary self.

> On a Columnar Self—
> How ample to rely
> In Tumult—or Extremity—
> How good the Certainty

That Lever cannot pry—
And Wedge cannot divide
Conviction—That Granitic Base—
Though None be on our Side—

Suffice Us—for a Crowd—
Ourself—and Rectitude—
And that Assembly—not far off
From furthest Spirit—God—[4]

Dickinson is sometimes much more socially hopeful than this, but even here the inward turn is away from an acknowledged crowd, and such acknowledgment, whether grim or not, of others who have an impact (as of levers and wedges) on the brave self is much more common in Dickinson than in Stevens. When Dickinson says (in poem 303) that the soul selects, from among many candidates, the company of one other soul, she testifies to an intense interest in the possibilities of the many candidates and to the importance of a possible communion with the selected one. In Stevens there is a campaign to wipe out the fact that the self's isolation is a removal from visible other persons—a campaign whereby they either become utterly ignorable or can somehow be shown to be not truly other.

The Stevens—I speak here and throughout this study not of the biographer's man but of the poet-in-the-poems, the man figured by the poetry—who emerges in the following chapters is a man with a profound concern for the intactness of his self, in conjunction with a profound aversion to the demands of interpersonal relations, demands which in his view threaten to puncture that intactness. Especially pressing appeals from other persons—for example, from persons in pain or from attractive women—provoke especially elaborate defenses, ranging from apparent obliviousness to explicit denial to sublimation. Stevens earnestly seeks to imply and believe that the solitary self has an ample, good life within reach, and that the absence of distinct other persons is not only undetrimental to this good life but essentially unimportant, if not indeed beneficial.

Fortunately, he is troubled enough by the reality of interpersonal needs and obligations to permit tantalizing glimpses of this reality in his poetry, and these glimpses are crucial in making us realize what he *doesn't* show us most of the time. This is what saves my study from being only a prosecution of omissions and evasions. Each of the first three chapters establishes Stevens' failure to deal with something—the suffering of others, the humanity of desirable women, the sheer presence of others—and then highlights the exceptional places where he does try to deal with the interpersonal, or at least to acknowledge the problem of dealing with it.

Meanwhile, there is a spirit of benevolence toward, and concern for, the reader in Stevens' poetry, and this spirit may be felt as the transformed expression of displaced energies which would, in a less solitary poet, have produced meditations on the failures and successes and mysteries of interpersonal relations. This proposition is the subject of my long final chapter. It is true, I sadly suppose, that the act of writing a poem is inherently a displacement of concern away from actual present persons in the writer's life; but I will argue that to say this does not relieve Stevens of his very lonely specialness.

Underlying my critique of Stevens is an intuitive truth which I assume my reader will accept, though he or she may not agree that I can appropriately base a critique of Stevens on it. It is that life requires more from us than epistemological and ontological meditation, and that interpersonal relations constitute the part of life that makes such meditation, no matter how alert and sensitive, inadequate. Ethical philosophers could be enlisted to try to lift this truth from the intuitive to the demonstrable, but I prefer to cite it as something we all know without proof. Living among other persons one must do more than feel, perceive, and describe. (Describing is a social act in some instances, and arguably in all instances to some degree; but it cannot in itself amount to a sufficient participation in the social realm of life.) We are born gregarious animals, so that even individuals more reclusive or reserved than Wallace Stevens are doomed to a lifetime of social involvements. Moreover, of course, these involvements always include problems of moral choice—even when life is at its most ordinary. (Who will decide what is for dinner tonight? Who will take the initiative in making sure the meal is ready at a reasonable hour? Who will cook? At the table, whose problems will be discussed? After dinner, will we only clean up the kitchen halfway, and if so, who will finish the job?) Social relations continuously and endlessly produce moral problems. We may be said to incur moral obligations also in relation to ourselves, and in relation to the planet Earth, and in relation to the gods (if any). But our relations with other people generate vivid and various and troubling moral difficulties which are less avoidable than other moral difficulties, harder to postpone or transmute, due to the presence of a separate active agent whose rights are disturbing because equal to our own. The other person in the room calls for actions beyond any imagining we can perform.

Poetry, if it is, as I believe, a means of understanding our most profound and essential human problems, may thus be expected to address the issues of social life. This is not to say that all poems must do so, or even that all poets must do so. But when a great poet avoids doing so through nearly all of a six-hundred-page oeuvre, this extended tour de force should be seen as an important puzzle: how can greatness coincide with such determined avoidance of interpersonal reality? Each of my first three chapters is haunted by this question, and chapter 4 pursues one kind of answer.

As I said earlier, this study is not biographical. It is about the poet *in* the poetry. Occasionally I turn to biographical details, and to Stevens' prose, to clarify and illustrate my argument and to enhance its plausibility, but my concern is with the poetry, not the life of the man in Hartford. Stevens was not a friendless man, and he was a husband and father; these facts in themselves make the man different from the poet in the poems. Much of the biographical evidence does suggest, however, that the isolation and alienation from others of the poet-in-the-poems reflects similar difficulties in the life of the man in Hartford. One recently illuminated case of such difficulty is his mostly epistolary relationship with José Rodriguez Feo, in which Stevens strove very touchingly—if also, finally, rather grotesquely—to create Feo in his own mind as a symbolic friend, both the son he never had and the self he might have been. This is persuasively brought out by Beverly Coyle and Alan Filreis in their introduction to *Secretaries of the Moon: The Letters of Wallace Stevens and José Rodriguez Feo*, where they trace Feo's frustrating struggle to really befriend an older man whose imagination "feared the necessary adjustments actual confrontation required."[5] For my project, though, biographical evidence is not essential: even if Stevens had been a wonderfully warm, candid, giving friend to many people, I would want to raise the same questions about his poetry (which would then, of course, seem even more bizarre in its limitations).

My approach is not chronological. In chapter 1 I do focus on Stevens' responses to the Depression and World War II, and in chapter 2 I point out differences between *Harmonium* and later poetry in relation to love and sex, but on the whole I don't see any basic change in Stevens' view of interpersonal experience across his career.[6]

As I proceed in this study, I sometimes compare Stevens with other poets—especially with Hardy in chapter 1, Dickinson in chapter 3, Frost and Ashbery in chapter 4. But I do not attempt to place Stevens in any systematic picture of the history of American poetry.

My project reflects no desire to make us stop loving Stevens. I think my love for him has indeed been strengthened in the process of understanding some of his limitations and my own attraction to those limitations. No doubt any mature love is built partly on such understanding: we love the vulnerabilities and shortcomings of the beloved, or at least we love to see how these are interlinked with the beloved's strengths and achievements. I do think that some lovers of Stevens have made overblown, infatuated claims for him, failing to register seriously his neglect of a vast dimension of our lives. We can learn to see his strangeness more truly.

Chapter One

STEVENS AND THE
SUFFERING OF OTHERS

S EVERAL KINDS of unhappiness are audible in the poetry of Wallace Stevens. There is the only partly acknowledged unhappiness of the poet as an individual troubled by loss of love and loss of youth, and there is the extensively thematized unhappiness of humanity in the modern world, humanity adrift in a universe that lacks transcendent meaning and confers upon us no purpose. To focus on Stevens' evocations of these two kinds of unhappiness is to find a basis for calling him a great poet of human suffering. And yet, stepping back from those evocations and remembering other writers' poems about human suffering, one hesitates: something is unsatisfactory in making such a claim for Stevens. He writes beautifully, though often covertly, about his own life's pain ("Red Loves Kit," "Farewell to Florida," "Bouquet of Belle Scavoir," and "World Without Peculiarity" are four of the poems that deserve to be cited), and he writes with endless resourcefulness about the special pain afflicting all modern persons at once as we confront the blankness of reality, of bare earth and evening without angels. But there is a third realm of suffering, consisting in the particular forms of pain experienced by particular human others—pain factored by their partial differentness from the observing self. Does Stevens face this dimension of reality in his poetry? How does he do so—and how does he avoid doing so?

Before tackling this problem, let us ask what poems by other poets of this century we might turn to so as to sharpen our sense of what Stevens has attempted or refrained from attempting in response to the suffering of others. My own list would include Robinson's "Eros Turannos" and "The Poor Relation"; Yeats' "Easter 1916"; Frost's "A Servant to Servants," "Home Burial," and "'Out, Out—'"; Eliot's "Portrait of a Lady" and "Preludes"; Wilfred Owen's battlefront poems; some of the proletarian portraits by Williams; Auden's "Musée des Beaux Arts" (a famous metaphorical framing of the problem itself); Muriel Rukeyser's "Boy with His Hair Cut Short"; Jarrell's "The Truth" and "The Woman at the Washington Zoo"; Larkin's "Deceptions" and "Mr. Bleaney"; Lowell's "A Mad Negro Soldier Confined at Munich"; Anthony Hecht's "'More Light! More Light!'"; Philip Levine's "Obscure" and "Blasting from Heaven"; Ginsberg's "Howl"; Lloyd Schwartz's "The Recital" and "Love"; Anne Winters' "Two Derelicts" and "The Street"; Alan Shapiro's "Rain" and "Happy Hour" . . . For me, though, Thomas Hardy is the poet who most comes to mind when I try to recall poems of this century that have registered convincing awareness of suffering in someone other than the speaker. Later in this essay I will draw examples from Hardy to show alternatives to Stevens' way of responding to the suffering of others.

First we need to consider where in Stevens' work human suffering can be seen as the experience of someone other than the poet. The instances will not be numerous, since Stevens' oeuvre is famously underpopulated with distinct individuals (whether happy or unhappy);[1] he feels most at home when he speaks for the entire species, using the pronouns *we* or *one*, or when the protagonist of a poem is a blatantly symbolic distillation of some aspect of The Self or The Mind (Hoon, Peter Quince, the floribund ascetic of "Landscape With Boat", the Well Dressed Man With a Beard, the Canon Aspirin, Professor Eucalyptus . . .). To be sure, in these preferences Stevens is participating in venerable traditions of lyric (as opposed to dramatic) verse, but he carries to an extreme lyric's tendency to exclude individualized others for the sake of focusing on the poet's self or The Self. His *Collected Poems* is not the book a reader might expect from the author of these appealing lines about what modern poetry requires:

> It has to be living, to learn the speech of the place.
> It has to face the men of the time and to meet
> The women of the time . . .
> > It must
> Be the finding of a satisfaction, and may
> Be of a man skating, a woman dancing, a woman
> Combing.[2]

Admittedly, to quote only these lines from "Of Modern Poetry" is to distort the poem by avoiding the lines where Stevens stresses the subjective and solitary quality of the poetic event as it occurs wholly within the mind, performed by and for the mind. Nevertheless, the lines quoted above have crucial force in the emotional effect of the poem. They seem to propose a tenderly accurate perception of the lives of individual human others as an obligation of the modern poem, an obligation whose respectful fulfillment will lead to satisfaction.[3] Surely it is hard to hear those lines without feeling that the satisfaction to be derived from the kind of poetry thus recommended will involve, or will at least facilitate, some amelioration of the relations between people, between the poet and the men and women who are to be faced and met.[4] Stevens undoubtedly knew, and intended, that such encouragement concerning interpersonal relationships (as a matter beyond the scope of the solitary mind's satisfaction with itself) would be a palpable component of the poem's emotional impact. He knew, moreover, that to give this lovely emphasis to poetry's capacity for the imaginative encountering of other persons was to invoke an available tradition in English and American poetry distinguishable from, though often co-present with, the tradition of the lyrical "I" who contemplates his own relation to life (Nature, time, memory, love, death) and distinguishable as well from the tradition of the representative speaker who can use the word "we" in uttering something true for all human beings. One kind of great precedent, in the work of achieving penetrating awareness of the lives of persons different from the poet, is of course provided by the dramatic monologues of Tennyson and Browning. But Wordsworth and Whitman are the poets whose efforts to recognize other persons give the cited lines of "Of Modern Poetry" their most resonant ancestry.

The repeated distinction between men and women in these lines may be heard as an allusion to, even an inheritance from, Walt Whitman, who again and again took pains to acknowledge gender difference as a sign of his willingness to see and respect all sorts of human differences.

> All seems beautiful to me,
> I can repeat over to men and women You have done such good to
>   me I would do the same to you,
> I will recruit for myself and you as I go,
> I will scatter myself among men and women as I go,
> I will toss a new gladness and roughness among them,
> Whoever denies me it shall not trouble me,
> Whoever accepts me he or she shall be blessed and shall bless me.[5]

> .   .   .   .   .

> Each of us inevitable,
> Each of us limitless—each of us with his or her right upon the earth,
> Each of us allow'd the eternal purports of the earth,
> Each of us here as divinely as any is here.[6]

As these examples indicate, Whitman's acknowledgments of different others are never far from his determined avowals of ultimate unity among all selves in their absolute equality of earthly sacredness. But I think Whitman's commitment to such phrases as "men and women" and "he or she" and "his or her right" serves to remind both him and us of his felt obligation to admire human life in its infinite variety (both sexes, all ages, all professions), because without such specificity in admiration the affirmations which Whitman urgently proposed would ring hollow, lacking the cogency supplied by texture and color and weight. A man skating, a woman dancing, a woman combing—these three glimpses in Stevens' poem constitute a distilled Whitmanian catalogue and stand for the possibility of respectful and even empathetic detailed observation of the lives of others, a possibility pursued and at least momentarily grasped many times in *Leaves of Grass*.[7]

That possibility is pursued and partly attained also in *Lyrical Ballads*. Wordsworth explains in the Preface of 1800 that he has abjured "personification of abstract ideas" in the poems: "I have wished to keep my Reader in the company of flesh and blood, persuaded that by so doing I shall interest him."[8] While we might judge that the realism of Wordsworth's depiction of characters such as Simon Lee, Martha Ray, and old Matthew has significant limitations, we can still agree that an attempt at vital awareness of the distinct experience of human others animates most of *Lyrical Ballads*. Betty Foy and her son in "The Idiot Boy," for instance, both manifest particularities of character which make them more than mere types, while we do not at all receive them as aspects or versions of Wordsworth's own identity. For readers of Stevens this achievement by the young Wordsworth should be troubling in view of the profound philosophical and temperamental affinities between the two poets, both of whom became intensely concerned, indeed obsessed, with identifying a happy relation between Nature and the imagination. Our experience of Wordsworth's vast attention to his own mind in *The Prelude* is protected from a sense that he is in a small exclusive way self-absorbed not only by his claim to represent the poetic power residing in every mind, but also by our recollection that he could, in *Lyrical Ballads*, present the distinct qualities of other selves. And when at the end of Book 4 of *The Prelude* Wordsworth reports his encounter with a tall soldier, a man wasted by illness, who returned to England three weeks earlier from a mission to the Tropic Islands, we do not feel that this dignified sufferer is merely a trope or device for furthering one of the poet's ideas.

I have belabored familiar points about Whitman and Wordsworth to support the idea that an attractive element of the credo in Stevens' "Of Modern Poetry"—the poet's undertaking to "face" and "meet" various other persons—has great precedents, particularly in the work of two poets who, in their resistance to transcendental supernaturalist mythologies, were deeply congenial to Stevens. For him, though, the undertaking turns out to be even more problematic than for these predecessors.

Yet there is some effort to face and meet others in Stevens' poetry. The effort is most starkly and awkwardly apparent in poems of the decade from 1936 to 1947, when Stevens could not ignore two huge sources of human suffering in the world outside his house: the Depression in America and, in Europe, totalitarian oppression and the ensuing world war. It was suffering that made human others inescapably noticeable to the poet. The suffering Stevens read about in newspapers persuaded him—against the current of profound self-concern and individualist hedonism (sometimes zestful, sometimes grim) which had striped *Harmonium* with lavish colors—that the separate experience of selves different from his own ought to be somehow engaged by a serious poet.[9] Ugly realities, with human others painfully involved, impinged upon Stevens' vision, and he fought his impulse to look away, finding indeed that to ignore them was too difficult:[10]

Who can think of the sun costuming clouds
When all people are shaken
Or of night, endazzled, proud,
When people awaken
And cry and cry for help?   (*CP* 139)

The poet's windows permitted sounds of pain to penetrate from the street, where unemployment afflicted millions of Americans. He did not respond by going out among the sufferers and encountering them as individuals, either actually or imaginatively—whereas Whitman, the wound-dresser in Civil War hospitals, did both.[11] But a response, Stevens felt, was called for.

He pondered this task most directly in two poems in *Ideas of Order* (1936), "Sad Strains of a Gay Waltz" and "Mozart, 1935."[12] These poems are burdened with the sense that suffering people need a new and appropriate performance by the poet; he ought to give them more than the cheap advice to "look / Within themselves" for joy, which is all that "A Fading of the Sun" (the poem quoted above) can come up with. In "Mozart, 1935," "The snow is falling / And the streets are full of cries." How shall the poet respond?

Poet, be seated at the piano.
Play the present, its hoo-hoo-hoo,
Its shoo-shoo-shoo, its ric-a-nic,
Its envious cachinnation.   (*CP* 131)

The job to be done is not an attractive one, as Stevens indicates by nonsense syllables whose vulgarity testifies to the miserable gulf between 1935 and the delicate sounds of Mozart. The nonsense syllables, moreover, erect a blank wall of sound between the poet and the real human cries in the street. To summarize those cries as "hoo-hoo-hoo" and equate this noise with "shoo-shoo-shoo" is to postpone the human seriousness of those cries. Notice that the noise of the present is characterized as "envious". If the "cachinnation" (loud harsh laughter) emanates from people who can't find work and can't feed their children, people whose "cries" fill the streets, the adjective selected seems tellingly unsympathetic. (Notice also the inclination to meld cries with laughter, as if from the poet's distance all human noises sound the same. More on this point later.) The poet-pianist is estranged from the street people, at least so long as he devotes himself to Mozart's "lucid souvenir of the past":

> If they throw stones upon the roof
> While you practice arpeggios,
> It is because they carry down the stairs
> A body in rags.
> Be seated at the piano.

The poem, especially in the above stanza, provides a startling intimation of a need for political relevance in art—startling, that is, from Stevens, who vigorously opposed demands for such relevance in many letters and in "The Noble Rider and the Sound of Words."[13] The pianist is summoned to "Strike the piercing chord" of a new music which will express the suffering of all those people whose losses have been symbolically aggregated into "A body in rags."[14]

There is an urgency in the summoning of the poet-pianist to his new work, urgency caused by the importunate quality of suffering when we cannot look away from it. We *can* dodge the apprehension of severe pain in others—and most of this chapter will examine methods for such dodging—but when it is immediately before our eyes, it produces not only fascination but also an instinctive (at any rate, deep and prerational) sense of imperiously required response. (In this respect the apprehension of suffering in others is like sexual desire for another person—a second kind of importuning of the self which generated great anxiety in Stevens. This will be the focus of chapter 2.) Admittedly our range of responses to vivid suffering in others includes noncompassionate responses, such as flight from the scene, passionate denial of the reality of what we have witnessed, and even sadistic desire to prolong or intensify the suffering. But none of these is a calm, relaxed response; my point is that severe pain undergone directly in front of a viewer normally jolts the viewer into a sense that something must quickly be done. In "Mozart, 1935" the stress of this sense of obligation is manifested both by the baldness of the terms of confrontation with suffering and by the effortful didacticism with which Stevens tries to control and cool the inflamed problem of injured others:

Be thou the voice,
Not you. Be thou, be thou
The voice of angry fear,
The voice of this besieging pain.

Be thou that wintry sound
As of the great wind howling,
By which sorrow is released,
Dismissed, absolved
In a starry placating.

A different poet—one more like Thomas Hardy, or more like William Carlos Williams, or more like Kenneth Fearing (a significant poet of social protest in the thirties)—having turned to face the "angry fear" of people, would feel that his poem's project must be to explore "this besieging pain" and to show forth its lineaments. Stevens, however, is interested not in writing about the street, but in writing about the problem of writing about the street. "Mozart, 1935" is a poem about poems that will do the work it does not itself undertake.[15] Stevens' earnest wish to maintain a distance from the turmoil of others' experience is reflected by his stern insistence on the word "thou," which is repeated four times in the two stanzas just quoted and returns as the final word of the poem. Stevens does not want the poet to be one person among others, a "you" among "yous." Indeed, he judges that for the poet-pianist to perform the new work, to strike the piercing chord, it will be necessary for him to adopt a status and a role larger and more central than mere individual selfhood: "Be thou the voice, / Not you." Stevens requires an artist abstracted from—and thus, we may suggest, protected from—the mess of injured egos and competing claims out there where "the streets are full of cries." When such a distance is preserved, a satisfactory outcome of the poet's effort to respond to those cries can be much more readily imagined by Stevens; the poem can arrive at "a starry placating" just five lines after "this besieging pain." The arrival can come so soon because the poet, functioning austerely as a "thou" (not a mere "you"), has stayed in generality, abstracting countless instances of suffering into simple terms—a body in rags, fear, pain, cries—whose generality renders them swiftly manageable.

But what then does Stevens' poet-pianist manage in response to the social conditions of 1935? What *is* a "starry placating"? Educated by other Stevens poems, we may presume it is a spirit of acceptance, in which the people's longings are calmed, though perhaps only provisionally and temporarily, that is, they are placated. It is acceptance of the human lot through acceptance of the natural universe—"Merely in living as and where we live," as Stevens puts it wistfully in the last line of "Esthétique du Mal" (*CP* 326)—this acceptance to be nurtured by the supreme fictions of poetry. "Starry" seems to mean "imaginary." We notice that this achievement of a starry placating is not to involve any attempt to change the social conditions that have brought others' pain to Stevens' attention. Sorrow is not to be remedied, nor even alleviated, but "released, / Dismissed, absolved . . . " We should wonder why suffering would need absolution—is it sinful? Has suffering come from a spiritual failure on the part of the suffering people? The poem is elusive about this, but it is sure that what the people need is a new way of thinking, not just food, shelter, jobs.

Stevens asserts this more fully (and more blandly, with less aliveness to pain) in "Sad Strains of a Gay Waltz":

There are these sudden mobs of men,

These sudden clouds of faces and arms,
An immense suppression, freed,
These voices crying without knowing for what,

Except to be happy, without knowing how,
Imposing forms they cannot describe,
Requiring order beyond their speech.   (*CP* 122)

The poem concludes with hopeful anticipation of a "harmonious skeptic," a poet-musician like the pianist in "Mozart, 1935," whose "skeptical music / / Will unite these figures of men" by showing them an "order" in which their lives make imaginative sense. Again, what I want to notice is the muffling of the apprehension of others' pain even as the poem proposes to acknowledge that pain. The speaker who perceives the unhappy people of the Depression as "These sudden clouds of faces and arms" may or may not be a compassionate person, but certainly appears unable or unwilling to perceive the suffering others as individuals, as differing persons whose dignity involves their individual qualities. Indeed, to view them as "clouds of faces and arms" is not to see them as whole persons at all. The sufferers are reduced to chimerical fragments from a nightmare, describable only by recourse to the surreal imagery of a cinematic special effect. Thus their having been "freed" from "suppression" seems an ominous and even regretted loosing of forces which ought to have been kept under wraps. The artist's response, meanwhile, will address itself not to the suffering "men" themselves but to "these figures of men." The necessity of imagining, which Stevens so beautifully defends and celebrates throughout his work, here serves as a buffer between the poet and the troublesome specificity of suffering people. Their reality is one of the realities Stevens is least willing to tolerate unless transformed—muffled and blurred—by the terms of his imagining.

The point here is not that Stevens ought to restrain or turn off his imagination in viewing suffering people and instead see only "things as they are," "nothing that is not there." After all, Stevens more than any other poet of this century has trained us to admit that *all* seeing is imaginative and to accept and even cherish the sense that our humanness is coterminous with our imaginative ability. The point is, rather, that more than one kind of imaginative act can be performed in response to a group of suffering people. To see *into* the emotional and spiritual life of a sufferer by an act of empathy (which may nourish sympathy; see note 22) is one imaginative response. To meld many sufferers together into a cloud of disembodied limbs is another sort of imaginative response, which confirms and reemphasizes the viewer's sense of estrangement from what he looks at.

The gap between this poet and the people he tries to acknowledge has been noticed by many critics, some inclined to justify and some inclined to censure.[16] One striking comment came from Robert Lowell in a 1947 review of *Transport to Summer*: "Perhaps Stevens is too much the leisured man of taste. As with Santayana, one feels that the tolerance and serenity are a little too blandly appropriated, that a man is able to be an imagination and the imagination able to be disinterested and urbane only because it is supported by industrial slaves."[17] This is a valuably intemperate challenge, jolting us into questions about the human beings who stand unseen around the edges of poems in which Stevens gazes upon pink and white carnations, pink and white dogwoods. Lowell suggests that there is more of a moral relation between those other persons and Stevens than Stevens cares to realize. It is this suspicion, which is really about a failure to imagine one's political reality, that spurs us to notice how the perception of others in poems like "Mozart, 1935" and "Sad Strains of a Gay Waltz" remains so distanced, so lacking in empirical substance, despite the poems' efforts to acknowledge suffering.

At this point my reader may fear that I intend merely a dogmatic Marxist attack on Wallace Stevens. But I am not a Marxist; and my moves toward a moral critique of Stevens should be understood as moves in resistance to what I feel as the immense attractiveness of Stevens' poetry—an attractiveness that has everything to do with Stevens' devotion to the potential sufficiency of the solitary self, free from any but the most abstract and ethereal moral requirements. Stevens' lifelong campaign for the enoughness of the solitary imagining self gives us consolations we often need in our loneliness—loneliness both social and cosmic—and in this respect Stevens' work fulfills his own ethical demand: "The purpose of poetry is to contribute to man's happiness"(*OP* 168).[18] But a price is paid for these special consolations, involving the failure to imaginatively engage the specific realities of other persons; and the moral problem in this failure becomes most disturbing when those other persons are in pain or distress. What I've begun to do is to examine the poetic means whereby Stevens pays this price.

In "Mozart, 1935" we felt Stevens instructing us that no concrete action could meaningfully relieve the pain of the people and that sorrow must rather be "Dismissed, absolved / In a starry placating." The fatalism here in regard to political history becomes explicit in "Idiom of the Hero," published in *Parts of a World* (1942); and the relevance of this fatalism to the question of Stevens' concern or lack of concern for the suffering of others may be considered in light of the following passage by Lucy Beckett in which the critic presents Stevens as a poet of compassion:

> Those who complain that he should have taken more notice of the horrifying events that were shaking the world at this time have failed to see that behind all his work, behind his search for a saving belief and the perseverance with which he used his mind and his imagination to find or make 'what will suffice', lay a compassion and an honesty that were the very opposite of complacent. The miseries of the Depression and of Europe in 1940 did not have to jolt Stevens out of one set of ideas and into another; they confirmed him in a sadness and a resolution that he had long ago arrived at from within himself. It should not be forgotten that in 1939 he was sixty years old, and a sane and wise man by any standards. His response to the war was not something new but something evolved from what was already old and familiar in his way of thought. When he wrote a short poem called "Idiom of the Hero" in a time mangled by dictators and deafened by their hysterical simplicities this is what emerged.[19]

Beckett then quotes "Idiom of the Hero" in its entirety:

IDIOM OF THE HERO

I heard two workers say, "This chaos
Will soon be ended."

This chaos will not be ended,
The red and the blue house blended,

Not ended, never and never ended,
The weak man mended,

The man that is poor at night
Attended

Like the man that is rich and right.
The great men will not be blended . . .

I am the poorest of all.
I know that I cannot be mended,

Out of the clouds, pomp of the air,
By which at least I am befriended. (*CP* 200)

For Lucy Beckett, it would seem, this poem is self-evidently exemplary of Stevens' compassionate concern for the suffering, both recent and imminent, of others (workers, the weak man, the poor man) in "This chaos" of economic and military dangers. But does the poem live up to Beckett's claim?

When the speaker of the poem turns to self-description in the last four lines, the note struck is not precisely one of compassion. Do we not hear rather a note of complacency and self-exculpating irony? "I am the poorest of all." Is he indeed? Would he not need a lot of gall to say so in front of those two workers? Who is this speaker who claims to be the poorest of all? Perhaps it is not the well-to-do Mr. Stevens (though the "I" of the poem's first two lines seems to be the poet more than it seems to be an abstract personage or ironized persona); the poem's title tells us to take the speech as a sample of utterance by "the hero"—that is, by a potentiality of the human spirit which sees reality rightly and can establish a healthy, undeluded relation with it. Very well, but can we admire this hero as much as his inventor does when he makes his play on the word "poor"? It is a playful turn, in that it shifts the meaning of "poor" from the economic realm to the spiritual realm where "poverty," defined by Stevens as everyone's status in a sheerly secular universe, is the central fact for his poetry to work with, a fact which can be only falsely and harmfully evaded by persons who believe in utopian creeds, whether socialist or fascist. Heroically divested of such delusions, the hero dwells firmly in the spiritual "poverty" no one can truly evade, and in this sense he is the poorest of all. And rather proud of it, proud of the clear thinking that has won him this status: "I know that I cannot be mended . . ." The nobility of his insight has made him, as it were, first among equals.

To shift focus from economic misfortune to universal spiritual aggrievedness by revaluating one word ("poorest") is to blur the difference between kinds of suffering, to rub away the distinction between one experience and another. Physical suffering (resulting from socioeconomic conditions) is made to seem no more than a subcategory of spiritual suffering, since the same adjective ("poor") describes the entire spectrum of such experience. The suffering worker's feeling is thus not importantly different from what Stevens (or "the hero") feels when he looks up at the blank sky beyond the clouds, except that Stevens understands the feeling of poverty more deeply than the worker does; and this superior understanding entitles the poet to a superlative level of impoverishment. Thus the word "poorest" confers upon the poet an elite status among sufferers at the same time as it elides the distinction between physical and spiritual suffering. This blurring together of different experiences is ironically at odds with the poem's ostensible denial of blending: "This chaos will not be ended, / The red and the blue house blended . . . The great men will not be blended . . ." Stevens denies the workers' hope for a political synthesis, a new political order which would wipe out the differences of socioeconomic injustice. At the spiritual level, though, as we have observed, a blending is indeed what Stevens has engineered, for the sake of his assertion that everyone in our century is fated to remain in the same chaos, the chaos of life without transcendent meaning. We are all permanent citizens in the egalitarian state of unsponsored godless existence.

That fatalism, alongside the blurring of disparate experiences, is the element of Stevens' response to others' suffering most apparent to us in "Idiom of the Hero." In denying that chaos will be ended, Stevens proceeds boldly to specify salvations that can never be achieved:

> The weak man mended,
>
> The man that is poor at night
> Attended
>
> Like the man that is rich and right.

A reader like Lucy Beckett hears a gentle pity in these lines, and perhaps not mistakenly—though to hear "right" so smoothly associated with "rich" should give such a reader pause. But we must notice Stevens' insistence on predicting unhappy outcomes. This is not a poem in which Stevens gazes upon phenomena in the present world and describes his imagination's interaction with them (except for the allusion to such interaction in the poem's closing reference to the friendly clouds). Rather it is a poem in which Stevens chooses to contemplate present sufferers generally in light of what he judges to be their disappointing political and economic future. This superimposition of future upon present reflects, I suggest, a lack of interest in, or a refusal to value, the present phenomena. A fatalistic perspective is a perspective which emphasizes an allegedly inevitable future at the expense of the present; the vitality of present phenomena (workers, weak man, poor man) appears less significant in the long shadow cast by destiny. A poem can involve fatalism and still resist this tenebrous tendency, as Hardy will remind us. But when fatalism declares itself as bluntly as it does in "Idiom of the Hero," the individual lives of others cannot win much attention. In a sense, fatalism can be understood as a second kind of blurring together of experiences: rather than blurring the difference between, say, a poor man's experience of poverty and Mr. Stevens' "poverty," fatalism is a diachronic blurring, a blurring-in-time, painting over the contours of present experience with the darker shapes of future experience.

Fatalism as a strategic response to the importunate demands of other lives also informs Stevens' "Burghers of Petty Death." Because of the romantic couple whose image seems to have prompted this poem (whether or not we conceive of them as still living and loving or dead and buried), I am reminded of Hardy's many poems about unhappy lovers, such as "The Last Leaf," "The Mound," "When Dead," "Best Times," "Beyond the Last Lamp"; and I am tempted to describe "Burghers of Petty Death" as a Hardy poem minus Hardy's compassion. The image of the man and woman in the poem (quoted here in full) is overwhelmed by the dark context Stevens establishes:

BURGHERS OF PETTY DEATH

These two by the stone wall
Are a slight part of death.
The grass is still green.

But there is a total death,
A devastation, a death of great height
And depth, covering all surfaces,
Filling the mind.

These are the small townsmen of death,
A man and a woman, like two leaves
That keep clinging to a tree,
Before winter freezes and grows black—

Of great height and depth
Without any feeling, an imperium of quiet,
In which a wasted figure, with an instrument,
Propounds blank final music.   (CP 362)

In the mere present of summer or autumn, "The grass is still green" for the man and woman, but a wintry future looms so vast over them that the poem cannot dwell with them on the grass but must stand away at a distance from which the lovers are only "the small townsmen

of death," and by the last stanza the man and woman have disappeared while the poem imagines an abstract absence and negation. In
Stevens' response to the two burghers by the stone wall, fatalism works
together with another strategy which we may call "dwarfing" or "min-
iaturization." For the individual others are not only seen to be "slight"
from the chronological perspective of their future in death, but also
from a cosmological perspective. The poem confronts an entire universe of mortality; death is seen to fill the world as it fills the mind that
contemplates it, and within this bleak panorama the particular man
and woman have been reduced to specks, two lingering leaves on a
tree, who seem smaller and more impermanent even than the two
"clods" who embrace at the edge of a field in "The Rock" (*CP* 525).
They are tiny in space as well as in time, and insofar as the poem
commits itself to perspectives from which this is true, the poem is relieved of any need to characterize the man and woman or to specify
their mortal hurts.

I have discussed four short poems ("Mozart, 1935," "Sad Strains of
a Gay Waltz," "Idiom of the Hero," and "Burghers of Petty Death") at
length so as to provide a basis for the four-point catalog of Stevens'
strategies outlined below. In referring to these modes of thought or
habits of mind as "strategies" I perhaps make Stevens' avoidance of
others' experience in his poetry sound more willful and schemed than
it was; but a strategy can be unconsciously employed. My proposition
is that the avoidance of vivid perception of other persons, endemic in
Stevens' work and especially noticeable when the other persons are
suffering, is accomplished in four ways:

1. *Merging* of individual others into one generalized image, so that the
distinctive traits of individuals can be ignored, as in "Mozart, 1935" ("A
body in rags") and "Sad Strains of a Gay Waltz" ("these sudden mobs of
men")—and notably in the image of the soldier, to be discussed later.

2. *Blurring* of various experiences together so that they can be summarily
described by a simple flattening term, because the varieties and gradations
of experience are not seen to matter; as in "Mozart, 1935," where all sorts of
suffering and anger are covered by the words "fear," "pain," and "cries,"
and as in the turn on "poor" in "Idiom of the Hero."

3. *Fatalistic foreseeing* whereby the present experience of others is deval-
ued via emphasis on their inevitable future, as in "Idiom of the Hero"
("This chaos will not be ended") and "Burghers of Petty Death."

4. *Dwarfing* or miniaturizing of others by viewing them as if from a great
distance and in a context much larger than individual life, as in "Burghers
of Petty Death."

As my discussion has already shown, the boundaries between these
four strategies are permeable, and a given passage might be taken as

a case of "merging" or "blurring" or both. Thus this sorting of reductive strategies may itself be reductive; but I think it helps clarify what Stevens (and many another writer as well) does when confronted by the too-disturbing sufferings of other persons. All four strategies move statement toward abstraction, away from the particulars of perception.

So far I have repeatedly implied that such abstracting prevents or cancels compassion, that sympathy and generality are fundamentally opposed. To construct such an opposition, however, is to require a dangerously limited notion of sympathy in which the capacity to *connect* many instances of suffering within a larger pattern could be forfeited. How wide can a poem's scope become before individuals merely disappear in the haze? A fascinating test case, for lovers of Stevens, is a passage in "To an Old Philosopher in Rome," where the poem's honored protagonist is a dozing old man on the brink of death, a man too weak for the trying work of individual distinctions. The poem seems to affirm that by grace of this condition the old man attains to a vast compassion for all human suffering; he finds

> the grandeur that you need
>
> In so much misery; and yet finding it
> Only in misery, the afflatus of ruin,
> Profound poetry of the poor and of the dead,
> As in the last drop of the deepest blood,
> As it falls from the heart and lies there to be seen,
>
> Even as the blood of an empire, it might be,
> For a citizen of heaven though still of Rome.
> It is poverty's speech that seeks us out the most.
> It is older than the oldest speech of Rome.
> This is the tragic accent of the scene.   (CP 509–10)

There is something mesmerizing (in rhythm and diction) about the passage—but is it a magnificently convincing avowal of concern for our afflicted species? Or is it a hypnotist's trick, a mix of pompous inflation and sentimental balderdash (think again of that last drop of blood that "lies there to be seen")? Stevens weaves the passage with words—misery, ruin, poor, dead, blood, poverty, tragic—that pull us toward the former judgment; but readers inclining toward this judgment should worry about the nearness of this old philosopher's state of mind to senility.

Other Stevens poems will make us return to this problem later. Now, though, I turn to Hardy, a poet often inclined toward fatalism, gloomy generality, and bitterly broad perspectives, but nevertheless a poet who can help us see a crucial relation between some powerfully affecting expressions of sympathy and specificity of perception. We will look at three poems in which Hardy reports the sufferings of others, beginning with "No Buyers," a poem which eschews the establishment of any philosophical context for the particular observation.[20]

No Buyers

A Street Scene

>A load of brushes and baskets and cradles and chairs
>   Labours along the street in the rain:
>With it a man, a woman, a pony with whiteybrown hairs.—
>   The man foots in front of the horse with a shambling sway
>   At a slower tread than a funeral train,
>   While to a dirge-like tune he chants his wares,
>Swinging a Turk's-head brush (in a drum-major's way
>   When the bandsmen march and play).
>
>A yard from the back of the man is the whiteybrown pony's nose:
>He mirrors his master in every item of pace and pose:
>   He stops when the man stops, without being told,
>   And seems to be eased by a pause; too plainly he's old,
>   Indeed, not strength enough shows
>   To steer the disjointed waggon straight,
>Which wriggles left and right in a rambling line,
>Deflected thus by its own warp and weight,
>And pushing the pony with it in each incline.
>
>   The woman walks on the pavement verge,
>   Parallel to the man:
>   She wears an apron white and wide in span,
>And carries a like Turk's-head, but more in nursing-wise:
>   Now and then she joins in his dirge,
>   But as if her thoughts were on distant things.
>   The rain clams her apron till it clings.—
>So, step by step, they move with their merchandize,
>   And nobody buys.

The two human figures appear humble and helpless and doomed, tramping in poverty toward death ("At a slower tread than a funeral train," as if already dead)—and yet the poem may be said to present life-size images of these people. Of course, many things about their lives remain unexplored; but what can be seen of them by the viewer in the street is offered as a sufficient matter for our attention. The poem devotes itself to the images of the man and the woman, and seeks no escape from the grimness they embody. No presiding explanation is advanced, no philosophical containment device is erected (except insofar as poetic form, and finally linguistic form itself, inevitably constitute walls between reality and reader; some contemporary criticism spins uninterestingly around this obvious inevitability). The two forlorn vendors and their pony march by very close to us. We observe them only for a minute, but during that minute Hardy makes us observe sharply—"The rain clams her apron till it clings"—and what he attempts is the opposite of blurring.

At the same time, Hardy's fatalism and his notorious "pessimism" are certainly palpable in "No Buyers," despite its disciplined devotion to detail. If the poem is read in the context of Hardy's oeuvre, its scene is shadowed in our gaze by his prevailing tendency to see all human beings as baffled, blind victims of time and circumstance. Besides, the idea of the vendors' doomedness is worked into the poem by (among other things) the word "dirge," by the way the pathetic animal mirrors the man, and above all by the climactic bitter brevity of the last line. So the poem's patient and energetic caring for detail is achieved in the teeth of the poet's own sense that the people observed are doomed: they are proletarians (not even burghers) of petty death. "No Buyers" is a poem in which fatalism, though present, is not allowed to blot or shrink or remove the human image. Elsewhere in Hardy's poetry, a fatalistic view sometimes comes suffused with a fatigue or despair which tends to drain or repulse the energy required for detailed apprehension of others' lives. The note of such fatigue is momentarily heard in "No Buyers" when Hardy says of the pony, "too plainly he's old." For the space of this phrase the poet seems wearied by the banality of his subject. There is a kind of emotional slide by which fatigue becomes disgust, and the phrase "too plainly" gives us a flicker of this possibility; the note struck is part of the chord that resounds in Stevens' poems of impatience and disgust, poems in which Stevens is wearied by the too plain mundanity of an unmythic world ("Gubbinal," "Loneliness in Jersey City," "The Common Life," "Long and Sluggish Lines"). But in "No Buyers" this weariness is overcome, without withdrawal from the depressing perception.

Thus in "No Buyers" Hardy makes a beginning, at least, on what Stevens identifies as the task of Modern Poetry: "to face the men of the time and to meet / The women of the time," even though they may be doomed, even though they may be banal or ugly in their doomed state. To have shown this, however, is not exactly to have shown that "No Buyers" is a compassionate poem; and if it is (as I feel) compassionate, there remains the question whether we would want to take it, in its rigorously visual, close-up portrayal of suffering others who constitute a seemingly inalterable and even untouchable spectacle, as a model for all poetry of compassion. But let me postpone these problems until I have brought in two more Hardy poems.

In "A Parting-Scene" Hardy again observes suffering strangers as they behave in a public situation, but here he lets himself acknowledge their misery more explicitly than he does in "No Buyers." The poem makes no claim to have completely unfurled their misery; it is a poem of limited ambition, not attempting to capitalize on its materials either by generalization or by dramatic portraiture. Yet within the small compass afforded by such casual brief exposure to others' lives as we experience in a railway waiting room, the poem looks hard at the pain of others and attributes significance to their pain.[21]

A PARTING-SCENE

    The two pale women cried,
  But the man seemed to suffer more,
    Which he strove hard to hide.
They stayed in the waiting-room, behind the door,
Till startled by the entering engine-roar,
As if they could not bear to have unfurled
Their misery to the eyes of all the world.

    A soldier and his young wife
  Were the couple; his mother the third,
    Who had seen the seams of life.
He was sailing for the East I later heard.
—They kissed long, but they did not speak a word;
Then, strained, he went. To the elder the wife in tears
'Too long; too long!' burst out. ('Twas for five years.)

Hardy keeps his distance from these sufferers—as we do usually keep our distance from weeping strangers who need no aid that we can offer—while still caring about their suffering enough to make it the poem's entire focus. We can imagine a poem that would tell us more about the particular soldier and his wife and his mother, and might cause us to care more about them as individuals. Hardy chooses, rather, a fidelity to the limitedness of the kind of encounter he describes. We feel that this is one of many parting-scenes which the speaker has witnessed or known about, and that it has not been possible, or convenient, for him to learn more about this particular family. "He was sailing for the East I later heard": Hardy (or the speaker) has perhaps not troubled to inquire after the soldier's fate, but on the other hand he has listened to and remembered what he has heard about that fate. To my mind (and here I reveal myself as a typical lover of Hardy's poetry), it is the very modesty of the poem's endeavor that makes such caring as it does evince so convincing and hence so affecting. The poem's tone of limited but real caring fulfills itself beautifully in the sober tenderness of the final parenthesis:

> To the elder the wife in tears
> 'Too long; too long!' burst out. ('Twas for five years.)

To the weeping wife it seems as if the soldier must be gone forever, but the poem keeps a cooler head. The poem knows that five years is not forever; indeed, it is not ten years; yet five years can be a terribly long time, and the poem knows this too. Both kinds of knowledge find expression in the parenthetical statement. The poem does not at all say "only five years"—it is too aware of, and concerned for, the people's suffering to say that—but the poem does deem it right to quietly indicate the finitude of what the wife exclaims against. Her outcry does not get the last word; yet it has been registered as the noteworthy expression of someone with her own special experience, not of merely "another weeping woman."

Thus far I have spoken of the poem "caring about" and being "concerned for" and "attributing significance to" the suffering of others, in order to fall shy of the less provable claim that the poem expresses compassion for the sufferers. Hardy does not say, "I wept for the poor lonely wife." Perhaps a reader could hear "A Parting-Scene" as spoken by a Hardy so grim and embittered as to be quite unmoved by the all-too-typical scene, citing the unhappy family as just one more of time's laughingstocks. But I cannot hear the poem in that way. I invite the reader to feel that the poem's sustained act of attention is respectful, respectfully alert to the signs of suffering, respectful because Hardy can tell that the pain is real and knows from his own life how it hurts; and that this respectful caring *about*, embodied by the entire poem, is here not separable from caring *for*. Recall the intuitive quality of the opening lines:

> The two pale women cried,
> But the man seemed to suffer more,
> Which he strove hard to hide.

The speaker here is attuned to grief not only by its outward signs but by manifestations subtler than tears. He experiences an inward awareness of the husband's suffering, for which we have the term empathy; and in this case I see no reason to pry empathy apart from sympathy as we characterize the speaker's feeling.[22] It is not as if the husband were considering draft evasion, in which case we would ask about Hardy taking sides. Where the question of approval versus disapproval is absent, empathy with a sufferer nourishes and indeed merges with sympathy for the sufferer. That is to say, we feel that

Hardy not only has an intimate sense of the family's suffering but regrets it and wishes it could be alleviated.

So I admire "A Parting-Scene" as a compassionate poem—notwithstanding the fact that it neither describes nor proposes any action to help the afflicted family—and I've suggested that its feeling for the suffering others is the more believable because it is not boundless. This is a poem that attains a calm perspective—"('Twas for five years.)"—on others' suffering without sacrificing either vivid perception of that suffering or the sympathy prompted by such vivid perception. "A Parting-Scene" does not maintain the stark close-up view that "No Buyers" maintains, yet still an important degree of specificity is achieved; we don't feel that we are merely glancing at *any* soldier, wife, mother. Hardy has partly stood apart from these sufferers, but he has not anesthetized his perception of them by any of the four strategies we noticed in Stevens. The ending of "A Parting-Scene" reflects Hardy's understanding that for a poem, or person, to become entirely immersed in the suffering of others could become unbearable. This understanding, which for Stevens is usually so urgent as to obliterate the special pleadings for sympathy that individuals always make, can be seen at work (but not exclusively in control) in another Hardy poem, "The Harbour Bridge."[23]

THE HARBOUR BRIDGE

From here, the quay, one looks above to mark
The bridge across the harbour, hanging dark
Against the day's-end sky, fair-green in glow
Over and under the middle archway's bow:
It draws its skeleton where the sun has set,
Yea, clear from cutwater to parapet;
On which mild glow, too, lines of rope and spar
   Trace themselves black as char.

Down here in shade we hear the painters shift
Against the bollards with a drowsy lift,
As moved by the incoming stealthy tide.
High up across the bridge the burghers glide
As cut black-paper portraits hastening on
In conversation none knows what upon:
Their sharp-edged lips move quickly word by word
   To speech that is not heard.

There trails the dreamful girl, who leans and stops,
There presses the practical woman to the shops,
There is a sailor, meeting his wife with a start,

And we, drawn nearer, judge they are keeping apart.
Both pause. She says: 'I've looked for you. I thought
We'd make it up.' Then no words can be caught.
At last: 'Won't you come home?' She moves still nigher:
  ' 'Tis comfortable, with a fire.'

'No,' he says gloomily. 'And, anyhow,
I can't give up the other woman now:
You should have talked like that in former days,
When I was last home.' They go different ways.
And the west dims, and yellow lamplights shine:
And soon above, like lamps more opaline,
White stars ghost forth, that care not for men's wives,
  Or any other lives.

The last four lines of "The Harbour Bridge" widen the poem's scope immensely: the camera (so to speak) pans away from the particular pair of unhappy people and zooms out so as to take in the vast dark sky which presides heartlessly over all earthly existence. To this extent we could be describing Stevens' "Burghers of Petty Death." But there is a drastic difference between the two poems in their responses to the vulnerable human others observed. To move with Hardy from his first to his third stanza is to participate in an inquisitive, riskily sensitive action, which is precisely what Stevens refuses to perform when he encounters suffering people. At the end of Hardy's first stanza we are still in an unpopulated world, regarding a landscape in terms of light and dark—a situation like that of many Stevens poems such as "The Poems of Our Climate," "Study of Two Pears," "The Common Life," "Of Hartford in a Purple Light." In these Stevens poems, the landscape gives an opportunity to ponder the relation between self and reality, without attention to any differences between the pondering self and other selves. In "The Harbour Bridge," though, Hardy cannot escape the realization that his landscape is populated with people who "go different ways." By the end of the second stanza the people on the bridge have become a compelling focus for Hardy's attention; the fact of their as-yet-unheard speech, with its individual possibilities, prompts recognition of their three-dimensionality: these burghers are more alive and troubling than the "cut black-paper portraits" to which distance would reduce them.

Hardy cannot keep his distance. The "we" of the second stanza (the pronoun seems significantly more immediate and involved than the "one" of the poem's first line) could mean Hardy and a companion, but may also be felt to mean Hardy and the reader, as if Hardy assumes the reader's shared interest in the specificities of other lives. In the third stanza we accompany Hardy and move close enough to distinguish personalities and then suddenly to eavesdrop.

> There is a sailor, meeting his wife with a start,
> And we, drawn nearer, judge they are keeping apart.

The husband and wife are estranged, and the conversation between them will be dispiriting, but with Hardy we are not allowed to self-protectively estrange ourselves from them; we are "drawn nearer" by the compelling force of our interest in the lives of others. Wallace Stevens might feel that we have violated the privacy of the unhappy spouses to no good purpose. But I think Hardy would answer that we have been reawakened, as we should be every day, to the severe need for what he called "loving-kindness" between persons who are too hurtfully "keeping apart." Admittedly the dialogue between sailor and wife has an essentialized quality: the presentation of this conjugal encounter is grimly efficient. But the scene is still poignant; it gives the sense that we have witnessed something real and disturbing.

Thus there is a kind of relief in the poem's final movement to a perspective from which the couple's pain becomes one tiny instance of human suffering. From the stars' perspective, indeed, the unhappy wife is not significantly different from happy wives, "Or any other lives." People are tiny phenomena whose experiences need not be distinguished and whose future, in a godless universe, must be dim. Hardy has recourse to distancing strategies like those of Stevens in order to emerge from this encounter with suffering others and complete his poem. He does not, either in action or in imagination, accompany the jilted wife to her lonely hearth. As in "A Parting-Scene," Hardy in "The Harbour Bridge" knows that to dwell unreservedly and continuously in awareness of others' suffering would be an intolerable oppression of self. But—again the crucial "but"—this knowledge has not destroyed his capacity to apprehend, and to be touched by, and to produce vivid images of, the specific sufferings of others. If the last line of "The Harbour Bridge" constitutes an escape for the sympathizer, it is an escape which has not wiped out the facts that provoked it.

We turned from Stevens to Hardy with a question about the moral significance of specificity (as opposed to generality and abstraction) in the apprehension and description of the lives of other human beings. Is specificity necessary for compassion? Can there be compassion without specific perception of the sufferer in his or her difference from others? Perhaps there is a real sense in which one can be moved with sympathy for all the children starving in Ethiopia or all the homeless people in Philadelphia or all the poor mortals who have ever

passed beneath the rain-stained vaults of Rome, without a vivid imagining of any one sufferer's special experience. Surely King Lear
achieves profoundly compassionate generality on the heath:

> Poor naked wretches, wheresoe'er you are,
> That bide the pelting of this pitiless storm,
> How shall your houseless heads and unfed sides,
> Your looped and windowed raggedness, defend you
> From seasons such as these? O, I have ta'en
> Too little care of this! Take physic, pomp;
> Expose thyself to feel what wretches feel,
> That thou may'st shake the superflux to them
> And show the heavens more just.   (3.4.28–36)

But such generalized compassion must always tremble near the brink
of sentimentality, which always involves simplification and blurring of
perception. When we judge that a reference to someone's suffering is
sentimental, we mean that the suffering has not been accurately *seen* in
its individuality, its complexity, its complex relations with other lives;
and thus that the sympathetic emotion proposed by the reference has
been prematurely summoned for the sake of pleasure derived from
the emotion itself or from proclamation of the emotion. (Lear's
speech, after all, is protected from this charge by a context of vivid
particulars, especially the unhappiness of his shivering Fool, which we
know Lear has perceived.) The action of mind which we choose to call
compassionate, as against sentimental, will be an arduously discriminating action.

At the same time, the negative connotation of *discrimination*—as in
questions of racism or sexism—should remind us that there is a component of compassion which opposes discrimination and sees through
differences to a shared humanity. But the perception of shared humanity tends to remain safely abstract and inert until it is reached by
way of the recognition of differences: Stevens appeals too easily and
too sweepingly to the idea of such sharing. What I hope to have shown
in discussing the three Hardy poems is that the element of compassion
in them, crucial to the poems' value (which is, of course, moral as well
as aesthetic), includes and depends on a considerable degree of specificity, reflecting earnest attentiveness in the observation of others'
unhappiness.

Specificity is thus intrinsic to a kind of compassion which seems decisively unsentimental, compassion which we feel ready to call "authentic" and "convincing." This is not to say, however, that specificity
of observation always generates such compassion. We can imagine an
exhaustively detailed description of a suffering person (in a medical

report, for example, or a legal brief) which would be devoid of sympathy, and there must be poetic analogues of such accounts. We may recall, for example, the clinical exactitude about violent deaths in the *Iliad*, where Homer's concern for human pain is sometimes hard to locate. Hardy in "No Buyers" may come as close to such a chilled bill of particulars detailing someone's misery as a great poet will ever come, staring so grimly at the rain-soaked street vendors. But look again at what Hardy sees when he focuses on the woman who, like her husband, carries a brush that no one will purchase:

> She wears an apron white and wide in span,
> And carries a like Turk's-head, but more in nursing-wise:
> > Now and then she joins in his dirge,
> > But as if her thoughts were on distant things.

Hardy makes us glimpse the possibility that this unknown woman is a mother, or has been a mother, or wishes to be a mother. And though he cannot, in his commitment to the visual impression in this poem (unlike the speculative and inquisitive attitude he allows himself in "The Harbour Bridge"), answer our questions about the woman's life elsewhere, he can still see her in a way that recognizes her touching need for a life elsewhere ("as if her thoughts were on distant things"), which is to say that Hardy is aware of a dimension in the woman's life that does not meet the eye, and that involves her unhappy consciousness of the inadequacy of her present life on the street. This sympathy—if the reader will now agree that such imaginative seeing is sympathetic and not merely curious—though it has not been inevitably *caused* by the specificity of Hardy's seeing, has been made more feasible by such specificity and is, in turn, reflected in the energy of such specificity. In other words, precise and detailed perception of suffering, while not alone sufficient to generate compassion (since compassion also requires an exertion of imagination), is both necessary for and conducive to the sort of compassion I've called "convincing," the sort of unvague, unmisty compassion one can imagine desiring to be the object of.

As we return now to Stevens, I may seem to have set up Hardy as compassionate hero in order to condemn Stevens as self-absorbed villain. Such a neatly symmetrical attack can be tempting. But to prefer one poet to another so simply would be to obscure what each poet gives us. Does Hardy in every way shine as poet of compassion? We ought to note that our examples from Hardy do not show either poet or speaker making any effort to *help* the unhappy people he observes, nor even meditating on the possibility of such effort. The passivity of Hardy's compassion reflects his fatalistic sense that the human condition cannot be greatly improved. Perhaps, though, we want a poetry of efficacious compassion, a poetry in which sympathy manifests itself (with whatever degree of success) in benevolent action. In such a poetry perhaps the speaker or a character would step forward and buy the vendors' brushes, console the separated family, befriend the abandoned wife. Hardy advocated "loving-kindness" and tried to practice it in life, but in his poetry he mostly described opportunities missed rather than opportunities seized. Wordsworth's "Simon Lee" and Whitman's "The Wound Dresser" come to mind, not to mention reams of didactic and inspirational verse. To the extent that we can imagine good poetry of active compassion, we will wish to qualify the nomination of Hardy as poet of compassion.

On behalf of Stevens, meanwhile, we should confess that when he evades exposure to the actualities of others' pain his activity is not sufficiently described by words like "self-absorbed" or "uncaring" because he is, at the same time, our benefactor, the provider of a kind of poetry we sometimes need: he speaks for the self exhausted or depressed or frightened by the endless suffering of others, the self that needs to withdraw from debilitated others so as to preserve its own vigor. We cannot constantly sympathize; this is a secular, practical truth implicitly acknowledged (as we have seen) by Hardy and rested upon, even (as we have suspected) cherished by Stevens.

Despite that sense of possible contamination from humanity's hurts, though, Stevens is, unlike Hardy, a poet committed to the belief that human life can fundamentally improve. The improvement, which is neither political nor economic, will flow from our eventual acceptance of earthly life without mythology. This sunny spiritual meliorism (most pointedly expressed in short poems such as "The Latest Freed Man," "How to Live. What to Do," "Evening Without Angels," "On the Road Home") has been received by countless readers as a great gift of hope from Stevens, as I noted earlier in connection with "Sad Strains of a Gay Waltz." In Stevens' mind, this hope comes wedded (or welded!) to the idea of a richly self-sufficient self, independent in the world, upon whom other lives can have no disturbing impact. The "moving nuns" around his "invulnerable" old philosopher in Rome are opaque phenomena demanding no conversation. For Stevens, isolation seems a necessary (and often not unpleasant) part of the price paid for secular spiritual well-being. His gestures toward a philosophical defense of the idea of absolute isolation will be discussed in chapter 3. When isolation is not fully attained, meanwhile, suffering others have to be somehow acknowledged, but Stevens wants to indicate that their pain can, at the spiritual level, be remedied or rendered tolerable.

Looking now at a few more examples of his response to suffering others, especially soldiers in war, we should not forget that our poet is laboring to sustain his great Stevensian consolation:

> It was in the earth only
> That he was at the bottom of things
> And of himself. There he could say
> Of this I am, this is the patriarch,
> This it is that answers when I ask,
> This is the mute, the final sculpture
> Around which silence lies on silence.
> This reposes alike in springtime
> And, armored and bronzed, in autumn.
>
> He said I had this that I could love,
> As one loves visible and responsive peace,
> As one loves one's own being,
> As one loves that which is the end
> And must be loved, as one loves that
> Of which one is a part as in a unity,
> A unity that is the life one loves,
> So that one lives all the lives that comprise it
> As the life of the fatal unity of war.   (*CP* 236)

These first two stanzas of "Yellow Afternoon" serve well as a declaration of the happiness Stevens believes in and recommends. But in the last line quoted, as well as in the third stanza (not quoted here), "Yellow Afternoon" becomes cryptic in ways that testify to threats against the "peace" and "unity" Stevens has described. The threat in the third stanza seems to be a woman whose love for the man has changed unhappily or vanished, reminding him of his own incompleteness; the passage is too murky for a more thorough paraphrase.[24] Equally murky, and even more undeveloped, is the reference to war:

> the life one loves,
> So that one lives all the lives that comprise it
> As the life of the fatal unity of war.

That last clause, with its grammatically peculiar "As," contributes no illumination to Stevens' evocation of the life of peace, and this failure helps us realize that the reference to war has been pushed into this poem of late 1939 only because the poet wants to indicate that his recommendation of an earth-loving repose does not simply ignore the violent deaths of thousands of people in the same winter.

The wish to accommodate war within an essentially affirmative vision of humanity's present and future led Stevens into other peculiar contortions, as we will soon see. In Stevens' very few references to suffering persons apart from the context of war (and apart from the poems already mentioned), though, there is often an unapologetic bluntness in response to pain. "Another Weeping Woman" is a poem that gives counsel to a grieving widow; Stevens confidently informs her that she grieves mistakenly, in that grief has blocked her imaginative life:

> Pour the unhappiness out
> From your too bitter heart,
> Which grieving will not sweeten.
>
> Poison grows in this dark.
> It is in the water of tears
> Its black blooms rise.   (CP 25)

To call the poem casually insensitive would probably be wrong, since the intensity of its concluding sentence about the need for imagination shows that the poet feels some sort of urgency, even if it is not the urgency of sympathy. But if we imagine the bereaved woman's feeling upon hearing Stevens' advice in the stanzas quoted above, we become more alert to the imperious tone of that advice with its suggestion that her grief is like a number of fluid ounces that need to be drained off. The widow might reply, "That's easy for you to say." And how would she feel about the poem's title? To be called "another weeping woman" is to be reduced to a small and replaceable instance of a too-familiar category—such reduction being one way of merging other people into a faceless composite—and there is a trace of dismissive exasperation in the title as well. Stevens apparently doesn't want to be exposed any longer to this woman's grief. As he coaches her to get it over with, he sounds awfully unpierced by the fact that she has been "pierced by a death."

In "A Thought Revolved" he cites a suffering woman as a brief and handy example of foolish religious faith. Here is the first stanza of the first section, entitled "The Mechanical Optimist":

> A lady dying of diabetes
> Listened to the radio,
> Catching the lesser dithyrambs.
> So heaven collects its bleating lambs.   (CP 184)

Tough talk like this shows up often in Stevens' poetry when he confronts his favorite old nemesis, religion, though seldom so clearly in response to the misfortune of another person. Such tough talk has been admired for being so far from sentimentality, so much the achievement of a bravely wintry mind able to face the fact that the dying woman is not en route to Christian paradise. In the second stanza of "The Mechanical Optimist," the focus on her continues to be relatively specific:

> Her useless bracelets fondly fluttered,
> Paddling the melodic swirls,
> The idea of god no longer sputtered
> At the roots of her indifferent curls.

Here Stevens seems willing to observe suffering without recourse to the abstracting strategies we identified earlier. By the standards of Stevens' oeuvre, at any rate, this brief portrait of a woman is rather close and vivid, not distanced and blurred. It is as if Stevens' certainty that her death is imminent, unavoidable and unquestionable (thus obviating any issue of moral interaction: she is beyond interaction), makes him willing to look carefully at her for a moment. There will not be a disturbing interval between her present and her inevitable future. Also, the woman is not seen to be in actual pain, either physical or psychological, in her last minutes, and this may be another reason why Stevens shies away from her into abstraction less promptly than we might have expected. But if the poem does not employ strategies of withdrawal (though to label the lady "The Mechanical Optimist" is a kind of distancing-by-categorizing, and the heavy rhyming may suggest a storybook unreality), it may still be, as a response to a woman dying of diabetes, more safely removed from the trouble of compassion than we would wish. In "The Mechanical Optimist," unlike Hardy's "No Buyers," close observation of another person's experience is mingled with, and governed by, an idea dear to the poet, namely, the unavailability of Christian faith to clear-sighted modern minds. Having selected a suffering person for her blindness to his governing idea, Stevens feels sanctioned in writing about her dying in an acerbic tone—"So heaven collects its bleating lambs"—strikingly different from the tone one would take in speaking of one's mother or sister or friend, and different also from Hardy's soberly respectful tone in speaking of glimpsed strangers.

Writing about "The Emperor of Ice Cream," Helen Vendler offers a justification of Stevens' toughness:

> The chill conveyed by the impersonal account conveys, better than any first-person expression of shock and pity and acknowledgment, the absolute necessity of the shock, and the pity, and the final unwilling acknowledgment of

a harsh truth. We have, says Stevens' two-stanza spatial structure, no choice in the matter: death and life coexist, side by side. We are shocked by the coarseness of this, and repelled by both the gross physicality of death and the animal greed of life. But in view of the inflexible order of this co-existence, mere "personal reaction" is not an adequate vehicle. The anguish of the poem is the anguish before the absolute predictability of emotion as well as the predictability of situation.[25]

If Vendler has earned her reference to "the anguish of the poem" (I'm not sure she has), we need to remember still that it is not the anguish of sympathy for suffering people. Grim realism, tending to harden under pressure from the fatalism of "absolute predictability," is in Vendler's account a value (because it is a way to truth) that justifies the abjuring of the "pity" and "personal reaction" which would only romanticize the truth. Vendler's account turns on a rather evasive phrase—"not an adequate vehicle"—but evidently suggests a reversal of the argument I have pursued in this chapter. Whereas I have contended that clear-eyed perception of another person's suffering is apt to foster compassion and that the expression of such perception is thus apt to reflect the presence of compassion in the speaker, Vendler's praise of "The Emperor of Ice Cream" implies that the only accurate seeing is chilly, impassive seeing, divested of "personal reaction," and that compassion fogs the air and softens harsh truths. In this view susceptibility to compassion tends to prevent the sort of seeing that I've wanted to identify as both the catalyst and the sign of compassion.

What we need is not a simple choice between these two views (I will allow that Vendler's view will rightly characterize some observers in some scenarios), but a sensitivity to the kind of specificity or accuracy achieved in poems recommended by each view. In the case of "The Emperor of Ice Cream," we should note that this is not, after all, a poem about suffering in the present; the woman on the bed is already dead, and is not apparently grieved for by anyone in the house. If pain and grief were present in the poem's characters, its tough, chilly attitude might seem (and be indeed!) not so much unsentimental as heartless. Besides, if we acknowledge that the dead woman *has* suffered, will we agree that the poem's "pitiless lamp" illuminates her with great accuracy and vividness? It does not shed any light on her face.

> If her horny feet protrude, they come
> To show how cold she is, and dumb.　　　　　　　　(*CP* 64)

The syntax of that sentence subordinates specific human fact to general conclusion—as if the human fact mattered only as evidence—in a way that epitomizes the same subordination we observed in "Burghers of Petty Death."

Another maneuver tried by Stevens in the cause of a tough-minded refusal of sentimentality is to make a context in which suffering can be called good. This turns out to be a version of the strategy, discussed earlier, of blurring experiences together: suffering is melted together with other intensities of human experience, including joy, and then the sum can be celebrated as the truth of human life freed from the cowardice and decrepitude of myth. Much of "Esthétique du Mal" involves this melting maneuver, and it is more explicitly performed in "On the Adequacy of Landscape" (*CP* 243). The poem contrasts cowardly, cerebral people who turn away from the glare of reality with brave people who are willing "to feel / The blood-red redness of the sun." The cowards lack the nerve to inhabit "the keenest diamond day / Of people sensible to pain," whereas the latter are brave enough each morning to "turn toward the cocks" who "wake, clawing at their beds / To be again." To experience life richly, the brave people must accept pain, and pain must always be inseparable from desire and satisfaction. What we need to note here is the inclination to conflate suffering with other sensations:

> So that he that suffers most desires
> The red bird most and the strongest sky—

As in some other poems—see for example the end of "On the Road Home" (*CP* 204)—Stevens deploys superlatives ("keenest," "sharpest," "most," "strongest") when he wants to recommend an attitude. The poem, in order to affirm the adequacy of a secular landscape, provides a philosophical basis for refusing to pity. If you're hurting (the poem implies), that proves you're alive; and you're lucky to be alive; hence, be glad that you're hurting. We may grant that there is a kind of truth in this exhortation while still feeling that such a poet would be the wrong person to turn to if we were particularly in pain. We do need a poet like Stevens who contrives to be undepressed by human suffering; but we need also poets "to whom the miseries of the world / Are misery, and will not let them rest," in the words of Keats' Moneta.[26] Or, since everyone must find some peace—whether in the consolation of philosophy or in the calm of artistic form—we need poets (such as Wilfred Owen) whose peace has not come too soon, too easily. There is a premature restfulness sought by Stevens when he suggests that miseries are significant as instances of intense sensation rather than as miseries. If his search for a philosophical tranquillity about all human experiences, including a readiness to be tranquil in our wounds, is the energy that carries Stevens to greatness, our gratitude should not keep us from watching anxiously to see whether benevolent tranquillity merges into indifference, which can in turn degenerate into ruthlessness.

The massive suffering of the Second World War brought the ultimate challenge to a poet insisting on the acceptability of earthly life. In "Martial Cadenza" he urges the value of an immediate awareness of perceptual reality:

> The present close, the present realized,
> Not the symbol but that for which the symbol stands,
> The vivid thing in the air that never changes,
> Though the air change.   (CP 238)

This "thing" that evades definition (no fewer than ten nouns or phrases are offered to name it in the sentence from which the quoted lines come) presents itself to Stevens as the evening star; writing at the end of 1939, he feels summoned to acknowledge that it shines not only on his own quiet street but also on Europe and the horrors of Europe's expanding war.

> What had this star to do with the world it lit,
> With the blank skies over England, over France
> And above the German camps? It looked apart.
> Yet it is this that shall maintain—

These lines allow into the poem the question of relevance: what does this poem about a star have to do with the human world, the social reality of bombing raids and armies clashing by night? Stevens answers with a confidence, like that in "Sad Strains of a Gay Waltz," about the people's need for a truthful music: "it is this that shall maintain." Without the poetry, and the eternal natural reality it responds to, there would be no human world. "Martial Cadenza" affirms values in both Nature and the imagination which will outlast any perturbation like war. (Hardy's version of this affirmation is "In Time of 'The Breaking of Nations'," but Hardy locates the enduring value in ordinary people, "a maid and her wight," rather than in an image as cleanly abstract as Stevens' star.) "Martial Cadenza" is deliberately a consoling and self-consoling poem:

> Only this evening I saw it again,
> At the beginning of winter, and I walked and talked
> Again, and lived and was again, and breathed again
> And moved again and flashed again, time flashed again.

Yet in the context of our questions about Stevens' capacity for sympathy, it is a consolation (like the "starry placating" in "Mozart, 1935") that emerges awfully smoothly after the reference to the war, as if sliding on wheels coldly greased; the poet, like his star, maintains himself so very far above those German camps and seems so little interested in what exactly is happening down there.

When Stevens does think about soldiers getting wounded and killed, he does not want to ponder the grisly variety of their sufferings. Instead he swiftly blurs their wounds into one wound and merges the men into one representative man.[27] In relation to this metahuman figure (the "central man" of "Asides on the Oboe," the "megalfrere" of "Chocorua to Its Neighbor"), any one man in pain is an infinitesimal aspect not to be distinguished from any other, and the sound he makes, like the sounds of the poor in "Mozart, 1935," can simply be called a cry. Groaning, cursing, roaring, screaming, retching—such ugly sounds of war disappear into the one word "cry." Thus the "collective being" who emerges in "Chocurua to Its Neighbor" can speak of

> The enlarging of the simplest soldier's cry
> In what I am, as he falls. Of what I am,
>
> The cry is part.   (*CP* 298)

The sound of individual pain, already both blurred by reduction to the word "cry" and diminished by attribution to the "simplest" soldier, vanishes into the cloud of collective identity. Can compassion survive all this abstraction?

Section VII of "Esthétique du Mal" brings our problem more dramatically into focus than anything else in Stevens' work, because here an explicit didactic insistence on the coalescence of a myriad cases of suffering is accompanied by a tenderness which many readers find beautifully compassionate.

> How red the rose that is the soldier's wound,
> The wounds of many soldiers, the wounds of all
> The soldiers that have fallen, red in blood,
> The soldier of time grown deathless in great size.
>
> A mountain in which no ease is ever found,
> Unless indifference to deeper death
> Is ease, stands in the dark, a shadows' hill,
> And there the soldier of time has deathless rest.
>
> Concentric circles of shadows, motionless
> Of their own part, yet moving on the wind,

Form mystical convolutions in the sleep
Of time's red soldier deathless on his bed.

The shadows of his fellows ring him round
In the high night, the summer breathes for them
Its fragrance, a heavy somnolence, and for him,
For the soldier of time, it breathes a summer sleep,

In which his wound is good because life was.
No part of him was ever part of death.
A woman smoothes her forehead with her hand
And the soldier of time lies calm beneath that stroke.   (*CP* 318–19)

Helen Vendler calls the rose metaphor "repellent," because it so blatantly fails to imagine the reality of bloody injuries; the torn viscera and severed limbs and smashed bones of war seem left out of the account. Vendler writes:

> Whatever the attitude of mind which can produce, in the twentieth century, the original conceit, it surely means that Stevens has averted his mind from the visual scene and has fixed it not on experience but on pious value. It is a betrayal of Stevens' most ambitious aesthetic to name death a summer sleep, to call a wound a rose, to palliate finality by a stroking hand, and to blur the tragic outline by a spell of Parnassian language.[28]

As this essay has abundantly indicated, I share Vendler's skepticism toward the generalizing strategy of "How red the rose." If my brother were wounded in war, I think the narcotic seductiveness of the poem would indeed feel repellently palliative, a sort of poetic Valium, an erasure of my brother's uniqueness by a rhetoric not different enough from the rhetoric of thoughtless patriotism. I would rather have my brother's elegy written by Thomas Hardy or Wilfred Owen, by a poet willing to look carefully at the sufferer's face, a poet who would never dream of saying "his wound is good because life was."

And yet there is, as Harold Bloom has maintained even while admitting Vendler's cogency, a poignancy about the "soldier of time" poem,[29] which somehow has not been dispelled by the complaint against the poem's idealizing generality:

> A woman smoothes her forehead with her hand
> And the soldier of time lies calm beneath that stroke.

I have repeatedly felt touched by those lines, and my feeling persuades me to retrieve the idea, warily entertained earlier, of a nonspecific compassion—even though my argument in general has been propelled by my sense that such an idea should not be embraced as a justification for Stevens' coldness. The poet who could write the two lines just quoted knows something of human suffering and human endurance, and he tenderly conveys the tenderness with which one person (a mother, a wife, a sister) can respond to another person's pain. If so, then Stevens' resistance to detailed realistic images of others' suffering must be less a matter of inability to see than a matter of unwillingness to contemplate: unwillingness to be gripped, trapped, depressed, engulfed by the importunate unhappiness of other people. Stevens may be thought of as a spokesman for the element in each of us that wants to walk out of the oppressively sad hospital into fresh air and solitude.

But as we have seen, he has not managed to ignore the hospital altogether. The presence in his work of references to the specific sufferings of others, notwithstanding the attenuated and evasive quality of these references, is an element in the greatness of Stevens. This element of resisted, partly unwilling recognition contributes a somber bass note to his melodies—a note which would not be provided merely by his many references to the universal "poverty" of life without God, or to the icy glitter of shaggy junipers, the perpetual adieu of mortal loss, the silence of a rat beside a dirty pond. There is pain in Stevens' world sharper than the constant diffused pain of being modern, and other people are, at times, all too vividly victimized in their special circumstances as soldiers or widows or frustrated lovers or unemployed workers, prompting Stevens to resort to his drastically de-individualizing maneuvers. The rare and endangered element in his work of undesired yet unescaped acknowledgment of others' suffering helps us discern in Stevens both a capacity for compassion and the power of his emotional need to repress or diminish facts which, by summoning compassion, alarmingly threaten his poetic and psychological equilibrium. Both findings deepen our sympathetic understanding of a poet whose own sympathy is so problematic.

Chapter Two

STEVENS AND HETEROSEXUAL LOVE

A T THE END of "Le Monocle de Mon Oncle," Stevens (or his avuncular spokesman) seems to dedicate himself to a career of studying love. Since the poem, notwithstanding its eva-siveness, has focused on an unhappy relationship between a man and a woman, the kind of love announced as the subject of the poet's ongo-ing inquiry seems to be heterosexual romantic love. The poet recalls the inadequacy of his intellectual effort in past years when he made a "lordly study" of mankind, and then turns to a more red-blooded endeavor:

> Like a rose rabbi, later, I pursued,
> And still pursue, the origin and course
> Of love, but until now I never knew
> That fluttering things have so distinct a shade.   (*CP* 17–18)

This has the ring of a promise, the promise of a pursuit in which we (insofar as we are romantics or would-be lovers, which is pretty far) would like to accompany Stevens. If it is a promise, though, it is a promise Stevens will not keep. In his later poetry there is amazingly little attention paid to the problems of love relationships between men and women.

Of course there have been other great poets who had very little to say about romantic love. Wordsworth, for example, was remarkably silent on the subject—and this silence reflects psychological similarities between him and Stevens. Both men placed great value on mental states achieved in solitude, states of calmness and of nondesirous joy. Wallace Stevens' poetry suggests that he was a man who resented being agitated by any other person, especially by a woman, and more especially by a woman who offered or expected romantic feeling or sexual desire. That resentment is the motive behind much of "Le Monocle de Mon Oncle," where Stevens permits himself to acknowl-edge and implicitly protest the tyrannical importunity of sexual de-sire: "If sex were all, then every trembling hand / Could make us squeak, like dolls, the wished-for words" (*CP* 17). In another mood, especially later in his career, Stevens was inclined to suggest that het-erosexual relations, rightly perceived, are either very simple or inex-plicable or both, hence not discussable, and not to be worked on:

> not balances
That we achieve but balances that happen,

As a man and woman meet and love forthwith.   (*CP* 386)

Of course, a reader accustomed to Stevens' poetry is not surprised
by his silence about problems of romantic/sexual relationships, since in
Stevens all subjects, all details of human experience, return like hom-
ing pigeons to the lonely birdhouse of his one great subject: the ways
in which imagination negotiates our relation with a reality not designed or sanctioned by any God. Everything Stevens mentions eventually finds its significance for him in connection with that negotiation.
He is incredibly skillful at ramifying the difficulties of the negotiation
so colorfully as to give the impression that his poetry answers to all of
human experience. Meanwhile he often does refer, fleetingly and tantalizingly, to romantic love. Romantic love becomes convenient for
him as a source of metaphors for his beloved conception of a passionate acceptance of one's own reality. But Stevens deliberately ignores or deftly avoids opportunities to consider romantic love as a
relationship between two distinct, separately subjective human beings.
I will examine that avoidance in some detail, because I think it has
been too blandly tolerated by critics of Stevens; then I will present
evidence that Stevens himself, especially but not only in early poems,
betrays an awareness that he is failing to deal with an important, painful, problematic area of experience, one in which moral error is notably possible. Thus the moral critique involved in my project has an
incipient existence in the work itself. We will emerge with a sense of
Stevens not so much as a man indifferent to love and to the moral
demands in love, but rather as a man intolerably disturbed by love and
its demands; not so much as a morally obtuse man, but as a frightened
man.

In his first volume Stevens was quite willing to refer to romantic/
sexual love within certain limits. One reason why *Harmonium* was
called hedonistic (by Yvor Winters, among others) is that several
poems in it recommend candid admission of and expression of sexual
desire. In "Cy Est Pourtraicte, Madame Ste Ursule, et les Unze Mille
Vierges" (*CP* 21–22) we are informed that God Himself, hearing
Ursula's tender prayer, "felt a subtle quiver, / That was not heavenly
love, / Or pity." God is feeling the bass of his being throb, like the
elders in "Peter Quince at the Clavier" or like Mon Oncle, who feels "A
deep up-pouring from some saltier well / Within me" (*CP* 13) when he
recalls his wife's youthful beauty. What Stevens wants us to approve
about such desire as God feels for Ursula is that it is real, and it is an

appreciation of something real, a woman as actual as radishes. It is not a feeling faked or disguised by a mythology, just as Ursula's love-message for her Lord is as much earthly ditty as it is prayer, free of mythology's formality: "This is not writ / In any book." "Last Looks at the Lilacs" addresses a man whose scientific attitude toward beauty, both natural and feminine, prevents him from appreciating the romantic reality of the woman at his side; Stevens mocks this nonlover for choosing a superficial, measuring sort of realism over a fully sensual perception and challenges him to

> say how it comes that you see
> Nothing but trash and that you no longer feel
> Her body quivering in the Floréal
>
> Toward the cool night and its fantastic star . . .   (CP 49)

Make your move, Stevens advises the man, because if you don't, another man will do so, as the "arrogantly male" representative of masculine desire, "the gold Don John, / Who will embrace her before summer comes." Note that the move Stevens calls for is a move in relation to the woman's body—she is said to be preeminently interested in the fact "that her nakedness is near"—not a move in an interaction understood to be more complexly human. When the short poems of *Harmonium* adopt an instructive or hortatory attitude, a right relation to beauty (beauty of woman or of Nature) is often presented as a delightfully simple affair.

The mistakenly reclusive dreamer addressed in "Hymn From a Watermelon Pavilion" is informed that "A feme may come, leaf-green, / Whose coming may give revel / Beyond revelries of sleep" (CP 89). In other words, wakefulness will lead to a rendezvous with a woman who will provide non-narcotic joy. The voice of the poem is very confident in its optimistic prediction as to what can happen when boy meets girl. Here, as in some other *Harmonium* poems, Stevens is so concerned with repudiating obsolete or cowardly illusions that he chooses not to notice ways in which sexual revelries can be painfully disturbing to a man who wants to be at peace with reality. A woman in such a poem (unlike the disturbing spouse in "Le Monocle de Mon Oncle") is a simple phenomenon and can be readily identified by one word, the archly archaic and dismissive word "feme." "A feme may come"—any feme, it seems, is likely to fill the bill. Similarly, Stevens feels no need to individualize the "prismy blonde" whom Crispin weds in section V of "The Comedian as the Letter C." She is defined sufficiently for Stevens by her impact upon Crispin's senses. She is "prismy," a sort of female

light show; she is an ingredient in her husband's feast of quotidian
pleasures:

> cream for the fig and silver for the cream,
> A blonde to tip the silver and to taste
> The rapey gouts.   (*CP* 42)

Were it not buried in one of Stevens' densest poems, this passage might be recognized as his most outspoken celebration of sexual
pleasure.

His most convincing expression of sexual desire, though, is in
"Peter Quince at the Clavier," where the red-eyed elders are be-
witched into a dissonant concerto of yearning by the sight of Susanna
bathing. Does this poem endow Susanna with human identity? Is she
more than just an attractive shape beside a garden pool? She at least
has a name, which is more than can be said for the other beauties
referred to so far (except Ursula). It is true that in section II of "Peter
Quince" Susanna is given a point of view. Her thoughts, though, are
awfully nebulous:

> She searched
> The touch of springs,
> And found
> Concealed imaginings.
> She sighed,
> For so much melody.   (*CP* 90)

So nebulous that we are certainly not encouraged to think of her as a
particular woman with a particular personality. Meanwhile, it is easy
to overlook the fact that the poet's reverie about Susanna is apparently
stimulated by the beauty of another woman, a present woman:

> what I feel,
> Here in this room, desiring you,
>
> Thinking of your blue-shadowed silk,
> Is music. It is like the strain
> Waked in the elders by Susanna.   (*CP* 90)

As I will explain later, I don't think the mere attribution of a blue
garment to this present figure (blue being associated with the imagination in Stevens' oeuvre) suffices as proof that the "you" is an aspect of
the speaker's mind rather than a woman, nor can I believe that Stevens
intended us to hear the passage only in that way. When the poet informs the woman in the blue dress that what he feels for her is music,
she might be forgiven if she replied, "Oh, is that so? Does this mean we

won't be going to bed together?" Also she might be wise to wonder whether this lover who claims to be thinking not exactly of *her* but of her blue-shadowed silk will be able and willing to give her the kind of personal attention she deserves.

Such thoughts on her part would, one feels, be unlikely to please Mr. Stevens (or Mr. Quince), if she were to voice them. Here I think it is apposite to quote a reminiscence by Naaman Corn, who was the chauffeur for the Stevenses on family outings:

> He didn't carry on any conversation with Mrs. Stevens much about something. She wouldn't talk on account of he would snap at her quickly. So she got where she just went in a shell, and she wouldn't say anything. One time I thought she couldn't talk because she never did say nothing, but I found out why. If every time you say something to a person, you're going to snap at them, they quit talking. They go underground. You could hear that, and you figured that's the reason why she clams up.[1]

With no one to help her in her victimization except "simpering Byzantines," Susanna has no chance to make her case against the guilty elders; trapped in a poem controlled by Peter Quince, she can only clam up and go underground.

By being so attractive, Susanna causes a lot of trouble, for the elders and for her Byzantines as well as for herself (even though "The fitful tracing of a portal" is a lullingly cleansed way of alluding to rape fantasies). The very simplicity and clarity of her appeal make her alarming, an unavoidable disturbance of the peace. In situations when our poet, or his male speaker, cannot for some reason commit himself to a decisive, simple sexual response to such a woman's appeal, he is inclined to propose revisions of her behavior, or reconceptions of her nature, so that her appeal will not be so bluntly sexual in its impact. Some sort of magic is needed to cloak her. In "O Florida, Venereal Soil," the feminine spirit of Florida is requested to make her desirability less boorish, more mysterious, more selectively exotic:

> Swiftly in the nights,
> In the porches of Key West,
> Behind the bougainvilleas,
> After the guitar is asleep,
> Lasciviously as the wind,
> You come tormenting,
> Insatiable . . .
>
> Donna, donna, dark,
> Stooping in indigo gown
> And cloudy constellations,

> Conceal yourself or disclose
> Fewest things to the lover—
> A hand that bears a thick-leaved fruit,
> A pungent bloom against your shade.   (*CP* 48)

Here the jaded male poet makes a request whose tone may be rather pathetic, yet at the same time we should see that he is trying to dictate the manner in which the dark female is to seduce him, and that what he doesn't want is a full and open encounter with her demanding self.

In a more mischievous mood, he gives instructions in "Floral Decorations for Bananas" whereby the too obviously sexual bananas—"These insolent, linear peels"—ought to be either replaced or disguised. The danger of blatant sexuality, however, turns out to be focused here not in hungry masculinity (as those phallic bananas might have indicated) but in teasing femininity: "The women will be all shanks / And bangles and slatted eyes" (*CP* 54). While this is a humorous poem, it is nonetheless a palpably uneasy expression of Stevens' fear of the force of female sexuality. He goes on to recommend an accommodation of those bananas which will make them less drastically noticeable, but the floral decorations meant to surround them have a moist vigor of their own which takes over the poem's last stanza and gets the last word:

> And deck the bananas in leaves
> Plucked from the Carib trees,
> Fibrous and dangling down,
> Oozing cantankerous gum
> Out of their purple maws,
> Darting out of their purple craws
> Their musky and tingling tongues.   (*CP* 54)

Female sexuality is felt to be something that can get out of hand, and drive a man crazy. Stevens' sense of feminine attractiveness as a terrible threat to a man's composure is reflected in this alarmingly discomposed remark from "The Noble Rider and the Sound of Words": "Democritus plucked his eye out because he could not look at a woman without thinking of her as a woman. If he had read a few of our novels, he would have torn himself to pieces."[2]

Purple romance generated by feminine attractions is sometimes pleasant because preferable to naked sexuality, but "Of Hartford in a Purple Light" indicates that it is even better to get away from women altogether if possible.

> A moment ago, light masculine,
> Working, with big hands, on the town,
> Arranged its heroic attitudes.

But now as in an amour of women
Purple sets purple round. Look, Master,
See the river, the railroad, the cathedral . . .

When male light fell on the naked back
Of the town, the river, the railroad were clear.
Now, every muscle slops away.   (*CP* 227)

In the feminized light of evening the speaker feels disarmed, indeed unmanned.

If the dangerous attractiveness of women cannot be avoided, or delicately controlled, moderated, redefined, then it will have to be somehow dissolved or spiritualized or sublimated. In "Anatomy of Monotony" Stevens speaks of how we are comforted on our mortal earth by the presence of other human bodies. Notice here how promptly we are shifted from an appreciation of those bodies to some vaguer object of desire:

other bodies come,
Twinning our phantasy and our device,
And apt in versatile motion, touch and sound
To make the body covetous in desire
Of the still finer, more implacable chords.   (*CP* 108)

Whatever those chords are, they have called us speedily away from what threatened to become a full-fledged celebration of attractive human bodies. Stevens here is surprisingly like the early Yeats in preferring to speak of "spaciousness and light" rather than actual nearby bodies.

When dream and magic (as in "O Florida, Venereal Soil," above, and "Two Figures in Dense Violet Night," below) are not available, art as such may be summoned to do the job of reconstituting the female to make her acceptable. Peter Quince uses the art of his own music at the clavier to establish a calm relation to the "clear viol" of Susanna's music of feminine beauty (*CP* 92). The title of "Anything is Beautiful If You Say It Is" refers to such a saving reconstitution achieved through language, and the poem's leading examples of a reality too depressing and alienating to take on its own terms are, in Irvin Ehrenpreis's words, two "indecent young women":[3]

Under the eglantine
The fretful concubine
Said, "Phooey! Phoo!"
She whispered, "Pfui!"

The demi-monde
On the mezzanine

Said, "Phooey!" too,
And a "Hey-de-i-do!"   (*CP* 211)

The poet seems confident that he has implied a connection between
the silliness of these young women—the insufficiency of their language—and their all-too-noticeable, glamorous (or pseudoglamorous)
femininity. He will turn away from their human fretfulness to scruti-
nize, with painterly gaze, unthreatening grapes, pears and cheese.

"So-and-So Reclining on Her Couch" beckons with an emphatically
physical image of a woman serving as an artist's model:

On her side, reclining on her elbow. . . .

She floats in air at the level of
The eye, completely anonymous,
Born, as she was, at twenty-one,

Without lineage or language, only
The curving of her hip, as motionless gesture,
Eyes dripping blue, so much to learn.   (*CP* 295)

Of course this female image turns out to be an occasion for a puzzling
meditation on the difference between a reality and a conception of
that reality. But unless we are excessively docile Stevensians, we must
feel that Stevens plays a dubious trick here in evoking a human character for a flickering moment and whisking her away into abstraction
the very next moment. We sense that in the case of viewing this young
woman, abstraction or artistic conception is not only inevitable—Stevens' perpetual assertion about all viewing—but nervously preferable
to any less mediated encounter with her reality. This twenty-one-year-
old blue-eyed woman whose image the male artist longs to reproduce
is a troublemaker because of her attractiveness. She must be rendered
abstract—for this purpose it helps that she is conceived as anonymous,
silent, lacking a past, and motionless—or else, if her individual humanity becomes noticeable, she must at that same moment be dismissed:
"Goodbye, / Mrs. Pappadopoulos, and thanks" (*CP* 296). The pleasing
humor of this ending should not make us miss the fact that this humor
helps the poet turn his back on a particular irritant, a female human
other.

When the mother of Mrs. Pappadopoulos was a lovely teenager, she
might have wandered around Key West and given Wallace Stevens
dreamy glimpses of an earthly paradise of gratified desire. Let us return to Florida for one more poem from *Harmonium*, the book in
which Stevens is most willing to admit he is aware of sexual need and
romantic love; "Two Figures in Dense Violet Night" provides one

more instance of the male requiring the female to be something other than merely a woman.[4] The poem begins with a hilarious complaint:

> I had as lief be embraced by the porter at the hotel
> As to get no more from the moonlight
> Than your moist hand.

Her hand is not enough. Is it that he wants the rest of her body too? Not tonight. Her physicality is not enough—or, it is too much.

> Be the voice of night and Florida in my ear.
> Use dusky words and dusky images.
> Darken your speech.

Now, this could sound like an invitation to quite a spicy interaction, albeit a rather crepuscular and verbal one, until we hear the next instruction to the not-yet-satisfactory mistress:

> Speak, even, as if I did not hear you speaking,
> But spoke for you perfectly in my thoughts,
> Conceiving words,
>
> As the night conceives the sea-sounds in silence . . .   (*CP* 86)

By this point the woman as woman, as human other, has disappeared, or will have done so if the speaker's wish is fulfilled. The poem is called "Two Figures in Dense Violet Night" but this comes to seem a deception, for when we peer into the poem's murk we see a man addressing an idea, a speaker creating via the art of his language an ideal mistress who will reside, not too moistly, only in his head.

A choir of Stevens scholars replies "*Of course* it's not a real woman, you fool! It's the interior paramour!" If you have studied Stevens, this objection to the drift of my argument has been in your mind all along. Stevens habitually imagines the animate principle in external reality as female when reality as a whole is felt to be beautiful and nurturing. This "woman" is his "inamorata" (see section XXVI of "An Ordinary Evening in New Haven") and appears in many poems. In "Six Significant Landscapes" her beauty is nocturnal and perhaps not safely removed from upsetting sexuality:

> The night is of the color
> Of a woman's arm:
> Night, the female,
> Obscure,
> Fragrant and supple,
> Conceals herself.
> A pool shines,

Like a bracelet
Shaken in a dance.   (*CP* 73–74)

In the wonderful late poem "The Woman in Sunshine," she has become reliably sublime in a daylit, reassuring way, offering a kind of
affection which, in being "the only love," promises to erase the dark
significance of sexual love. Here is the whole poem.

THE WOMAN IN SUNSHINE

It is only that this warmth and movement are like
The warmth and movement of a woman.

It is not that there is any image in the air
Nor the beginning nor end of a form:

It is empty. But a woman in threadless gold
Burns us with brushings of her dress

And a dissociated abundance of being,
More definite for what she is—

Because she is disembodied,
Bearing the odors of the summer fields,

Confessing the taciturn and yet indifferent,
Invisibly clear, the only love.   (*CP* 445)

Reading Stevens we learn to think of this ethereal female as a pro-
jection of the poet's mind. As Frank Doggett writes:

> She is best understood as an embodiment of an attitude toward the content
> of objective experience. The attitude is often that of a longing suddenly
> realized by a vivid image of woman. . . .
>   When reality is configured by myth, the miscellany of things on every side
> becomes one world conjoined by a latent centrality of being; its shifting
> appearances are held together by a figure of reality or nature. The woman
> as mother or as inamorata reflects this sense of person felt within the reality
> of the world, derived perhaps from a projection of self but always known to
> be something apart—intimate but elusive, continually desired and never
> truly attained.[5]

Insofar as this female presence is understood to be a creation of the
poet's mind she may be called the interior paramour, that is, the nourishing power of the poet's imagination. A sophisticated Stevens reader
becomes completely accustomed to images of this woman-who-is-not-
a-real-woman-but-a-principle-or-presence (whether "out there" or in
the imaginer's head) and may scorn the more naive reader who tries
to find real women in the poems.

Stevens himself would perhaps disdain my literal-minded argument on behalf of the actual human women glimpsed in his poetry. He would feel amused pity for readers who find the wrong kind of solace in his "Final Soliloquy of the Interior Paramour." Readers who worry about the strength and value of their love relationships with other people feel a powerful attraction in the matching of the word "together" with the word "enough" in the poem's ending: "We make a dwelling in the evening air, / In which being there together is enough" (CP 524). Alas, it is not a man and a woman who live together in this poem; it is not two persons; the title of "Final Soliloquy of the Interior Paramour" makes this clear.[6] Note, however, that if the poem is looked at without its title, a reader can justifiably feel invited to think of two persons who have joined in love. And in many Stevens poems, including those I have discussed thus far and most of those I will soon speak of, the female lover is not so decisively dehumanized, nor the idea of an actual human lover so firmly repudiated, as the title of this particular poem requires.

I think we are wrong to so readily accept the notion that Stevens can evoke a beautiful "woman" in poem after poem and mean "only" an idea, a conception, an attitude, a principle, but not an actual woman. My argument is that you cannot describe something as "a woman" without meaning something about actual women. Metaphors are not innocent in either direction. When you say that A is like B, you reveal something about your sense of A and your sense of B as actualities in your experience. Stevens' critics, fascinated by the metaphysical meaning of his female presences, have indulged him too gently in accepting them as only metaphysical. Critics sometimes go to absurd lengths to let Stevens escape from moral implications in this way. Here, for example, is Eugene Paul Nassar on "Peter Quince at the Clavier":

> "Peter Quince" is really a poem about the imaginative faculty, its seasons and its value. It is not a poem about love between the sexes, nor in any way about relations between people. It is, rather, about the poet in solitude carrying on his sometime love affair with his "interior paramour," she who brings forth each "spring" children of desire that of necessity must be raped in "autumn." "Peter Quince" is an "amoral" poem in that it does not deal with moral problems at all, but with the inevitable cycle of creation and destruction that is the life of the poetic mind. The skeptical poet has his own obligations to his poems, the "Susannas" he creates, which are antithetical to the obligations that obtain in the love of one person for another.[7]

To some extent, I'm afraid, Stevens would endorse Nassar's rather repellent interpretation. Yet consider: Stevens knew perfectly well, when he was writing his stanzas about Susanna and the elders, that he was causing us to think about (among other things, yes, but first and most vividly) an actual vulnerable woman and actual lustful old men and actual sexual molestation. Stevens was choosing to affect our ways of thinking about such people and such events. If he tells us the story of an attempted rape in an imaginative context that guides us toward accepting the event as inevitable and even conducive to poetic creation, as Nassar suggests, then Stevens is doing something that has moral implications for which he bears some moral responsibility. Similarly, whenever he speaks to us metaphorically in terms of romantic love, sexuality, or femininity, *one* of the things he is doing is describing, and influencing (or seeking to influence) our understanding of interpersonal love, actual sex, and real-life women. When he writes in "Adagia" (*OP* 165), "A poet looks at the world as a man looks at a woman," he proposes to explain something about the relation between poet and world by analogy with what he assumes to be the more obvious relation between a man and a woman. A sexually desirable woman? The analogy doesn't explicitly include this meaning but does deliberately call it to mind. Stevens' confidence in the analogy, and his tone of approval, are not shaken by the fact that the analogy locates all human subjectivity and agency in the male hero.[8] As before, whether he encourages us to focus on this truth or not, Stevens is partly writing about people.

It is on that basis that I have seen fit to discuss Stevens' habitual failure or refusal to present images of mutual love or two-way relationship between individual men and women; and on that basis I maintain that my point is not vaporized by the objection that Stevens does not (primarily) intend to refer to real women in many of his references to femininity. Besides, as Helen Vendler has persuasively argued, Stevens' veiling of his references to sex and love has hidden his study of sexual desire and romantic/sexual emotions more effectively than he himself ultimately must have intended.[9]

The pattern I have shown is one of consistent failure by Stevens to describe the female other as a fully human individual, as a separate subjectivity, an independent actor and perceiver outside his own mind. This has held true across a spectrum of attitudes toward love, from aggressively candid sexuality at one extreme to ontological mystery at the other extreme. Stevens is not inclined to pay steady attention to real women in writing of romantic/sexual love. Real women cause problems; they impinge. They impinge upon the male poet's freedom by exciting an animal desire which is too simple and vulgar, unimaginative and therefore deathly, or by calling for delusory romantic revisions of desire, which are also deathly when they pull him too far from reality. And, more importantly, women impinge upon the male poet's crucial sense of his own sufficiency and essential humanity by being noticeably different people. In this regard Stevens' resistance to the fact of attractive women as separate human beings is one aspect of the larger subject of his resistance to the fact that human beings are different from each other at all.[10] (This point will return near the end of this chapter, and again in chapter 3.)

There is something frustrating about an analysis that essentially demonstrates an absence. I have repeatedly shown that a complexly human woman or a complexly human heterosexual relationship does not appear in Stevens in places where one might have hoped for such an appearance. One reason for presenting this kind of analysis is that it can help us resist the centripetal pull of a powerful writer whose artistic charisma may otherwise lure readers into the feeling that he has said "all there is to say." But it is more satisfying to be shown things that are present in a set of poems. So I return to my assertion that Stevens does acknowledge, here and there, the possibility of moral failure and failure of spirit in relating to the female other, and even acknowledges the likelihood that he himself has thus failed. Such acknowledgment finds its way into the poetry in expressions of anxiety and remorse.

In 1907, years before he became a serious poet and two years before his marriage in 1909, Stevens in his journal tried to coach himself into more gentle relations with people:

> I must be gallant. One loses too much in going under the surface. Besides, it is all what one imagines, there. Take a lacquered cheek—why not let it go at that? . . . I must think well of people. After all, they are only people.[11]

Several essential aspects of Stevens may be glimpsed here: his attraction to surfaces (particularly female surfaces), his fear of the depths in others, his courage in developing a response to dissatisfaction, his desire to be benevolent, and his potential misanthropy. The journal entry was not, to be sure, intended as a guide in choosing and living with a spouse, but it reflects attitudes that would tend, over a long period, to prevent the development of happy mutual understanding in a marriage. A decorous truce is the best version of relationship the entry would seem to predict. As the years passed, the marriage of Wallace and Elsie declined into a condition of polite estrangement.[12] Mostly Stevens seems not to have blamed himself for this; but notes of anxiety and regret, and even perhaps remorse, which cannot be heard as unconnected to the marriage once one knows something about it, are occasionally audible in the poetry, when Stevens admits that something is incomplete in the relation between the (male) self and the female other. Some startlingly relevant examples appear in *Opus Post-*

humous—in poems Stevens chose to omit from the works published during his lifetime.

First, though, some examples from *The Collected Poems*. The feeling that there could perhaps have been more in a relationship with a woman may be felt to cause the furtive poignancy of a few unexpected moments in late poems, as in "The Bouquet," where section II ends with,

> The sun is secretly shining on a wall.
> One remembers a woman standing in such a dress.   *(CP 450)*

The beautiful late poem "Prologues to What Is Possible" ends hauntingly with a reference to "The way a look or a touch reveals its unexpected magnitudes" *(CP 517)*. Haunting because we sense that the aged poet is himself haunted by a feeling of magnitudes beneath the looks of persons, magnitudes which he never sufficiently explored because he never sufficiently expected them. A person can never deeply know another person, Stevens seems to have assured himself too readily; a man can never fully know a woman. This fatalism is caught in three lines from "The Pure Good of Theory":

> It is never the thing but the version of the thing:
> The fragrance of the woman not her self,
> Her self in her manner not the solid block . . .   *(CP 332)*

Of course, that idea could be accompanied by strenuous efforts to apprehend a woman's reality by way of "versions"—but it is not. "Bouquet of Belle Scavoir," one of the poems ostensibly not about a real woman, expresses frustration at the unavailability of a direct encounter with the female spirit: "It is she that he wants, to look at directly, / Someone before him to see and to know" *(CP 232)*. My claim is that these lines cannot be wholly untainted with sadness about what occurs in actual relationships between women and men, relationships in which a woman may not be looked at as directly as she should be looked at. "The form of her in something else / Is not enough," Stevens says about the female spirit, but he feels just the opposite when an actual woman appears. Indeed the entire current of his thought that presses toward direct encounter with the thing itself—"Let's see the very thing and nothing else" *(CP 373)*—can seem sadly spurious when we notice how hard he tries to ignore the possibility that one of the phenomena directly confronting the "freed man" may be an attractive woman.

In "The Hand as a Being" our man is "Too conscious of too many things at once"—perhaps he has culpably failed to focus on what matters—but he is rescued from this unhappy and unsociable condition by "the naked, nameless dame":

Her hand took his and drew him near to her.
Her hair fell on him and the mi-bird flew

To the ruddier bushes at the garden's end.
Of her, of her alone, at last he knew
And lay beside her underneath the tree.   (*CP* 271)

What interests me in those lines is the implication that the man needs
to relinquish the mi-bird, the demon of his self-absorption, a symbol of
his Hoonlike solipsism, in order to enter into loving relationship with
the woman. Here (though of course we are invited to agree that the
naked, nameless dame is to be deemed not a human individual but a
sense of life itself) Stevens seems to know something that he does not
usually admit.

He probably thinks that the same healthy relinquishing of ego is
what allows the happy ending of the importantly bold poem of regret
called "World Without Peculiarity," so that the problem of "The hat-
ing woman" (a startling reference to his wife, apparently) is cured by
a unifying of his spirit with the maternal earth. But what we should see
in this is a radical retreat from actual interpersonal trouble toward the
peaceful privacy of solitude. An earlier poem, "Yellow Afternoon,"
ends strangely with what seems to be an account of failure to accept
relationship with the female other. The man in "Yellow Afternoon"
has been feeling his love for the earth, for earthly reality. Then:

The thought that he had found all this
Among men, in a woman—she caught his breath—
But he came back as one comes back from the sun
To lie on one's bed in the dark, close to a face
Without eyes or mouth, that looks at one and speaks.   (*CP* 237)

Undoubtedly Stevens is up to something metaphysical there, as many
a critic will tell us, but I suggest that what we feel in those lines is a
cryptic confession of a man's cowardly withdrawal from the woman
back into the private dark of the self. The poem audibly and syntac-
tically shies away from the woman as soon as her startling power is
recalled.

A more explicit warning of the cost involved in becoming phi-
losophically self-sufficient arrives refreshingly at the end of section
XII of "Esthétique du Mal," after the poet has hypothesized a world
free from pain because free from knowledge of others and from
desire:

Yes, but
What lover has one in such rocks, what woman,
However known, at the centre of the heart?   (*CP* 323)

The poignancy of this section, ending as it does with the above lines, depends on our realizing that the "woman" much missed here is indeed a woman, not an abstract principle or sense of life. And the phrase "However known" tacitly admits the existence of a variety of ways of knowing a beloved woman, some ways perhaps embarrassingly preferable to others.

The short poem "Arrival at the Waldorf" is probably Stevens' most direct expression in *The Collected Poems* of guilt about a love relationship. The traveling poet has escaped back into the cool hotel of his imagination, away from the disturbances of rampant social life. He is safe at the Waldorf, but has brought guilt in his baggage:

> This arrival in the wild country of the soul,
> All approaches gone, being completely there,
>
> Where the wild poem is a substitute
> For the woman one loves or ought to love,
> One wild rhapsody a fake for another.   (*CP* 240–41)

I think Stevens exercised more daring, more courage in writing "Arrival at the Waldorf" than in writing many a poem that bravely faces up to the nonexistence of God. As we read a collection of poetry so cleansed of personal relationships that impose complicated moral problems, we ought to feel jolted when we come across that reference to "the woman one loves or ought to love," the woman who is being avoided by the guest at the Waldorf.

Opus Posthumous, though, is a less exclusive hotel, and in its corridors we get several further glimpses of troublingly human women. In the last year of his life, Stevens talked to his friend Stephen Langton about his periods of silence, "what he called 'lapses of grace' . . . when he put aside writing poetry entirely. He said nevertheless the desire to write was gnawing at him all the time. He tried to do without it to make life a little more livable personally, with his wife, I think."[13] This biographical scrap sheds a little light on the peculiar poem "Red Loves Kit," which Stevens published in a magazine in 1924 and never chose to republish. After "Red Loves Kit" Stevens published nothing for six years. It is a poem about the failure of his marriage—"such /Unhappy love reveals vast blemishes" (*OP* 31)—and about the husband's retirement from the marital battlefield into a mental realm where the interpersonal blemishes need not be exposed. His daily life has been darkened by his wife's unjust accusations: "Her words accuse you of adulteries / That sack the sun, though metaphysical." Stevens' metaphysical adulteries were those between him and his interior paramour, trysting poetically at the Waldorf of his creative imagination. Though the poem labors to construct an exoneration for the husband and then an imaginative escape into gaudy melancholy ("It will be fecund in rapt curios"), the main accomplishment of "Red Loves Kit" is to acknowledge, in remarkable detail, problems of relationship between a real woman and a real man. From the start of the poem the speaker is already convinced that these problems have become insoluble:

> Your yes her no, your no her yes. The words
> Make little difference, for being wrong
> And wronging her, if only as she thinks,
> You never can be right. (OP 30)

Despite a title by which the poet tries to push this couple sardonically away from himself, Red and Kit are more revealingly human than any pair of ex-lovers or unhappy lovers imagined by Stevens after "Le Monocle de Mon Oncle."[14] Stevens would not give this accomplishment a home in *The Collected Poems*.

Let me cite two more poems exiled into *Opus Posthumous*. Stevens never published the following early poem, written around 1919 or 1920:

ROMANCE FOR A DEMOISELLE LYING IN THE GRASS

> It is grass.
> It is monotonous.
>
> The monotony
> Is like your port which conceals
> All your characters
> And their desires.
>
> I might make many images of this
> And twang nobler notes
> Of larger sentiment.
>
> But I invoke the monotony of monotonics
> Free from images and change.
>
> Why should I savor love
> With tragedy or comedy?
>
> Clasp me,
> Delicatest machine. (OP 23)

Here Stevens tries to be funny about the male speaker's no-nonsense desire for sex uncomplicated by sentiment, by "tragedy or comedy." The striking thing about this joke poem is that it acknowledges, by rejecting, what so much of Stevens' poetry refuses to acknowledge at all, namely, the existence of a complicated and different inner life within another person, specifically a desirable woman: "All your characters / And their desires." A 1934 poem, "One of Those Hibiscuses of Damozels," while obviously humorous in the repetitions by which it celebrates the elusiveness of the young woman's essence, becomes in its third and fourth stanzas a surprisingly plaintive protestation of inability to see her reality behind or amid her decorative attractions:

ONE OF THOSE HIBISCUSES OF DAMOZELS

She was all of her airs and, for all of her airs,
She was all of her airs and ears and hairs,
Her pearly ears, her jeweler's ears
And the painted hairs that composed her hair.

In spite of her airs, that's what she was. She was all
Of her airs, as surely cologne as that she was bone
Was what she was and flesh, sure enough, but airs;
Rather rings than fingers, rather fingers than hands.

How could you ever, how could think that you saw her,
Knew her, how could you see the woman that wore the beads,
The ball-like beads, the bazzling and the bangling beads
Or hear her step in the way she walked?

This was not how she walked for she walked in a way
And the way was more than the walk and was hard to see.
You saw the eye-blue, sky-blue, eye-blue, and the powdered ears
And the cheeks like flower-pots under her hair.   (*OP* 74)

Protestation of inability—"how could you see the woman that wore the beads"—here seems not safely distinct from confession of failure—"the way was more than the walk and was hard to see." Less is at stake than in "Red Loves Kit," but what is at stake involves more than just a solitary man; no critic can plausibly claim that this damozel is Nature or the beauty of reality as a whole. Stevens here has had to confront an actual woman with eyes and ears and airs, and he has controlled the confrontation by reveling in the insistence that her physical appearance (let alone her inner reality) is too complex to assimilate. Though he distanced her further by labeling the poem one of "Five Grotesque Pieces," the sociable reader is still prompted to wonder about sisters of this damozel who might be more visible, and lure the poet out of the safety of his suave bafflement.

If she does have a sister in *The Collected Poems*, it is Vincentine in "The Apostrophe to Vincentine." Vincentine manages to overcome or survive the dehumanization (via idealization) implied by the poem's title. She outlives the first two stanzas in which the *Harmonium* poet reports his admiration for her as object (first, a quasi-divine and superhuman object; second, a physical and subhuman object). Then, with an assertion of personhood that stands out as heroic in the solitude of the Stevens cosmos, Vincentine enlarges the lover's perceptions in stanzas III and IV:

III

Then you came walking,
In a group
Of human others,
Voluble.
Yes: you came walking,
Vincentine.
Yes: you came talking.

IV

And what I knew you felt
Came then.
Monotonous earth I saw become
Illimitable spheres of you,
And that white animal, so lean,
Turned Vincentine,
Turned heavenly Vincentine,
And that white animal, so lean,
Turned heavenly, heavenly Vincentine.   (*CP* 53)

A real-life Vincentine would not feel that her individuality had been exhaustively described by those lines, but this poem, its playfulness notwithstanding, shows Stevens making room for the idea that the beloved is a human other, voluble rather than silent, her speech requiring an adjustment in his perception of her, because it is generated out of her illimitable selfhood, so that "what I knew you felt," though the phrase sounds confident, has become a less simple matter than before. On the other hand, the poet is not at peace with this recognition, as Helen Vendler has observed in commenting on the repetitions of the final stanza. (By "brutality" Vendler refers to Stevens' insistence on the physicality of the beloved.)

> Brutality and apotheosis end in a stalemate. We remember Vincentine at least as powerfully in her repellent incarnation as a white animal so lean as in her named and transfigured state, brunette, dressed, walking, talking, and feeling. The poem shows us a mind willing and welcoming the decor of thought and fancy, while unable to rid itself of primal reductiveness and visual disgust.[15]

Where are we led by our finding that a woman like Vincentine, who briefly wins respect as an independent person, is so endangered and so rare among the many female presences in Stevens' work? We have to recognize that Stevens mainly proposed a way of seeing and an attitude toward seeing that are not conducive to, nor concerned with, seeing into another person—into her mind, into her heart. This latter kind of seeing, which when successful we call sympathy or empathy, is achieved in the mysterious effort of mutual relationship. Participation in mutual relationship is neither passive nor stable: both participants are always in relative motion, and in this intimate motion they see one another shiftingly in various human lights. Wallace Stevens' strongest reaction to that agitating dance is—despite all his efforts to approve theoretically of change—a desire to sit still and gaze upon a panorama of surfaces, enjoying his mind's play with them, a play in which a lovely woman can be regarded as no more interesting than a tree or cloud, no more personal than the moon. Denis Donoghue has remarked: "As long as the imagination can grasp an object, the nature of the object does not matter, because its chief purpose, in Stevens' eyes, is to disclose the power of the imagination."[16]

It is as if Stevens decided, over and over, that he had enough trouble accepting himself, his humanity in an indifferent and disturbing universe, without adding to his problem the maddening further dimension which arises from the differences between people. "World Without Peculiarity" amounts to a confession of this refusal to deal with interpersonal strains as important realities. Working out a philosophical approval of the ontological reality of one man—himself—was hard enough, and seemed to him more essential than the problems of diplomacy ("Your yes her no, your no her yes") generated by acknowledging that one man's needs and feelings may not be another man's and that one woman's may be something else again.[17] We, meanwhile, may suspect that part of why Stevens' self-acceptance (as an imaginer existing temporarily on earth) seemed to him so problematic and so urgent was because of the painful loneliness fostered by his inclination to look away from human differences as revealed in human relationships.

Within his general objection to human differences, Stevens felt a visceral objection to sexuality itself,[18] as we have noticed in poems such as "Floral Decorations for Bananas" and as Vendler has suggested in connection with "The Apostrophe to Vincentine." The objection to sexuality is the most vivid manifestation of the objection to difference, because the fact of gender is the most vivid reminder that one man alone is not self-sufficient, is not *the* human being, and cannot achieve a sense of completeness in any lasting reliable way. The limitedness, the inadequacy, the poverty of unaccommodated man on earth is painfully visible, for Stevens, when man actually touches woman and finds only temporary and incomplete satisfaction.

> They sang desiring an object that was near,
> In face of which desire no longer moved,
> Nor made of itself that which it could not find . . .   (*CP* 376)

Despite the many evocations of static fulfillment proffered in other lines from "Credences of Summer," those ellipsis dots in the above quotation mark Stevens' rueful awareness of the endlessness of desire. His unhappiness about this—unhappiness containing a portion of anger—causes stanza XXII of "Like Decorations in a Nigger Cemetery" to sound more like a curse than a blessing:

> The comedy of hollow sounds derives
> From truth and not from satire on our lives.
> Clog, therefore, purple Jack and crimson Jill.   (*CP* 154)

The purple of romance needs to be included in the recommended dance to help disguise the mere poor physicality of coupling or clogging. (To "clog" can mean to hinder, impede, obstruct; also, to satiate, surfeit, cloy; what Jack and Jill must do together will be irredeemably physical and unavoidably associated with hollowness.)

The evenhandedness of the phrase "purple Jack and crimson Jill" (and indeed the fact that in this case it is not Jill who is romantically empurpled nor Jack who is red-bloodedly carnal) provides occasion for agreeing with the reader who may have wished (many pages ago!) to point out that Stevens mostly doesn't individualize men as characters any more than he does women. For example, the great captain is no more human and no less symbolic than the maiden Bawda whom he weds in the "mystic marriage in Catawba" ("Notes Toward a Supreme Fiction": "It Must Give Pleasure" IV):

> The great captain loved the ever-hill Catawba
> And therefore married Bawda, whom he found there,
> And Bawda loved the captain as she loved the sun.
>
> They married well because the marriage-place
> Was what they loved. It was neither heaven nor hell.
> They were love's characters come face to face.   (*CP* 401)

Here Stevens' concern is to urge that each partner should marry real life, earthly reality, and love that reality in each other, or each other insofar as they are part of that reality. We feel Stevens' strong impulse to transfer (though he would not accept this verb) the focus of loving attention from the human lover to the environment, to Catawba. The male figure is as neglected, as reduced to a symbolic role, as the female figure. Thus there is a haunting touch of irony in the claim that they have "come face to face." They have no actual faces that we are helped to imagine, any more than Ozymandias and Nanzia Nunzio in another of Stevens' symbolic weddings ("It Must Change" VIII).

However, I would argue that a male reader of Stevens has more chances to feel represented, offered a complex image of self, than a female reader has. And this is not solely a matter of the male reader's being able to identify comfortably with the speaker of, say, a poem without characters like "The Man Whose Pharynx Was Bad" (*CP* 96) because the speaker is understood to be Mr. Wallace Stevens. The male reader, after all, "the ignorant man, alone," is the one who has a chance to marry "the sensual, pearly spouse" of life itself in "The Sense of the Sleight-of-Hand Man" (*CP* 222). He can enjoy identifying with the creativity of Ozymandias, notwithstanding Ozymandias' facelessness, when Ozymandias imaginatively weaves the "fictive covering" and makes the "spirit's diamond coronal" for his trembling passive bride, "the woman stripped more nakedly / Than nakedness . . ."(*CP* 396)[19] The male reader can discover himself on many pages of Stevens, in the image of a centrally important human being, even if the characterization is unelaborated. He can be the old sailor imaginatively catching tigers in red weather in "Disillusionment of Ten O'Clock" (*CP* 66) or the latest freed man getting up in the morning (*CP* 204–205) or the Englishman dying in Florence (*CP* 148–49) or the furious rabbi, the crying chieftain, and their central man in slouching pantaloons in "It Must Be Abstract" (*CP* 389) or Andrew Jackson Something and his grandfather in "The Lack of Repose" (*CP* 303). The solitary human being is typically conceived of by Stevens as male.[20] In Stevens, as many quotations in this chapter have shown, femininity is insistently associated with something being looked at rather than someone looking. No room is left for a woman's subjectivity by the man who writes, "A poet looks at the world as a man looks at a woman" (*OP* 165).

For him, a woman is at best a means, a means to facilitate a man's at-homeness in the world. This feeling, reflected in some of the poems discussed above, such as "The Hand as a Being," can also be detected in the following lines from "The Common Life," which complain against an unimaginative view of experience:

In this light a man is a result,
A demonstration, and a woman,
Without rose and without violet,

The shadows that are absent from Euclid,
Is not a woman for a man. (*CP* 221)

When things are put right, a woman will be profoundly useful for a man.

It is true that one of Stevens' first, most important, and perhaps most charming solitary protagonists is a woman, the brooder of "Sunday Morning." But even if we do not feel that the poet's relation to her in the poem is patronizing (as can be argued), Stevens was reluctant, as we see in a letter of 1928, to admit that her serious thinking could be connected with her femininity: "This is not essentially a woman's meditation on religion and the meaning of life. It is anybody's meditation."[21] In the world of his poetry, a believable woman with so much going on in her mind is intolerable. At the other end of Stevens' career we meet Penelope in "The World as Meditation" (*CP* 520). Is she a woman credited with a complex human mind and heart and with a challenging equity in the love relationship? The poem famously equivocates about the humanity of Penelope and Ulysses—"was it Ulysses? Or was it only the warmth of the sun / On her pillow?"—but surely only a very jaded Stevensian theorist can read this poem without feeling touched by the sense of yearning human lovers, and especially by the humanity of Penelope in her solitude:

She would talk a little to herself as she combed her hair,
Repeating his name with its patient syllables,
Never forgetting him that kept coming constantly so near. (*CP* 521)

That is why I see "The World as Meditation" as an extraordinary poem for Wallace Stevens to have achieved, and as one of his greatest poems.[22] What we need sadly to notice, though, is the condition in which Stevens has imagined his lovers, the condition in which he is willing to think about them and particularly about Penelope's humanly subjective (albeit passively waiting) self. Stevens selects the poignancy of solitude, caught between nostalgia for what once occurred ("they had met") and the perpetual incipience of what might occur if Ulysses ever gets home again. At the end of his great lonely oeuvre, Stevens is still unwilling to deal with that meeting.

Chapter Three

STEVENS AND SOLITUDE

The human

Revery is a solitude in which
We compose these propositions . . .

(*CP* 355)

I N CHAPTERS 1 and 2 we considered Stevens' treatment of two
special categories of interpersonal experience, and in both chapters we encountered the possibility that his evasions and denials
were based—cogently or not—on a sweeping claim that ultimately
there can be no true exchange of experience between any two human
beings, regardless of sexual attraction or the pull of sympathy. The
present chapter is intended to uncover and confront this premise
more directly.

References to solitude, and evocations of loneliness as emotional response to solitude, appear so chronically in Wallace Stevens' poetry
that the reader comes to expect them and perhaps to accept them
uncritically, since the poet usually seems so confident that the solitude
he alludes to is an undeniable fact of everyone's life and is, moreover,
an essential component (cause, effect, or both) of the poverty/revery
which he identifies as the modern human condition. I want to argue
that in his insistence on solitude Stevens takes too much for granted,
and that occasionally he lets the poetry admit that he has done so.[1]

If each of us is alone in the world—as is no doubt true *in some sense*—
the nature of our aloneness, the degree to which it is inviolable, remains a complicated matter. Like Stevens, we carry on every day, talking and writing, helping and competing and fighting and loving, as if
there were indeed elaborate and important connections between ourselves and other persons. It may be true to say that at the same time we
are, in some sense, alone, but everything depends on exploring that
"sense" and distinguishing it from other possible meanings. Stevens
often preferred to simplify the matter with radical assertions and
broad implications that mix together four different meanings of the
word *solitude*. We need to resist this mixing in order to resist Stevens'
inclination (in most, but not all, of his work) to present solitude as not

only necessary but good. We need to resist his inclination, I think, in order to locate and guard an opening which does exist in his poetry, an opening for the possibility of moral and convivial interaction with other persons. Without a belief in this possibility, both human life and poetry (the two are finally not separable for Stevens) are grotesquely diminished. So I feel, and I will suggest that Stevens some of the time felt so too.

To say that a person is "alone" can mean more than one thing. It can mean, simply, that no other person is physically present in the room, or in the house, or walking alongside our protagonist. More significantly, *alone* can mean that regardless of physical proximity or separation there is no emotional bond connecting the self with others in love or friendship or affiliation. Further, there is the philosophical idea of the inevitable solitude of each mind isolated within the shell of its imagining: one cannot know or connect with the other person, because one has only one's own imaginative perception of that person. This idea, which shows up often in Stevens, is an ontological proposition more radical than a statement of emotional aloneness; the latter condition can be deemed remediable (find a lover, find a friend, create the bond), except when it is seen as an effect of the irremediable condition of isolation within one's own mind. Finally, a fourth meaning of *alone* is important for Stevens: all humanity is alone in the universe without a god watching over us.

> We live in an old chaos of the sun,
> Or old dependency of day and night,
> Or island solitude, unsponsored, free,
> Of that wide water, inescapable.   (*CP* 70)

The third and fourth kinds of solitude, which we may call ontological and cosmic, have been involved in so many commentaries on Stevens that a reader might suppose all references by Stevens to solitude are explainable in philosophical or antitheological terms. But in the world Stevens describes, the more practical, remediable kinds of solitude (physical and emotional aloneness) also signify. As we have seen in the preceding chapters, some of the poetry acknowledges that the pain of isolation, and also the pleasure of isolation, arise in a life in which solitude *can* be altered, relieved, escaped, or relinquished.[2] This truth, however, is deeply disturbing to Stevens—because if people *can* be together, then a host of vexing questions about *how* they should be together (questions that vex the Eliot of "La Figlia Che Piange") come clamorously into the picture. These are questions Stevens mostly does not wish to address in poetry; they threaten to complicate unbearably the finding of "what will suffice" for unreligious twentieth-century life, which is the great task Stevens assigned himself. Hence, Stevens was inclined to invite us to conflate all four kinds of aloneness into one condition, that condition to be unquestioningly acknowledged as a philosophical and/or (the haziness of this "and/or" is Stevens', not mine) post-Christian inevitability. He was comforted by the implication that a man physically alone and emotionally alone is really just an obvious illustration or literalization of the constant reality of man's ontological and cosmic aloneness, and that a person's wishes for relationship with other persons are thus misguided and not susceptible of fulfillment by any act of will.

Because of the conflative tendency just described, it is hard to show in a given instance that the solitude at issue is practical and remediable, since Stevens will usually have made it easy to interpret the solitude as absolute, a result not of misfortune or choice but of a principle of human existence. In the famously and beautifully tantalizing late poem "The World as Meditation," we are led to yearn for the reunion of loyal lovers, Penelope and Ulysses, and we are moved by the way the poem honors Penelope's loving patience and hope and fidelity:

> She has composed, so long, a self with which to welcome him,
> Companion to his self for her, which she imagined,
> Two in a deep-founded sheltering, friend and dear friend.   (*CP* 521)

The stanza includes, but is not controlled by, the idea that the lover can know only her imagined recreation of the beloved; this idea does not prevent the stanza, and other phrases in the poem, from conveying a powerful auspicious sense of the real possibility that these lovers can, with good fortune, be together. Indeed at one point the poem affirms that they have come together: "Yet they had met, / Friend and dear friend and a planet's encouragement." If so, then we would seem to be dealing with a world in which solitude need not be total or permanent and may be escaped. However, Stevens undoes this romantic encouragement in two ways. First, he counterbalances "they had met" with the final stanza's implication that the meeting must remain forever potential, not actual:

> She would talk a little to herself as she combed her hair,
> Repeating his name with its patient syllables,
> Never forgetting him that kept coming constantly so near.

Second, he counteracts our sense of the human individuality of Penelope and Ulysses—a sense which the poem has deliberately solicited—with an elusive but dominant sense that Penelope and Ulysses are not persons but elements of a metaphor about the relation between the imagination and a sense of life on earth as livable and beneficent and good.[3] By these means Stevens has given a wonderfully affecting picture of that relation, but we must notice that he has managed to do this in a way that seems to discredit the possibility of actual contact between human lovers present to one another in a complex interaction. No sooner does he give us Penelope and Ulysses as individual human lovers than he takes them away, resolving them into principles or forces, shutting them within the vehicle of his metaphor, so that their separation comes to seem a given in the nature of earthly life. Thus Stevens evades the mystery of the togetherness of two persons.

It is an evasion that might be felt as very consoling by a person, a reader, alone against his or her will. "There is really no other way to be," the poem says to such a reader. Because of his need to provide such consolation (even if the need is not candidly confessed), Stevens is a great poet of solitude—of practical solitude, the kind that a particular person can choose by avoiding other persons, the kind also that he or she can feel chosen by if other persons are avoiding him or her. Stevens is a poet of both happy chosen aloneness and loneliness. These emotional realities had sufficient force in his spirit to survive his tendency to sublimate them into philosophical universals. Loneliness informs especially the poems concerning a female beloved, an "inamorata" whose status as individual person is nearly always rendered dubious, like the status of Ulysses.[4] Loneliness also finds expression in a few misanthropic poems such as "Loneliness in Jersey City" and "Outside of Wedlock" (*OP* 76). In "Palace of the Babies" Stevens' protagonist is isolated from a community of people who sleep peacefully together thanks to their shared faith in angels, "Drawn close by dreams of fledgling wing . . . because night nursed them in its fold." The loneliness afflicting this unreligious protagonist is not an inevitable ontological condition, since it has been escaped by the "babies" in their communal palace.

> Night nursed not him in whose dark mind
> The clambering wings of birds of black revolved,
> Making harsh torment of the solitude.
>
> The walker in the moonlight walked alone,
> And in his heart his disbelief lay cold.
> His broad-brimmed hat came close upon his eyes.   (*CP* 77)

As Milton J. Bates has observed, this character's inability to see what the others see results from a choice made, a choice arising from individual personality: "The disbeliever trims his thinking to the cut of his hat; he will not expose his eyes to illusory 'moonlight.' Besides restricting his vision, his mental haberdashery leaves him isolated and, ironically, benighted."[5]

But Stevens is more willing to allow the experience of practical solitude to be manifest as something desirable and commendable than as something regrettable or unwisely sought.[6] The desire to find such solitude desirable is what animates "Gallant Château," whose speaker tries to affirm an inner life from which other persons, who *might* have been disturbingly present, now are absent.

GALLANT CHATEAU

Is it bad to have come here
And to have found the bed empty?

One might have found tragic hair,
Bitter eyes, hands hostile and cold.

There might have been a light on a book
Lighting a pitiless verse or two.

There might have been the immense solitude
Of the wind upon the curtains.

Pitiless verse? A few words tuned
And tuned and tuned and tuned.

It is good. The bed is empty,
The curtains are stiff and prim and still.   (*CP* 161)

In this cryptic poem Stevens evokes a gallantry, a nobility achieved by the person who can tolerate the absence of others. Within his windless interior (a château built by the same architect who designed the spiritual hotel of "Arrival at the Waldorf"), this hero recognizes the undesirability of others with their disquieting hair, eyes, hands; he has closed the window, or chosen a shuttered room, so that the only presences are his own thoughts and the poetry that is his private, solitary labor.[7] By sequestering himself the imaginer has bravely, or stoically, sharpened his focus on his ongoing imaginative work ("tuned and tuned and tuned").

Similarly, the man most profoundly attuned to earthly existence, which he rediscovers after a trip to the moon in section VII of "Extracts From Addresses to the Academy of Fine Ideas," will be a man undistracted by any woman:

And then returning from the moon, if one breathed
The cold evening, without any scent or the shade
Of any woman, . . .

. . . if then
One breathed the cold evening, the deepest inhalation
Would come from that return to the subtle centre.   (*CP* 258)

Celebrating this healthy respiration, Stevens finds it necessary to explicitly quarantine his patient away from "the shade / Of any woman," as if exposure to her (and to questions about how to relate to her) would inevitably induce shortness of breath and damage or even destroy the breather's at-homeness on earth. It may be objected that Stevens has hypothesized "the exactest poverty," a condition thoroughly divested of contingent earthly pleasures (such as romantic love and maternal love), and that this hypothesizing of an extreme case is the reason why no woman is allowed into the protagonist's experience. But what I point out is that the poem contrives to suggest that the inhalation achieved in the absence of any woman is deeper than if she were present.

"Anglais Mort à Florence" laments the diminishment and final loss of its protagonist's power to "stand alone" not only physically but spiritually, as the time approaches when he must merge into the majesty of death.

> He stood at last by God's help and the police;
> But he remembered the time when he stood alone.
> He yielded himself to that single majesty;
>
> But he remembered the time when he stood alone,
> When to be and delight to be seemed to be one,
> Before the colors deepened and grew small.   (CP 149)

I think the presence of the police is enough to suggest that this Englishman dying in Florence is relinquishing a social aloneness chosen in a world of possible human contacts, and not merely the perpetual unchosen aloneness of every separate consciousness. What matters in this moving poem is the fierce pride about self-sufficient solitude, pride that makes the help of other people (represented here only by policemen who pose no threat of intimacy) tolerable only as a last resort.[8]

This strong feeling that the self's best hours can come only with drastic separation from other selves emerges often when Stevens tries to describe a happy state. (But not always; see sections V and XII of "Esthétique du Mal," discussed later in this chapter.) For Crispin, the minds of others are contaminants to be washed away:

> What was the purpose of his pilgrimage,
> Whatever shape it took in Crispin's mind,
> If not, when all is said, to drive away
> The shadow of his fellows from the skies,
> And, from their stale intelligence released,
> To make a new intelligence prevail?   (CP 37)

All fools must be slaughtered before the mind can lay by its trouble
and marry itself to the health of summer, season of ripe centered vitality.[9] In "Sailing After Lunch," in order to feel a refreshed romantic
relation to life one will need to be alone,

> To expunge all people and be a pupil
> Of the gorgeous wheel and so to give
> That slight transcendence to the dirty sail,
> By light, the way one feels, sharp white,
> And then rush brightly through the summer air.　　　　(CP 121)

Those lines can be heard as jubilantly hopeful or pathetically wistful.
Either way, I note again that if other people need to be expunged—
surely there is violent emotion behind the choice of this verb, though
the poem does not address this emotion—then they must be, in some
important way, not absent.

In another mood, when the self cannot muster the energy to rush
brightly through the summer air alone, the world is a "dwindled
sphere" in which others cannot be avoided and contact with their in-
glorious actuality is associated with the encroachment of death:

> Each person completely touches us
> With what he is and as he is,
> In the stale grandeur of annihilation.　　　　(CP 505)

One way to deal with the discomfort caused by other selves rubbing
against one's own is to assert that such rubbing is an illusion, that contact between persons is ultimately impossible, because the world is
meditation. We noted this proposition as one of the meanings proffered by "The World as Meditation," and the idea—solipsism as inevitable, whether prison or palace—can be pointed out in many Stevens
poems, such as "Tea at the Palaz of Hoon" and "Hymn From a Watermelon Pavilion"; but, interestingly, it is almost never taken up as an
issue to be debated. Instead it is allowed to coast along as an assumption (whose philosophical basis Stevens could have found in Nietzsche
or Walter Pater or F. H. Bradley, among others),[10] and then occasionally, in passages to be discussed later, gets undercut radically. Relationship or nonrelationship with other persons is a topic about which
Stevens likes to be impressively decisive or swiftly cryptic; he prefers
not to focus on it as an issue.

"The Poem That Took the Place of a Mountain" is a late poem that
keeps aloft, in a spirit of sober pride, the idea of ontological (inevitable,
unchosen) solitude as a beneficent condition which can be accepted
with grace and courage, much the way "Gallant Château" affirmed an
acceptance of practical solitude by means of the endless tuning of po-

etry. A poem gives the protagonist a private world (not a château this time but, with a greater sense of there being nothing else, a mountain) in which to fulfill himself and rest:

> It reminded him how he had needed
> A place to go to in his own direction,
>
> How he had recomposed the pines,
> Shifted the rocks and picked his way among clouds,
>
> For the outlook that would be right,
> Where he would be complete in an unexplained completion:
>
> The exact rock where his inexactnesses
> Would discover, at last, the view toward which they had edged,
>
> Where he could lie and, gazing down at the sea,
> Recognize his unique and solitary home.   (*CP* 512)

Stevens here takes for granted both the rightness and the necessity of the word "solitary" in the last line; the poem contains no argued reason why his mountainside could not be populated by neighbors, friends and lovers (or, if we must defer to the idea that all experience is imagined, then versions of neighbors, versions of friends, versions of lovers). Nor does the poem's celebration of individuality demand the word *solitary*, for the uniqueness of a man's imaginative existence does not presuppose its removal from other unique imaginative existences. In other words, the poem could have celebrated the poet's creative difference from others without erasing all others from the scene. So the protagonist's home is characterized as solitary because of Stevens' pressing desire to connect satisfaction with the idea of inevitable solitude.

"It reminded him how he had needed / A place to go to in his own direction"—and emphatically *not* in someone else's direction (his own father's, or Eliot's, or William Carlos Williams' for example). Despite this implication, which to my ear is unmistakable, there is a reply to what I have said about "The Poem That Took the Place of a Mountain," a reply which many praisers and interpreters of Stevens would volunteer, calling upon the idea that the poem's protagonist is not just Wallace Stevens, nor indeed any one man, but rather a representative person, a figure representing all human beings, each of whom lives out essentially the same life on the "mountain" of his or her own imagining. According to this idea, since all imaginers participate in the same fundamental process, the important thing is to describe that process ("How he had recomposed the pines" and so forth) without getting distracted by tiny differences between individual instances of The

Person, The Poet. After all, the essential experience of all others (neighbors, friends, lovers, and presumably enemies too) will be implicit in the account of the protagonist's experience; hence they are in effect subsumed into the one figure of the imaginer.[11] His solitude in the poem's last line must then be understood not as a social condition but a cosmic one.

For Stevens, a great attraction of this idea is that it permits him to write about only one person, a solitary self, while taking credit for writing about all selves. He can place one actor alone on stage and still bill the play as a vast extravaganza, a "world" or "planet." He can claim to express all of society by showing one mind working:

> The whirling noise

> Of a multitude dwindles, all said,
> To his breath that lies awake at night.   (*CP* 171)

This sentence from section XII of "The Man With the Blue Guitar" may be felt to express a courageously existentialist sense of how each individual, in his or her own struggle toward understanding and health, epitomizes and thus in a way lives for, and chooses for, all of humanity as it seeks its as-yet-undefined earthly sufficiency. But let us not swallow too quickly the reductiveness of the sentence quoted. How much is buried in the phrase "all said"? The whirling noise of the multitude of persons is composed of many voices, some of them— Stalin, Hitler, Roosevelt, John Steinbeck, T. S. Eliot, Greta Garbo, Ethel Waters, Rita Hayworth—sounding rather different from that of the poet lying awake in Connecticut. It must be a drastic dwindling whereby this rich human cacophony comes to be expressed in the breath of the solitary man.

What we need warily to notice here is the comfortable cooperation between two ideas whose logical relation is at best elusive and seems indeed to be a relation of contradiction: the idea of centrality (there is an essence common to all persons, which can be metaphorically imagined as one man, a "central man," "Who in a million diamonds sums us up"),[12] and the idea of ontological solitude (each person is essentially alone forever). The centrality idea, we may concede, partly arises from and promotes a true spirit of humanist solidarity—as we saw in chapter 1, an ultimate test of this proposition is provided by the "soldier of time" section in "Esthétique du Mal," which is poignant for Harold Bloom and maudlin for Helen Vendler—but it is also an idea very convenient for a writer who dislikes the range of problems that develop whenever two or more persons are in any sense together or present in the same scene. The "central man," by being everyone, succeeds in being alone:

He breathed in crystal-pointed change the whole
Experience of night, as if he breathed
A consciousness from solitude, inhaled
A freedom out of silver-shaping size,
Against the whole experience of day.   (*CP* 298)

These lines from "Chocorua to Its Neighbor" describe a manlike being who arises from the minds of all men, "beyond their life, yet of themselves / Excluding by his largeness their defaults" (*CP* 299). Stevens endows this figure with an aura of sublime cleanness ("crystal-pointed," "silver-shaping"), and the quoted stanza rather candidly indicates why: the animating oxygen of this figure's existence derives "from solitude"; he has been cleansed of the countless irritating, small distinctions among persons. Such distinctions, of whatever flavor or tendency, are felt by the voice of the poem to be objectionable facts, "defaults" which need to be excluded for the sake of the central figure's high freedom and radiance. Pungencies such as those of "the roller of big cigars" (*CP* 64) and "the negro undertaker" (*CP* 47) seem to have been scrubbed from his superbody. There are phrases in "Chocorua to Its Neighbor" that could be cited to argue that the "megalfrere" *includes* and somehow elevates all individual selves, but what I want to take note of is that Stevens finds it both necessary and pleasurable to express the nobility of the central figure in terms of exclusivity and isolation. Again I suggest that if you desire a landscape in which one man can be somehow very important while he stands peacefully alone, safe from the whirling noise of other people, an attractive strategy is to declare that your solitary man somehow contains or represents all those whose particularity you have wiped away.

In section VIII of "Things of August," Stevens postulates a happy epiphany of the union of all selves in the central man, "the impersonal person"; but as the word "impersonal" and the reference to "a solitude of the self" and the invocations of timelessness and forgetfulness all reveal, the emotional goal of the epiphany is not really a uniting of many selves together but rather a vanishing of other selves, a relief from multiplicity. Thus it is nearly impossible to imagine another person sitting beside Stevens on the park bench:

When was it that the particles became
The whole man, that tempers and beliefs became
Temper and belief and that differences lost
Difference and were one? It had to be
In the presence of a solitude of the self,
An expanse and the abstraction of an expanse,
A zone of time without the ticking of clocks,

A color that moved us with forgetfulness.
When was it that we heard the voice of union?

Was it as we sat in the park and the archaic form
Of a woman with a cloud on her shoulder rose
Against the trees and then against the sky
And the sense of the archaic touched us at once
In a movement of the outlines of similarity?
We resembled one another at the sight.
The forgetful color of the autumn day
Was full of these archaic forms, giants
Of sense, evoking one thing in many men,
Evoking an archaic space, vanishing
In the space, leaving an outline of the size
Of the impersonal person, the wanderer,
The father, the ancestor, the bearded peer,
The total of human shadows bright as glass.   (*CP* 494)

Stevens postulates union and inclusion, but in fact wants a purity "bright as glass" via exclusion.

The contradiction between the two artificially yoked impulses here can be seen more sharply with the help of D. H. Lawrence in his wonderfully ambivalent and partly sarcastic overview of Whitman. Lawrence praises Whitman's openness to encounter (a very un-Stevensian aspect of Whitman), but can't bear Whitman's claim to incorporate whatever he encounters:

> All that false exuberance. All those lists of things boiled in one pudding-cloth! No, no!
> I don't want all those things inside me, thank you.
> "I reject nothing," says Walt.
> If that is so, one might be a pipe open at both ends, so everything runs through.
> Post-mortem effects.
> "I embrace ALL," says Whitman. "I weave all things into myself."
> Do you really! There can't be much left of *you* when you've done. When you've cooked the awful pudding of One Identity.[13]

To make one's soul the great American melting pot, Lawrence sees, is to make an infinite alloy in which no soul or self can be significantly itself. Lawrence goes on to contend that Whitman's effort, in this regard, is not only unappealing but basically mistaken about what one's soul is for: "The soul wishes to keep clean and whole. The soul's deepest will is to preserve its own integrity, against the mind and the whole mass of disintegrating forces."[14] This yearning for separate intactness is, as we have seen, a strong force in Stevens, but he sometimes wanted to disguise or evade—or, at his best, to counteract—the isolationist and even misanthropic tendency of this yearning by way of Whitmanesque notions of a self that could include all selves. Emotionally, though he lacked Lawrence's zest for soul-shaping conflict between selves, Stevens was still closer to the radical individualism of Lawrence than to the euphorically expansive panhumanism of Whitman. But Stevens had important misgivings about the costs, moral and emotional, of solitary individualism, and these misgivings contribute crucially to the value of his poetry, as I will argue in the second half of this chapter.

First let me give one further example of the mystification Stevens floats into when he needs to skirt the issue of whether a person should try to be *with* others or not. In the second section of "The Sail of Ulysses," Stevens describes a beneficent state of mind which seems to amount to a mood of deep confidence in one's own perceptions and ideas. The comfort of this state of mind is expressed, in the fifth, sixth and seventh lines of the section, as comfort provided by a loving friend. But Stevens permits this metaphor only under auspices established by the section's first two lines, which insist that the "luminous companion" is *only* metaphorical, not a human other:

There is a human loneliness,
A part of space and solitude,
In which knowledge cannot be denied,
In which nothing of knowledge fails,
The luminous companion, the hand,
The fortifying arm, the profound
Response, the completely answering voice,
That which is more than anything else
The right within us and about us,
Joined, the triumphant vigor, felt,
The inner direction on which we depend,
That which keeps us the little that we are,
The aid of greatness to be and the force.   (*OP* 100)

As with the phrase "unique and solitary home" at the end of the "The Poem That Took the Place of a Mountain," there is something gratuitous about the emphasis on "loneliness" and "solitude" in the section's opening lines. Behind these lines lie the vague but pervasive convictions of ontological solitude (you can't know me; I can't know you; hence there can be no real contact between us) and cosmic solitude (no God watches over us) that are given a largely uncontested sovereignty in Stevens' oeuvre.[15] Why, after all, could the condition "In which knowledge cannot be denied" not be characterized without reference to solitude? Why indeed could the condition not be imagined as in some way a social condition? Once again Stevens has touchingly expressed a desire for a human touch ("the hand, / The fortifying arm") in terms that imply a premature relinquishing of the possibility that such touching can take place between two persons.

If the account I have so far given were the whole story of Stevens' relation to the subject of solitude, he would still, I suppose, be a great poet of the subject, because of the depth of feeling in most of the poems I've mentioned, such as "Anglais Mort à Florence" ("he remembered the time when he stood alone"). But the greatness would be of a very narrow kind. Since the aversion to human company runs so deep in Stevens,[16] some readers have thought it right to honor him by admiring his consistency, suggesting that he departs from his declaration of the self's aloneness, and from approval of that aloneness, only in negligible aberrations. Helen Vendler writes:

> Solitude, not society, is his subject as poet, whatever he may have felt as man, and he remains always a poet of "the organic consolation, the complete / Society of the spirit when it is / Alone."[17]

And of "Notes Toward a Supreme Fiction," Vendler remarks:

> One signal claim relinquished by the poem is any overt social or human connection. The introduction, as Stevens tells us . . . , has "nothing to do with Mr. Church" to whom the poem is dedicated—it is addressed to the interior paramour, and signifies Stevens' final acceptance of his remorseless, if involuntary, isolation from the human world . . . In ceasing to attempt the poetry of human relation, Stevens becomes, paradoxically, most human.[18]

But these statements by Vendler wrap up the subject too quickly. She is attracted to the stoicism in Stevens, and thus perhaps disinclined to attach any importance to the moments when Stevens realizes that his removal from other persons is unsatisfactory and, moreover, unnecessary. He does have such moments, and they make him more interesting than a poet who settles for the idea that the self is always and inevitably alone. Just as part of Stevens knew that a wounded soldier experiences something sharper than the general *mal* of secular existence, and that a beautiful woman amounts to more than either a physical stimulus or a sublime idea, part of Stevens knew that solitude is not the whole story.

Another famously isolated poet, Emily Dickinson, also knew this. Before turning to evidence that Stevens felt human interaction (and here I mean interaction more significant than mere blind friction and irritating imposition) to be possible—a truth fleetingly acknowledged in the phrase "Yet they had met" in "The World as Meditation"—it may be helpful to see that this possibility is not always relinquished even in a poetry so stringently devoted to truths of deprivation as to sometimes make Stevens' "poverty" seem by comparison a very tranquil and tolerable condition.

Dickinson, like Stevens, dwells mainly on the absence of some fulfillment associated with the image of a beloved other; and though for Dickinson the other is often divine (God or Christ), he is also often a human lover who is somehow out of reach. As we have seen, Stevens frequently responds to such isolation from a desirable other by implying that it can bring a fulfillment preferable to the fulfillment of contact with the other. Another move, made by Stevens in sadly beautiful poems such as "Ghosts as Cocoons," "The Hand as a Being," "Debris of Life and Mind," and "The Woman in Sunshine," is to transform the appeal of an actual woman (so disturbingly physical and other) into the munificence of a feminine spirit or "sense" which can be satisfyingly present to him in a rightly imagined natural landscape. A similar preference for an imagined lover over a real and available one can be found in some Dickinson poems too (see for instance poems 518 and 679 in Johnson's edition), which is not surprising, since she like Stevens is above all in love with her own power of imagination. However, a great strength in Dickinson's work is her piercing expression of the pain of separation from the beloved, pain which often replaces or overwhelms the pleasures of sublimation. (I think especially of poems 509, 511, 523, 570, 640, 725, 734.) There is a candor in this which is not among Stevens' chief virtues. Stevens is gripped by the wish that poetry, as a way of life, can eventually smooth away all pain or at least make it thoroughly tolerable. In Dickinson there is, instead, a fierce sense of the satisfaction of poetry as something that competes with, but does not expunge, the agony of loneliness.

Moreover—and this is the point we need here—the agony of loneliness in Dickinson is pain in response to a felt *possibility* that has remained unrealized for the yearning lover. Despite her profound awareness of gulfs between persons, Dickinson knows that meaningful contact can occur; one's solitude is not ontologically pure, and that is why it can be excruciating. Dickinson's delicate allowance for the possibility of contact between minds can be traced in meditative poems such as "I measure every Grief I meet" (561) and "His mind of man, a secret makes" (1663).[19] But her more frankly credulous (if I can use the word without pejorative connotation) testimony to the reality of human interaction comes in love poems. Here is poem 568:

We learned the Whole of Love—
The Alphabet—the Words—

A Chapter—then the mighty Book—
Then—Revelation closed—

But in Each Other's eyes
An Ignorance beheld—
Diviner than the Childhood's—
And each to each, a Child—

Attempted to expound
What Neither—understood—
Alas, that Wisdom is so large—
And Truth—so manifold![20]

The lovers in this poem may remain largely unknown to one another, or in any case there is much that remains unknown to them, but the poem does not posit this ignorance as the only important truth about their encounter. Instead the poem expresses excitement about the variety and richness of the truths that inform their relationship—excitement both about truths already learned (in the action of the first stanza) and truths not yet grasped. The encounter between two persons here has not been a mere brutal bumping nor has it been merely a new proof of the self's isolation; the encounter has been, rather, productive and invigorating. It has produced a shared learning from the Book of Love, and a discovery of each other's remaining ignorance, and a childlike optimistic effort to push ahead into new understanding. Admittedly, the poem laments—"Alas"—the infinity of what needs to be known about relationship, but the note of lament is less important to the poem's tone than the note of wonder. Two persons have found remarkable things in each other, and they feel that much more may still be found.

In "I could suffice for Him, I knew—" (643), Dickinson presents the possibility of profound interaction not so much as a wonderful exploration but more as an alarming challenge. Profound interaction is very much a possibility, offering a kind of wholeness in which one's special incompleteness, cherished in solitude, will be given up; the proposition calls for the most delicate weighing, precisely because a kind of union, or conjunction, with the other person is drastically feasible.

I could suffice for Him, I knew—
He—could suffice for Me—
Yet Hesitating Fractions—Both
Surveyed Infinity—

"Would I be Whole" He sudden broached—
My syllable rebelled—

'Twas face to face with Nature—forced—
'Twas face to face with God—

Withdrew the Sun—to Other Wests—
Withdrew the furthest Star
Before Decision—stooped to speech—
And then—be audibler

The Answer of the Sea unto
The Motion of the Moon—
Herself adjust Her Tides—unto—
Could I—do else—with Mine?[21]

The metaphor of sea responding helplessly to moon may imply that love has succeeded in destroying the speaker's autonomy (though I think a less violent, more playful reading is solicited by the last stanza's account of whispered acquiescence). If so, still this loss is counterbalanced by the promise of mutual sufficing, and both results reflect the reality of the contact between persons. Dickinson's poem "Again—his voice is at the door—" (663) blazes with the thrill of such contact as an experience that deepens minute by minute. (The poem apparently narrates her first meeting with Reverend Charles Wadsworth in Amherst in 1860.)[22] Their conversation and their stroll together are so charged with meaning and joy for both persons (the poem assumes this mutuality of feeling) that they begin with a shy, anxious sounding of each other's depths—depths which are *not* unfathomable—and proceed into a condition so manifestly shared that the word *alone* becomes an opportunity for jubilant irony.

We talk in *careless*—and in *toss*—
A kind of *plummet* strain—
Each—sounding—shyly—
Just—how—deep—
The *other's* one—had been—

We *walk*—I leave my Dog—at home—
A *tender—thoughtful* Moon
Goes with us—just a little way—
And—then—we are *alone*—

Alone—if *Angels* are "alone"—
First time they *try* the *sky*!
Alone—if those "veiled faces"—be—
We cannot *count*—on High![23]

This exaltation is social; the two people have provided each other with a certainty that they are not alone. (Meanwhile the speaker's poor dog *is* alone, left behind. The physical dog's delightful absence helps confirm our sense that the poem deals with the actual mutual presence of two persons.)

The point of showing that Dickinson could so confidently express the reality of important interaction between persons is not to prove that she is more honest than Stevens or greater than Stevens. She may be both—especially if, as I suppose, self-awareness about, and energetic engagement with, the whole range of one's strong emotions are likely constituents of greatness. But my purpose here is only to establish that a poet for whom separation and deprivation were profoundly necessary subjects still made room in her work for experiences which reveal that separation and deprivation are not absolute universal conditions. Dickinson was less of a theorist than Stevens—though Stevens was aware that theory hardens truth into falsehood and that "It can never be satisfied, the mind, never" (*CP* 247)—and more willing to live in and endure the emotions that generated each poem. Though Dickinson is a teacher, she is not a systematic teacher. Dickinson did not take upon herself a prophetic task, a project of explaining how life can be wisely lived, and her poems do not try to add up to such an explanation. Stevens' kind of greatness is inseparable from his efforts to do such prophetic, explanatory work for his entire culture; for this purpose his poems would, he hoped, gather into a harmonious whole. The project—though he pursued it with wonderful fluctuations and ambiguous undulations—pressed him to convert personal and temporary experiences, such as loneliness, estrangement, and solitude, into universal truths. Concomitantly, each poem, though it might have been prompted by a particular experience, was under pressure to show itself as *the* poem, an instance of the same perpetually reenacted dance of imagination with reality. In view of these ambitions and pressures, we can see why a man who often experienced a wide gap between himself and other persons (and often cherished the gap) might write poems implying that the self is always and everywhere alone.

However, Stevens occasionally does acknowledge the countertruth that we have seen vividly affirmed by Dickinson. Passages quoted earlier in this chapter—from "Anglais Mort à Florence," "The Comedian as the Letter C," "Sailing After Lunch," and "Lebensweisheitspielerei"—show a regretful and grudging acknowledgment by Stevens that contact with others can happen (though not necessarily at a depth of emotional significance) if it is not successfully avoided.

What about less negative acknowledgments? Stevens' edginess about the subject, and his edgy admission that it *is* a subject, can be heard in a letter to Barbara Church in 1952. He explains that he does not want a summer vacation trip—"I have never liked going to the places to which other people go or doing the things they do"—but soon he adds:

> The truth is that one gets out of contact with people during the summer and feels the immense need (of which one is not conscious in other seasons) of people for other people, a thing that has been in my thoughts for a long time, in one form or another. I suppose there's a word for it. Poe liked to analyze his feelings in crowds. What I have in mind is not the old idea that the world without other people would be unbearable, but almost that: the pull between people.[24]

We notice that he holds open the possibility that the world without other people could be bearable, but at least there is a recognition here of a magnetism between persons in summer. In his poetry a comparably unimpassioned suggestion that something good might arise from social interaction comes cryptically in section XLIX of "Like Decorations in a Nigger Cemetery":

> It needed the heavy nights of drenching weather
> To make him return to people, to find among them
> Whatever it was that he found in their absence,
> A pleasure, an indulgence, an infatuation.   (*CP* 158)

Rainstorms, spoiling the sunny landscape enjoyed by solitary men in poems like "Sailing After Lunch" and "Nomad Exquisite," drive this protagonist toward social life. The passage does not go so far as to declare that "among them" means "by way of relationship with them," though, nor does the passage affirm that the return to people leads to benefits unavailable in solitude.

In "Wild Ducks, People and Distances" Stevens recognizes a value in the presence of others, but it is a bleak and chilly value. To live in a socialized world of villages is to be protected from the starkness of the gap between humanity and nature ("a place / That is not our own and, much more, not ourselves" [*CP* 383]), protection needful because we are not Snow Men and cannot participate in the wild ducks' unreflective unambivalent "migrations to solitude." The socialized man has to live in

> The weather of other lives, from which there could
>
> Be no migrating. It was that they were there
> That held the distances off: the villages
> Held off the final, fatal distances,
> Between us and the place in which we stood.   (*CP* 329)

Not exactly an anthem to municipal festivity! Stevens is profoundly wary about hoping for too much from other people.[25]

This wariness is matched by his defensiveness about the hopes or demands for a social content that other people might bring to his poetry. In his essay "Effects of Analogy" (1948), Stevens argues energetically that a poet is chosen by his subject and thus cannot be fairly expected to take up another subject. Significantly, Stevens proposes to rehabilitate the image of the ivory tower in defending the integrity of an isolated poet committed to his own "congenital" subject, which may not be, Stevens pointedly insists, "the community and other people":

> The truth is that a man's sense of the world dictates his subjects to him and that this sense is derived from his personality, his temperament, over which he has little control and possibly none, except superficially. It is not a literary problem. It is the problem of his mind and nerves. These sayings are another form of the saying that poets are born not made. A poet writes of twilight because he shrinks from noon-day. He writes about the country because he dislikes the city . . . So seen, the poet and his subject are inseparable. There are stresses that he invites; there are stresses that he avoids. . . .
>
> Recently, a very great deal has been said about the relation of the poet to his community and to other people, and as the propaganda on behalf of the community and other people gathers momentum a great deal more will be said. But if a poet's subject is congenital this is beside the point. Or is it? The ivory tower was offensive if the man who lived in it wrote, there, of himself for himself. It was not offensive if he used it because he could do nothing without concentration, as no one can, and because, there, he could most effectively struggle to get at his subject, even if his subject happened to be the community and other people, and nothing else.[26]

Stevens is quite persuasively excusing himself from the job of writing about human relationships; at the same time, though, he suggests that the poet should not write solely "of himself for himself," and that there *is* a poetry of "the community and other people" for someone to write.[27]

The fifth section of "Esthétique du Mal" is a startling attempt to write that poetry, or at least to incorporate that poetry's material within the author's secular vision. "Esthétique du Mal" is a disjointed and somewhat evasive poem and thus disappointing as a whole, but in some of its oddities Stevens breaks free from the sleek ensolacings of his habitual manner. Section V surprises the Stevensian reader by focusing on love in a spirit that is neither defensively sardonic nor defensively sublimatory. Stevens here has the courage to summarize a great realm of human experience which his poetry has studiously dodged. For once, the actuality celebrated is not a matter of relation between a lone viewer and trees or ducks but of relations between persons.

> Softly let all true sympathizers come,
> Without the inventions of sorrow or the sob
> Beyond invention. Within what we permit,
> Within the actual, the warm, the near,
> So great a unity, that it is bliss,
> Ties us to those we love. For this familiar,
> This brother even in the father's eye,
> This brother half-spoken in the mother's throat
> And these regalia, these things disclosed,
> These nebulous brilliancies in the smallest look
> Of the being's deepest darling, we forego
> Lament, willingly forfeit the ai-ai
>
> Of parades in the obscurer selvages.   (CP 317)

For a moment here, with this ode to family intimacy, Stevens ventures to write the poetry he was not born to write. His critics are understandably nonplussed. Harold Bloom calls the section "amazingly tender" and congestedly remarks, "I do not think that the judgment of any critic here can be purely cognitive in its determinations, and I for one am very moved."[28] Helen Vendler, however, calls the speaker of section V "this mawkish votary of love" and notes that its most intense language is devoted to the divinities ("distant heads," "golden forms") that have supposedly been foregone.[29] I would have to agree that section V is not Stevens' finest hour in terms of richness, resonance, complexity of emotional truth. He treads very gingerly in this realm of human intimacy, as if sensing that his poetry is not at home here, protecting himself from the glare of all it has neglected by means of rhetorical difficulties ("This brother half-spoken in the mother's throat," "the services / Of central sense"). Still, he does not shy away from such phrases as "dear relation," "Be near me, come closer, touch my hand"—nor does he contrive to imply that these relations are illusory.

> Be near me, come closer, touch my hand, phrases
> Compounded of dear relation, spoken twice,
> Once by the lips, once by the services
> Of central sense, these minutiae mean more
> Than clouds, benevolences, distant heads.   (CP 317)

At this point Stevens harnesses his celebration of family love to his tireless campaign against religion, and we ride back into normal Stevens country for the remainder of section V. But we have seen an acknowledgment of the reality and value of "dear relation" which Stevens' more typical poetry should not make us forget.

If the acknowledgment is awkwardly generalized, and generalized in a way open to the charge of triteness, this is not only further evidence (along with the rarity of references to "dear relation" in Stevens) that human interaction is not a congenital subject for him; it is also an important reminder to us that there is much work to be done in exploring the nature of this "in-bar" realm where "true sympathizers" interact. The inadequacy of section V is valuable because it helps us wake up to the fact that the world of Stevens' poetry is not our whole world. (Only a great poet can put us under a spell from which we thus need to wake.) We notice that it is not enough to say "So great a unity, that it is bliss, / Ties us to those we love." The loves that we experience are not continuously blissful and are in fact checkered with fear, mistrust, jealousy, vanity, competition, rage, and weariness. Where there is unity in family love, it is an interesting kind of unity that incorporates and transcends such discords. One of the poetries we need, a poetry not feasible for Stevens, is a poetry that explores such entanglement.

Since Stevens' death in 1955, the postmodern reaction to modernism has of course involved much turning toward the personal and the local—one thinks immediately of *Heart's Needle* by Snodgrass, *Life Studies* by Lowell, *Kaddish* by Ginsberg, and other autobiographical poems by poets such as Roethke, Berryman, Plath, Sexton, Rich—in search of truths scanted by the austerities and grandeurs of Yeats, Eliot, Pound and Stevens. Family relationships have become a standard subject in American poetry, so much so that in some cases we should wonder whether the subject serves as an evasion of issues outside the troubled family house, issues of citizenship and the fate of the culture that the modernist poets presumed to address. No doubt we need both kinds of poetry, or many kinds indeed, and may watch hopefully for the poet who can write convincingly about interpersonal relationships *and* about the entire culture, or tide of history, in which those relationships take shape. At this point I want simply to name a few poems which I value for their insights into the entanglement of family relations: "My Papa's Waltz" by Theodore Roethke, "Dunbarton" by Robert Lowell, "Golden State" and "Confessional" by Frank Bidart, "Sign for My Father, Who Stressed the Bunt" by David Bottoms, "Miami" by Daniel Mark Epstein, "Switchblade" by Michael Ryan, "My Father's Leaving" by Ira Sadoff, "Astronomy Lesson" by Alan Shapiro, "Looking at a Photograph of My Father at My Age" by Jeffrey Skinner, "The Body" by C.K. Williams.[30] (Probably because I am a son, I have chosen poems by and about sons.) In the light shed by such poems, Stevens' cherished ideal of a clean, lucid solitude can appear a frail fantasy. Juxtaposition of any of these poems with section V of "Esthétique du Mal" suggests that to be really embedded in what Stevens calls "the actual, the warm, the near" is to forego the solitary hauteur that can bequeath lofty statements about the difference between in-bar and ex-bar. In other words, as I suggested earlier in connection with Stevens' poems of "the central man," there is a profound link between Stevens' grandly noble aspirations, both for his poetry and for post-Christian humanity, and his attraction to the idea of solitude. A self enmeshed with other selves cannot so easily be imagined as triumphing over the grief of mortality, the nostalgia of religion, and "the whole experience of day".

An early triumpher in Steven's oeuvre was the happy persona named Hoon, whose delicious solipsism in "Tea at the Palaz of Hoon" (1921) was unthreatened by the presence of a "you" for whom loneliness was a significant problem:

Not less because in purple I descended
The western day through what you called
The loneliest air, not less was I myself.   (*CP* 65)

The "you" cannot figure in the rest of the poem because, as Hoon explains, "I was the world in which I walked, and what I saw / Or heard or felt came not but from myself . . ." No pressures from other lives can make Hoon's experience of tea or the ocean any different. By 1935, however, Stevens could perform (though with painful ambivalence) a repudiation of the persona whose solipsism no longer sufficed:

Too many waltzes have ended. And then
There's that mountain-minded Hoon,
For whom desire was never that of the waltz,

Who found all form and order in solitude,
For whom the shapes were never the figures of men.
Now, for him, his forms have vanished.   (*CP* 121)

The shapes Hoon created in solitude have dissolved, along with outmoded communal forms ("waltzes"), under pressure from new realities that are inescapably social: "There are these sudden mobs of men . . ." Stevens assigns himself the work of finding an alternative to the too-safe poetry of solitude. But like "The Circus Animals' Desertion," in which Yeats assigns himself the work of a demythologized psychological realism, "Sad Strains of a Gay Waltz" is an essentially grim poem by a poet bravely trying to go against his grain. Besides what we have already examined, there is very little in Stevens' oeuvre after 1935 (or before) which can be called poetry of human relations, whether socio-political or "dear." One short poem of 1935, "Re-statement of Romance," will deserve to be noticed as an importantly unusual case.

First, however, let us look at a strange section of "Esthétique du Mal" which can be used as a summary, a touchingly contorted summary, of both the currents in Stevens that we have observed: the strong gravitation toward solitude and the occasional countervailing recognition that relationship with another person is possible and desirable. Section XII amounts to a confession of inability to write the poetry of true sympathy adumbrated by section V, followed by an outcry against this inability. Section XII purports to develop a logical philosophical argument, but the logic becomes spurious, I think, exactly where Stevens wants to reject the demands of relationship. Here are the first two of the section's three stanzas:

> He disposes the world in categories, thus:
> The peopled and the unpeopled. In both, he is
> Alone. But in the peopled world, there is,
> Besides the people, his knowledge of them. In
> The unpeopled, there is his knowledge of himself.
> Which is more desperate in the moments when
> The will demands that what he thinks be true?
>
> Is it himself in them that he knows or they
> In him? If it is himself in them, they have
> No secret from him. If it is they in him,
> He has no secret from them. This knowledge
> Of them and of himself destroys both worlds,
> Except when he escapes from it. To be
> Alone is not to know them or himself.   (*CP* 323)

The first and second worlds ("The peopled and the unpeopled") both give the protagonist a life of solitude, but these solitudes are unsatisfactory ("desperate") apparently due to the pain of knowing that perception ("what he thinks") may not be reality ("true"). As far as section XII is concerned, such pain is equally desperate in both the social realm and the individual realm. In other words, Stevens no sooner acknowledges the difference between the self's inner world and the social world than he develops an argument in which this difference doesn't matter. In this context there is no question of committing oneself to interaction in the social world, because the "peopled" category is significant only as an impediment to a happy kind of solitude. The middle stanza argues that the acknowledgment of other people is a pollution which renders not only the social world but also the inner world unbearable, uninhabitable. Why? Apparently because, to be tolerable, these two worlds must maintain very firm boundaries, whereas once the self grows aware of its similarity to or connection with other people its Iron Curtain becomes horribly permeable; the condition of having "no secret" from another person elicits fear and revulsion. We must wonder what has happened to the gap between perception and reality in this fear, since there is no sense here that a self might be safely fortified by its difference from others' "knowledge" of him. The argument is cryptic and willful though it manages (in language more devoid of imagery than any other passage of equal length in Stevens) to sound like logical discourse. The neurotic, fearful energy underlying section XII becomes most visible in the extremism of the following declaration: "This knowledge / Of them and of himself destroys both worlds, / Except when he escapes from it." Nothing in the argument has justified such an unqualified identification of intimacy ("no secret") with destruction.

The element of sophistry in the writing continues into the third stanza with the pseudological opening phrase "This creates" which could be rewritten more honestly as "What I crave is" (or, "What he craves is"):

This creates a third world without knowledge,
In which no one peers, in which the will makes no
Demands. It accepts whatever is as true,
Including pain, which, otherwise, is false.
In the third world, then, there is no pain. Yes, but
What lover has one in such rocks, what woman,
However known, at the centre of the heart?   (CP 323)

Stevens wants an escape from the kinds of un-solitude, or frighteningly imperfect solitude, produced by awareness of other people, and his solution is this very underdefined "third world," where the mind is apparently purely passive and so indiscriminately tolerant (something like Yeats' old Chinamen in "Lapis Lazuli," but less animate than they) that other persons cannot destabilize it. This life is presumably to be associated with the "paradise unknown" of those who live "Completely physical in a physical world" (CP 325), but in section XII Stevens has not shown that this life is superior to a vegetable existence. Fortunately, there is a redeeming turn at the end of section XII (as we noted in the preceding chapter) which gives the whole section some emotional weight. As if suffocated by the aridity of his own putative logic, Stevens breaks free into the truth of emotion, acknowledging his yearning for human love: "Yes, but / What lover has one in such rocks, what woman, / However known, at the centre of the heart?" Harold Bloom comments: "For Stevens, another crucial self-recognition is recorded in the rhetorical question . . . that must be answered, 'no lover, no woman,' despite whatever knowledge has been attained."[31] For our examination of Stevens' devotion to solitude and his impulse to protect this devotion via the idea that solitude is an ontological inevitability, the interjected phrase "However known" is important because it can be heard as an implicit rejection of that idea. "However known" is an exasperated dismissal of the endless dubiety about interpersonal contact ("But was it Ulysses?") that turns out to be self-fulfilling prevention of such contact. There *is* a way in which a loved woman can be "at the centre of the heart" of the lover; the complications and imperfections of such human intimacy do not render it unreal. This is a brave, if brief, admission by Stevens; its emotional honesty is what Denis Donoghue calls "the saving pressure and the saving grace of Stevens' later poems."[32]

There remains one mid-career poem to consider in which Stevens comes as close as he can to a real examination of human intimacy. Less sanctimonious than section V of "Esthétique du Mal," less equivocal than "The World as Meditation," and not private and tendentious like "Red Loves Kit," (*OP* 31), "Re-statement of Romance" is Stevens' most promising approach to the great subject of interpersonal relations.[33] The fact that it has been neglected by critics—it is not mentioned at all in the important studies by Helen Vendler, Harold Bloom, Milton J. Bates, Frank Doggett, and Lucy Beckett, and barely mentioned by Joseph Riddel—no doubt reflects their willingness to be guided by the poet's own emphases.

From one point of view, "Re-statement of Romance" is less about a relation between two human beings than about the relation—or in a way the nonrelation—between them and their natural environment. The poem declares that night is not filled with haunting spiritual presences (this is one more version of Stevens' tireless insistence that earth is, fortunately, not a world designed with us in mind), and proceeds to assert that awareness of this truth about night is somehow enabling for the two persons in their encounter. As is often the case with Stevens, he gives us not an argument but a magisterial assertion, relying on his charisma for cogency.

RE-STATEMENT OF ROMANCE

The night knows nothing of the chants of night.
It is what it is as I am what I am:
And in perceiving this I best perceive myself

And you. Only we two may interchange
Each in the other what each has to give.
Only we two are one, not you and night,

Nor night and I, but you and I, alone,
So much alone, so deeply by ourselves,
So far beyond the casual solitudes,

That night is only the background of our selves,
Supremely true each to its separate self,
In the pale light that each upon the other throws.   (*CP* 146)

As usual, Stevens is amazingly optimistic about the benefits to be derived from relinquishment of religion and supernaturalism. What is
extremely unusual here is that the benefit emerges as an effect not
only upon a solitary perceiving self but upon the relationship between
two selves. As if to dramatize his plunge into the treacherous waters of
interpersonal relations, Stevens makes the poem leap a stanza break in
order to get from "myself" to "you." Then comes a sentence bearing
an idea radically out of harmony with the rest of Stevens' work and
indeed perhaps with the rest of this same poem. "Only we two may
interchange / Each in the other what each has to give." Coming from
Stevens this is a shocking acknowledgment of something complex and
valuable that occurs in the relationship of two persons. For a moment
vast new vistas of subject matter can be glimpsed. Ronald Sukenick
comments unperturbedly on the poem: "Ego in relation with responsive ego transcends alien reality."[34] But we should not let Stevens slide
away from the idea as if it were just one more variation on a summer
day. After all, to take seriously the importance of ego in relation with
responsive ego is to imagine the speaker of "The Idea of Order at Key
West" (*CP* 128) turning away from the safely distant singer "striding
there alone" in order to converse with Ramon Fernandez, a Ramon no
longer pale and silent but vital and vocal in the give-and-take of
friendship.

But many Stevens scholars will say I am imposing my own wishes
upon "Re-statement of Romance." Admittedly the remainder of the
poem does perform a strategic withdrawal from the risky radicalism
of "Only we two may interchange / Each in the other what each has to
give." Stevens next employs one of his most regrettable rhetorical
tricks (see *CP* 93, 171, 253, 255, 335, 392, 506, 532, and *OP* 48, among
other instances), the trick of declaring two things to be one: "Only we
two are one." Apparently the statement means that the two human
beings are the same kind of thing, human, while nature ("night") is not

human. At the same time, to say "we two are one" is to shift the poem away from any interest in the valuable difference between the two persons ("what each has to give"). Moreover, concern with "interchange" is firmly discouraged by the third stanza's stress on aloneness. Here the assertion seems to be that by giving up a haunted or spiritualized natural environment, in which one's cosmic solitude would be mistakenly understood as "casual," contingent, not absolute and permanent, modern romantics can achieve a profoundly healthy awareness of selfhood ("Supremely true each to its separate self").

This deepened aloneness is achieved, though, "In the pale light that each upon the other throws." The poem's last line does not regain the courage of its fourth and fifth lines, but at least allows that one's most authentic selfhood is somehow fostered by the felt presence of another person's perceptions of one. Even this, while not the examination of "interchange" that the poem for a moment seemed willing to embark upon, is a remarkable concession for Wallace Stevens to make.[35]

"Re-statement of Romance," we may say, opens a big door just a crack and then quickly shuts it.[36] If so, then are we pointing out merely a temperamental omission (every poet omits: we don't go to Eliot for a sense of joy, or to Milton for comedy, or to Pope for the darknesses of the psyche, or to Shelley for the life of the body) or a disastrous failure, a lack that vitiates the oeuvre? Answers to such evaluative questions always depend on the needs of a given reader. How intensely and how constantly do I need poetry that deals with, or at least moves in the world of, human relationships? And how much, on the other hand, do I need poetry, like so much of Stevens', that encourages and validates the solitary experience of the separate individual? My feelings fluctuate, as Stevens would say they must—"He never felt twice the same about the flecked river."[37] But it has seemed important to me to show not only Stevens' strenuous omission of the great subject of interpersonal experience, but the fleeting indications that he was conscious of this as a great omission. These indications can help us hear our poet as an often worried man, worried by the loneliness which he tried to deny or redefine as fortunate necessity. We can hear the sad half-falsehood of the often-quoted confession in his "Adagia": "Life is an affair of people not of places. But for me life is an affair of places and that is the trouble" (OP 158). Stevens knows he has trouble here, but he wants it to be a simple and unalterable kind of trouble. For him, though, life was partly an affair of people (as we have seen in "Esthétique du Mal" V and XII, "Sad Strains of a Gay Waltz," "Re-statement of Romance," and elsewhere), troublingly so. To see that it was disentangles us from those ensolacings of his that are too sleekly solitary. Moreover, to see that Stevens—whose thinking we admire despite its omissions—sometimes recognized the importance of a realm of experience he could not explore is to feel strengthened in our own sense of the importance of human "interchange" as we watch for its negotiations in the engaging and troubling work of others.

Chapter Four

STEVENS AND THE READER

ACH of the preceding chapters has mainly found—albeit with affecting qualifications and exceptions—an objectionable withdrawal in Stevens' poetry from caring about (being interested in and being kindly disposed toward) individual other persons. Though I have tried to be more analytic than moralistic, certainly my project could be called a moral critique of Stevens, notwithstanding my attempts along the way to acknowledge my delight in much of his poetry. But all along I have been bothered by the sensation of ignoring a special defense of Stevens that might be offered, a defense in which the delight I have occasionally acknowledged would somehow provide an answer to my own critique.

Conscience reminds me of many occasions in my life, ever since 1970, when I felt bleak, lonesome, lost—often due to some trouble in relationships with other people—and took in hand a volume of Stevens' poetry. In those moments—on a bus or train, in a café or restaurant or empty house—it seemed as though only Stevens would suffice to comfort me and buoy me up, relieving my mood of anxiety or frustration or self-doubt. Hardy, or Frost, or Eliot, or Auden wouldn't do; what I needed was Stevens. Undoubtedly this has to do with my personality and is to some extent (as we say when criticism gives up) merely a matter of taste; yet I have persistently the sense that there are demonstrable special qualities in Stevens' poetry which evoke in many readers besides myself a set of grateful feelings more specific and coherent than the whole range of feelings that can be involved when we say, for example, "I love Keats" or "I love Yeats".[1] The feelings evoked by Stevens that I have in mind may be provisionally summarized by saying that they come together into a sense of being befriended by Stevens. If the case can be made that Stevens' poetry does indeed evoke a special sense of being befriended, then this truth about Stevens would seem—on the level of immediate intuitive response—to comprise an answer to the accusation, in my preceding chapters, that Stevens has largely failed to care about other people in his poetry. "Certainly he has cared," we may be moved to reply, "he has cared about *us*."

To what extent can Stevens be rescued from complaints about his coldness, his implicit misanthropy and his profound estrangement from persons ignored or merely glimpsed *in* his poems by exposition of a warm and kind attitude toward persons addressed *by* his poems? In other words, can we contend that sympathy and virtue and benevolence in Stevens' relation to the reader atone for, or counterbalance, or somehow erase the significance of the drastic meagerness of these qualities in his relation to the sufferers and women and other fellow citizens who so thinly populate his poetry?

The obvious problem with the contention is that the relation between poet and reader, as achieved by means of the printed poetry, is a relation between two persons only in a special and limited sense. It is not a relation between two persons present to one another; the poem stands between them. Each develops a relation to the poem which implies an attitude toward the other person, using the poem to imagine the other; but the two persons never meet. It is as if the poem were an apartment designed by the poet for a tenant he has never met; when the tenant arrives and explores the premises, wondering about the designer's intentions, the poet has long since gone off to another wing of the complex. Moreover, of course, the relation between poet and reader is one of giving and receiving rather than of mutual give-and-take. Unlike the human relations discussed in the preceding chapters, which are distinguished by at least the possibility of a balancing reciprocity, the relation between poet and reader is not logically a two-way interaction, since the poet cannot, in the arena of the poem itself, be acted upon by the reader. (This is not a point about geographical separation. If I could go to Hartford and have tea with Mr. Stevens, I might conceivably establish a friendly relation with the author of the poems, but this would not amount to a relation with the author *in* the poems.)

Thus it is only by means of a certain mumbo-jumbo that we can arrange to speak of the relation between poet and reader as a human encounter in which one person befriends another. A poet who in his or her poems is good to the reader is not a person doing good to another human being like, say, your friend who listens and talks to you for eight hours when you have suddenly realized that your marriage is in trouble. To feel befriended by the poet in the poems is to enjoy an illusion. But this illusion is crucial to the value of Stevens.

Befriended—will this expression suffice? And can an author so cool, fastidious, disdainful and secretive really be seen as friendly, even when his poems reject or sabotage our confidence in, or belittle all our experiences of, comradeship outside books? Many statements I make in this chapter about Stevens' relation to the reader will indeed be statements one might make in praising a friend—though in comparison to what one might say of one's best friend or a close friend these statements must remain rather pale and thin. In sum they may establish a sense of what Stevens offers the reader as a valuable but very limited kind of friendship. The term *befriended* seems helpful in evoking limitations which make the word *friend*, with its richness and even (for E. M. Forster among others)[2] sacredness, seem unearned here. *Befriended* connotes receipt of benevolence from above, from someone who is somehow better off or stronger, and who reaches out across a social gap.

Stevens nearly always contrives to sound like a man calmer, wiser, and thus older than we are, presenting an utterance that is a consciously stylized performance. This is true when his tone is wry, arch or rueful as in many *Harmonium* poems (though the early work contains arguable exceptions, such as "Domination of Black," "Gray Room," "Depression Before Spring"), and more unmistakably true throughout the later work. His characteristic voice attains the proud poise of the rabbi, a figure of the poet, portrayed in "Things of August":

> The thinker as reader reads what has been written.
> He wears the words he reads to look upon
> Within his being,
>
> A crown within him of crispest diamonds,
> A reddened garment falling to his feet,
> A hand of light to turn the page,
>
> A finger with a ring to guide his eye
> From line to line, as we lie on the grass and listen
> To that which has no speech,
>
> The voluble intentions of the symbols,
> The ghostly celebrations of the picnic,
> The secretions of insight.   (*CP* 492)

We who lie on the grass and listen are not on the rabbi's chosen level, and what we hear is not speech in the ordinary social sense.

However, what is missing from this passage about the rabbi and from many of Stevens' other explicit portrayals of the poet/scholar/thinker is acknowledgment precisely of the element of personal benevolence that is to be our focus. Along with the idea of Stevens as "befriender" of the reader, another word has repeatedly proposed itself to me: *uncle*. Stevens as the reader's uncle, as a Favorite Uncle? I will risk the vulgarity of this metaphor in trying to sort out reasons why readers feel helped and pleased in the special relation that Stevens develops with them. No doubt the uncles of my own readers are a heterogeneous group and the phrase "favorite uncle" cannot be relied on to conjure up the same figure in each reader's mind. But I ask the reader to think of one archetypal kind of uncle, as seen through the eyes of a nephew or niece perhaps ten years old: an uncle who visits frequently but usually doesn't stay long, who always offers amusement and a sly, winking benevolence, though retaining too a certain dignified distance, whose life apart from his charming avuncular behavior we cannot quite imagine; an uncle who dispenses advice abundantly but cryptically, so that we learn to listen with a pleasant tentativeness, knowing that today's advice is apt to be mysteriously revised (though not rescinded) by tomorrow's. He says, "Phoebus is dead, ephebe" (*CP* 381). He says, "Infant, it is enough in life / To speak of what you see" (*CP* 365). He says, "Some things, niño, some things are like this, / That instantly and in themselves they are gay / And you and I are such things . . ." (*CP* 248). He says, "Piece the world together, boys, but not with your hands" (*CP* 192). He says, "I say now, Fernando, that on that day / The mind roamed as a moth roams . . ." (*CP* 22). He says, "Mesdames, it is not enough to be reconciled / Before the strange . . ." (*OP* 50). We listen with the cautious smile of a nephew or niece who has learned that no single piece of wisdom will be allowed to harden into bronze fixity (but that there is, nevertheless, a figure in the carpet). Uncle Wallace will always bring a curio or puzzle from his pockets, something not utterly new—it will be recognizably his kind of surprise—but enough of a fresh variation to keep us blinking, engaged, invigorated (though not thrilled, amazed, appalled, awed, or galvanized into action, Uncle Wallace is not such a disturbing visitor, as I will observe in detail later). He cares about us enough to exert himself over and over in the performances that will elicit from us these rather moderate, but pleasurable and salubrious, responses.

The metaphor begins to crumble. ("They will get it straight one day at the Sorbonne"[*CP* 406].) There are poems and passages in Stevens which may be felt to rebuke the metaphor; for instance, someone might object that the confrontation with death in "The Auroras of Autumn"—

Shall we be found hanging in the trees next spring?
Of what disaster is this the imminence:
Bare limbs, bare trees and a wind as sharp as salt?   (*CP* 419)

—is nothing like what an uncle would say to a young niece or nephew. But as Stevens instructs us, a metaphor need not be satisfactory in every respect so long as it "gives / Sounds passing through sudden rightnesses" (*CP* 240): "The squirming facts exceed the squamous mind, / If one may say so. And yet relation appears" (*CP* 215). The Favorite Uncle notion is one device for specifying the way in which readers may feel, with whatever degree of irrationality, that Stevens has conveyed in his poems a benevolent concern for us—each of us, not just humanity in the aggregate—as fellow human beings, and that the poetry thus embodies a model for one good (while limited) kind of interpersonal relationship.

The issue here involves the reader's emotional response to poetry more explicitly than many of the issues taken on by criticism (for example, the identification of Stevens' attitude toward God, or toward Emerson—though no good analysis of these problems could be uninfluenced by the analyst's emotional experience of the poetry), and thus it carries me into commentary more obviously impressionistic than most critical commentary. Before considering the set of qualities which tend, I will claim, to elicit in Stevens' reader a sense of befriendedness, we should ask whether there are some more objective indexes whereby we can analyze Stevens' attitude toward the reader.

How can a poet show in his poems that he cares about and cares for the reader? *Cares about* and *cares for*—the verbs are meant to include the cluster of feelings and attitudes we look for in a friend: he knows us, he pays attention to us, he respects, admires, and likes us, he desires our welfare. The poet will have to behave in some special fashion to be distinguished on these grounds, because I take it as self-evident that every poet—I do not say every writer, because I allow the arguable exception of the diarist[3]—is interested in the reader, in some reader, even if the desired reader has never entered the poet's life and, sadly, may never do so.[4] Emily Dickinson did not burn her poems; at the end of her life she left them neatly waiting. Hence I am disturbed by a line in Stevens' poem "The Planet on the Table" (written near the end of his career), in which he contemplates his *Collected Poems*: "It was not important that they survive" (*CP* 532). The line strikes a false note; or else, it is to be heard as a phase of the satisfied mood which the poem expresses, the mood of a famous old man who knows, after all, that his work will indeed survive. In this mood Stevens gravitates toward the sense of radical self-sufficiency which has always been such a strong magnet in his life of wishing and thinking, and implies that the only important relation has been between himself and his imagination (or, between the creative and receptive aspects of his imagination), while publication has not mattered. This attraction to the idea of a self suffi-cient unto itself inclined Stevens to emphasize the solitude of the reader in the few poems where reading is explicitly mentioned and to evoke a oneness of reader with book, hence of reader with writer, as if no relation between two different human beings were involved. (More on this point soon.) Accordingly we should not expect an abundance of obvious explicit evidence in the poetry (as distinct from his essays and letters) of Stevens especially caring about and caring for his reader.

Again, what would constitute such explicit evidence? It would come in three forms: (1) in the form of statements about the reader, and reading, in the poems, (2) in the form of direct address to the reader, and (3) in the form of detailed images of the lives of persons like the reader. Considering first the third form of evidence, we quickly recall that this is not Stevens' territory: the preceding chapters have stressed the extreme scarcity of Stevens' references to the actualities of specific human lives. (Perhaps, though, when it is a question of showing interest in the *reader* rather than more broadly in "others," there are not many great poets who go much beyond Stevens in this form of evidence, that is, who write in detail about the lives of such people as read serious poetry.)[5]

Then what about direct address to the reader? We do not find in Stevens anything so barefaced and alarmingly warm as this in Whitman:

> When you read these I that was visible am become invisible,
> Now it is you, compact, visible, realizing my poems, seeking me,
> Fancying how happy you were if I could be with you and become
>   your comrade;
> Be it as if I were with you. (Be not too certain but I am now with you.)[6]

The absence of such salutations in Stevens should not be attributed to his greater skepticism about language's power to bridge the gaps between selves; in fact Stevens shares with Whitman an amazing serenity about the power of language to capture and convey truths of feeling (though they be constantly shifting), a serenity that separates both Whitman and Stevens from postmodern anxiety about the poetic medium itself. Stevens prefers not to provoke such eye-to-eye confrontations with the reader for the emotional reasons discussed in chapter 3; to directly solicit the reader's support or sympathy or even attention would be to betray an incompleteness of the imagining self which Stevens almost never cares to admit. He will not openly acknowledge the presence (as imagined by him) of the reader's mind finding its way through the poem. The brash, presuming confessional intimacy of Nabokov's Humbert Humbert (if I may reach into the realm of prose fiction for a moment), summoning the reader to engage with the writer's full personality, is decidedly un-Stevensian:

> Knowing me by now, the reader can easily imagine how dusty and hot I got, trying to catch a glimpse of nymphets (alas, always remote) playing in Central Park, and how repulsed I was by the glitter of deodorized career girls that a gay dog in one of the offices kept unloading upon me.[7]

And yet, if we read this sentence from *Lolita* side by side with certain Stevens poems that reveal both sexual desire and the nearness of desire to disgust, we find the two voices, Stevens and Humbert, remarkably similar. I am thinking of "Floral Decorations for Bananas" (*CP* 53), "Depression Before Spring" (*CP* 63), "Metropolitan Melancholy" (*OP* 32), and the first section of "It Must Change" in "Notes Toward a Supreme Fiction"(*CP* 389). The point is that Stevens achieves an insinuation—as if to say, "*You* know how I feel"—without the direct statements of a less embarrassable man like Humbert. (As a persona, of course, Humbert partly protected Nabokov from embarrassment.) To explain how Stevens achieves his insinuations of familiarity between himself and the reader is not easy; it is a factor in the mystery we are exploring. The key to such insinuation, clearly, is the presumption of similarity between reader and writer, the presumption that the reader's fund of psychological experience resembles the writer's. (Admittedly this presumed resemblance is limited in Stevens by the attitude of avuncular seniority noted above.) When a writer thus presumes, we may notice the presuming tone as much as we notice whatever is being declared, and whether we notice it or not we are affected by the confidence of the presuming; if we admire other aspects of the writer's work, we are apt to feel flattered, or touched, by his or her conviction that we are alike. Stevens' presumption of similarity between himself and the reader (which reflects his aversion to the reality of personal peculiarity) will prove to be an essential element of his "befriending," as we shall see.

While presuming that the reader is like a younger version of himself, Stevens avoids a Whitmanesque seizing of the reader's lapels. There are some poems in which a sort of stand-in for the reader is directly addressed—as ephebe, infant, niño, boys, Fernando, etc. (see the passages quoted earlier in this chapter). In each case, though, it can be argued that the addressee is not the reader per se but either an aspect of the poet's mind or a player in the small drama out of which the speaker speaks. Stevens (like most poets most of the time, to be sure) shields himself from the glare of open address to the reader as "you" or "reader."

What about imperatives not addressed to any designated listener? Many of Stevens' poems dole out instructions and give assignments; how often do we feel that the student being instructed is the reader?

Jot these milky matters down.   (*CP* 144)

From oriole to crow, note the decline
In music.   (*CP* 154)

The baroque poet may see him as still a man
As Virgil, abstract. But see him for yourself,
The fictive man.   (*CP* 335)

. . . what we say of the future must portend,

Be alive with its own seemings . . .   (*CP* 346)

Regard the invalid personality
Instead, outcast, without the will to power . . .   (*CP* 368)

Let's see the very thing and nothing else.   (*CP* 373)

Suppose this was the root of everything.   (*CP* 460)

Again, each of these imperatives might be interpreted as directed by the poet to himself or to part of himself. But the persuasive didactic element in Stevens' poetry, of which such imperatives are only one symptom, gradually conveys the sense that he actively seeks and desires an acquiescence on our part, and this tends to counteract his emphasis on the entirely sufficient solitary self. The poet is not indifferent to us; his befriending of us may take the manner of a riddling and mercurial mentor, but he is not such an austere teacher as to say, "Here is the truth, take it or leave it." He exerts himself to win our interest and trust.

The sentence I have just written, of course, is a broad claim that could be made about all great poets, though they exert themselves with interesting variations of demeanor and temperature. The special flavor of Stevens' interest in the reader will, I hope, emerge cumulatively from this chapter's observations.

What does Stevens have to say about the reader and reading as such? There are some seven or eight poems or passages which refer to reading and a reader, as distinguished from the many references to the poet and the composing of poetry. As I noted earlier, Stevens is disinclined to describe reading as an encounter with an alien mind, the mind of a different person. Instead he uses rhetoric and metaphor to build accounts of reading which are happily undisturbed by difference, accounts in which the gap between poet and reader is somehow healed. In "Academic Discourse at Havana" he says of the poet:

As part of nature he is part of us.
His rarities are ours: may they be fit
And reconcile us to our selves in those
True reconcilings, dark, pacific words,
And the adroiter harmonies of their fall.   (*CP* 144)

The view of poetry as a project of reconciliation is espoused here with such thoroughgoing wistfulness as to include a reconciling of poet with readers that is not just a reaching of agreement but a merging. To say "As part of nature he is part of us" is to affirm the naturalness (earthliness, freedom from illusory transcendental sanctions) of both poet and reader in a way that lumps them together within nature, the poet encompassed by his readers, implicit within them. "His rarities are ours"—in this brazenly simplifying equation we hear Stevens' yearning for escape from peculiarity, from the problems of being a certain man with a certain troubling wife and troubling daughter and certain troubling memories. If the poet's rarities are shared by all of us, then of course they are not rarities at all and the poet seems to enjoy a union with "us," a union whose emotional appeal significantly resembles that of his union with his terrestrial environment on a yellow afternoon in autumn:

> He said I had this that I could love,
> As one loves visible and responsive peace,
> As one loves one's own being,
> As one loves that which is the end
> And must be loved, as one loves that
> Of which one is a part as in a unity,
> A unity that is the life one loves . . .   (CP 236)

These incantatory lines, comforting the listener with the word *love* seven times in seven lines, try to lull us, along with the poet, into an uncritical state of mind, a forgetting of the differences between self and world, or self and other.

To arrive at such a "unity," Stevens was all too willing to forego, in nearly all of his poetry, any specific reference to his own life (wife, daughter, friends, job), and thus to offer himself to the reader as someone older and wiser than, but otherwise hardly distinguishable from, the reader—a good man with no shape. In his *Materia Poetica*, published in 1940, Stevens declared: "The poet confers his identity on the reader. He cannot do this if he intrudes personally."[8] We are called upon to agree that there is a kind of identity that is not personal. Stevens' wish to exclude the problem of personal difference from the relationship between poet and reader leads him into maneuvers whose goal is to create a sense of poet and reader as identical, and these maneuvers, observed with a proper skepticism, involve the mere trickery of double-talk. In "Of Modern Poetry," Stevens contrives to bring the word "audience" into the poem without allowing it to represent listeners separable from the poet, as he says that the poem must

> like an insatiable actor, slowly and
> With meditation, speak words that in the ear,
> In the delicatest ear of the mind, repeat,
> Exactly, that which it wants to hear, at the sound
> Of which, an invisible audience listens,
> Not to the play, but to itself, expressed

In an emotion as of two people, as of two
Emotions becoming one.   (*CP* 240)

Critics may explain these lines as a statement about the poet's mind
satisfying itself, but the fact remains that Stevens has used the theater
metaphor to give the impression that he has dealt with the relation
between poet and reader, while at the same time implying that this is
only a relation between aspects of one thing.

In "The House Was Quiet and the World Was Calm" it is the author, rather than the audience, who is invisible except for a possible
ambiguity of the word "scholar," which may be felt to suggest author
as well as reader. The poem's second line asserts that "The reader
became the book," and soon we are told:

The words were spoken as if there was no book,
Except that the reader leaned above the page,

Wanted to lean, wanted much most to be
The scholar to whom his book is true, to whom

The summer night is like a perfection of thought.   (*CP* 358)

The book's author, a ghostly presence in the word "scholar" and also
perhaps in the word "spoken," melts into the reader through these
lines, and the melting effect is reinforced by a flurry of sedative Stevensian equations at the end of the poem:

The truth in a calm world,
In which there is no other meaning, itself

Is calm, itself is summer and night, itself
Is the reader leaning late and reading there.   (*CP* 359)

Similarly in "Things of August" V, quoted earlier, the rabbi's act of
reading seems (despite the presence of the "we" who "lie on the grass
and listen") so fully to internalize the text as to make it an emanation
from, or crystallization of, the reader's own being:

The thinker as reader reads what has been written.
He wears the words he reads to look upon
Within his being,

A crown within him of crispest diamonds . . .   (*CP* 492)

Here the words *thinker* and *reader*, and the submerged word *poet* are
trying to become synonyms.

In the beautiful poem "Large Red Man Reading," Stevens does not
resort to double-talk, but here too we are encouraged to feel that The
Reader is also The Poet, for the returning ghosts have come, after all,

"to hear *his* phrases, / As he sat there reading, aloud, the great blue tabulae" (*CP* 423; emphasis added). The poem is a great affirmation of both earthly life and poetry, proclaiming Stevens' happy sense that poetry is what gives life to life, poetry being for him not only the written words but the imaginative energy (represented here by the Red Man's reading aloud) that emblazons the "outlines of being" not only with emotional significance but with color, shape, and size. In this broadened, unaristocratic conception of poetry, every imaginer is a poet. Reading being an imaginative activity, the reader is a composer, a poet—splendid! But in accepting this pleasant idea, we must not slip into accepting the more mystical idea which we have seen Stevens smuggling into his poems of reading, namely that the reader is *the* poet. To say that the reader is a kind of poet is one thing: this allows for the presence of another poet, "the poet," who can then interact, across difference, with his or her reader. But to say that the reader *is* *the poet*, as Stevens implies, is to shut down the whole issue of how the poet relates to us—teaching, consoling, demanding, teasing, negotiating and so on—by the quackery of instant healing.

You, my reader, have just read my sentence ending with the phrase "the quackery of instant healing." Perhaps you have already formulated an opinion about the sentence and the phrase. First, though, it must have been necessary for you to imagine what I meant—and this entailed imagining yourself as me. To read one of my sentences is to pretend, provisionally, to be me, to be the one who would mean those words. To this extent Stevens implies a truth in implying an identity between reader and writer. But of course there always comes, in the flicker of an instant, the divorce (or trial separation): you step back and consider whether the word "quackery" is quite fair, whether it is too outlandish, and so forth. We are a tempestuous couple, dear, marrying and unmarrying and remarrying with the prodigious energy generated by the problem of being partly similar but not the same. Wolfgang Iser summarizes such marital tension this way:

> As we read, there occurs an artificial division of our personality, because we take as a theme for ourselves something that we are not. Consequently when reading we operate on different levels. For although we may be thinking the thoughts of someone else, what we are will not disappear completely—it will merely remain a more or less powerful virtual force. Thus, in reading there are these two levels—the alien "me" and the real, virtual "me"—which are never completely cut off from each other. Indeed, we can only make someone else's thoughts into an absorbing theme for ourselves, provided the virtual background of our own personality can adapt to it.[9]

Stevens does not want to engage this problem of adaptation across the difference between poet and reader. He finds it too alarming, just

as Vincentine is alarming in section III of "The Apostrophe to Vincentine," where she briefly steps forward as a separate self with an
internal life uncontrolled by the poem's idealizations:

> Then you came walking,
> In a group
> Of human others,
> Voluble.
> Yes: you came walking,
> Vincentine.
> Yes: you came talking.   (*CP* 53)

The poet quickly retires from encounter with such otherness, just as
he avoids any account of reading that would focus on the meeting of
two different minds.

As a result, Stevens' poetry of reading gives us little help in the effort to show that his work expresses interest in us, and caring for us, as
human others. The reader poems contribute only a hazy valorizing of
the act of reading: we see that Stevens feels reading is a good thing, so
we feel approved. This is a limited point, but it is already a difference
between Stevens and poets who imply that we should be doing something else besides reading. (I think of Browning urging us to vigorous
risk-taking; Whitman calling us out to the open road; Eliot advising
contemplative stillness and prayer; Ted Hughes challenging us to confront our animality; Robert Bly summoning us to explore the unconscious.) What remains is to show why I (and perhaps you) can feel that
Stevens likes and cares about his reader not just as reader but as person, not just as an approved abstract role-player but as a respected
individual.

Every poem projects a likely reader and a desirable reader (the two
will coincide if the poet is optimistic enough). My suggestion is that in
the case of Stevens' poetry, the reader—if indeed he or she sufficiently
resembles Stevens' implied reader—can, to an unusual degree, not
only feel that he or she is the desired reader for the poems but enjoy
the illusion that Stevens particularly likes and cares about him or her.
The imagined befriending is not passionate, but it gives certain valuable gifts, and gives them reliably, however moderately. Most of this
chapter will be an exposition of seven features of Stevens' poetry that
collectively generate this valuable illusion.

However, at this juncture it seems necessary to acknowledge once
again the logical vulnerability of an argument based so squarely on the
reader's (*this* reader's) emotional responses. Two difficulties naturally
threaten the procedure. First there is, of course, the matter-of-taste
problem: *De gustibus non est disputandum.* As with any aesthetic judgment of value (as in a book review, for example), the declaration that

"Stevens makes us feel X" strays beyond the comfort of provability, and my own reader, whose similarity to me I may have mistakenly presumed, is always free to reply "No, he doesn't. I feel Z." I may say that Stevens' production of a great many short poems whose themes echo each other is "generous," but my reader may call it "vainly redundant." The point can be argued but not positively disposed of. However, this must never become a paralyzing difficulty, because a criticism drained of emotional and valuative responses is soon grotesquely impoverished; poetry is neither written nor read (nor written about) for the sake of what is logically demonstrable.

The second difficulty, more important here, lies in the difference between being pleased and being befriended. To be befriended is a more specific experience than to be pleased; a person may please us in many ways without making us feel befriended. The problem is not solely one of intention. A person may please us without intending to, whereas befriending is an intentional action. But it is also true that a person may try to please us, and indeed try to make us feel befriended, without succeeding in either.

I choose not to be distracted by the interminable issue of intentionality here. My assumption is that if intelligent and initiated readers very frequently respond to a poet's work with a certain happy feeling, the inducing of that feeling is part of the poet's purpose. Of course this assumption depends on the sensitivity of the reader, a reader who, for example, is not entirely cheered by a fundamentally bitter poem. We can construct a case in which the assumption is unreliable; we can cite long-standing misinterpretations, such as those of poems by Robert Frost which have ignored the poems' yearning for death; we can remind ourselves that some of a writer's purposes are so unconscious that their status as "intentions" is dubious; and we can argue that the inducing of certain specifiable responses in a reader may be too narrow a conception of what a poet attempts. However, none of these objections seems fruitful here. My task is to show that Stevens induces a certain response which includes a sense of this inducing having been intentional. If we feel befriended by him, we feel that he has meant to befriend us; and I am not concerned with doubting this intuitive assumption.

The difficulty I wish to acknowledge here is that of specifying certain feelings as feelings of being befriended. In the absence of the relatively direct kinds of evidence discussed earlier, the sort of evidence in the poetry to be adduced hereafter is mostly hard to distinguish from evidence which supports merely the very broad statement that Stevens pleases us. He pleases us, yes, in various ways, but is this not merely the sort of pleasing accomplished by a professional entertainer, or a remote and austere orator, by a grand performer uninterested in us as individuals?

These acknowledged difficulties will not be dissolved in my discussion, but I think they will be made less and less irksome by the truth that will emerge from it concerning Stevens' work.

My list of seven features does not pretend to encompass all the felicities and glories of Stevens' poetry. Nor does the list claim logical inevitability: another critic could organize the subject differently and name ten or sixteen features, perhaps splitting my categories into subcategories. Or fewer categories might be posited; for each of my seven overlaps with at least one other on the list.

Also, I want to acknowledge that most of the points on my list are familiar touchstones of Stevens criticism, though they have not been coordinated in the way I intend. Only in the case of the seventh and last feature, Holiday from Responsibility, will I need an extensive discussion—because it is, of these seven points, the one least emphasized in Stevens criticism, and the one most disturbing in light of the ethical concern that has pervaded the preceding chapters.

I present the list now with summary statements about each point. This will be followed by a section containing examples and amplifying remarks.

1. SPEAKING FOR US
This is the most objectively demonstrable item on the list. Stevens uses the pronouns we (our, us) and one frequently in an explicit claim to speak of experience which he shares with all human beings, or at least with all those who can be imagined reading his poems. This use of we and one occurs actually in fewer than half of the poems, but the generalizing involved tends to make these occurrences eminently quotable and memorable for any reader pursuing Stevens' main ideas; and thus the voice saying "we" and "one," presuming similarity between speaker and reader, can seem to be the essential Stevens voice. This presumption of similarity has the effect of summoning the reader into a sense of close alliance with the poet (though this effect is interdependent with the effects of the other features I enumerate: John Ashbery can say "we" hundreds of times without evoking the same feeling of interpersonal relatedness). Intimacy is not quite an acceptable word for what is felt, since a fastidious hauteur nearly always keeps the poet at a calm distance from us[10]—he is never looking straight into our eyes—and yet the cumulative effect of the "we" and "one" passages calls the word intimacy to mind. We hear the voice of a man persuasively implying that in basic ways he is like us and knows us well.

2. HUMOR

Stevens is often funny in a dry, sly manner and occasionally in a louder, or even (briefly) a boisterous manner. Even when his humor is expressed by outlandish gestures such as his famous nonsense words and his raiding of other languages (Ohoyaho, tink and tank and tunk-a-tunk-tunk, zay-zay and a-zay, ithy oonts and long-haired plomets, oh beau caboose, turbulent Schlemihl, a lost blague, lingua franca et jocundissima . . .), it is not comedy for just anyone, for the common citizen on the street. A casual reader attracted by an apparently comic title like "The Paltry Nude Starts on a Spring Voyage" or "The Revolutionists Stop for Orangeade" soon feels chastened by the initial opacity of the poems; but the initiated reader can respond with a knowing smile.[11] Stevens conveys his confidence that *we* will divine when he is being funny and will know how to enjoy it; his humor implies a respect for his sensitive audience of aficionados.

3. GAME-PLAYING

Stevens displays a repertoire of habitual maneuvers which provide entertainment not for just anyone but for the initiated reader, a reader who is not merely an educated student of poetry but a Stevensian. This is a more particular matter than can be expressed by saying that Stevens has a distinct and difficult style. Thousands of pages written about Stevens are palpably energized by a sense of having found the key or keys to a wonderful treasury of riddles. References (not quite systematic but addictively almost systematic) to color, to the seasons, to weather, to sun and moon, to birds, to Florida and other tropical zones, to a female spirit; and reliance on crucially nuanced words such as *poverty, solitude, sense, central,* and *hero*; and manipulations of syntax; and radically abbreviated or hidden narratives;[12] and odd, oblique relations between poems and their titles—these are some of Stevens' habitual maneuvers. They have a flashy quality of showmanship, because they allow surprises of speed and efficiency in expressing an idea or feeling by way of fast transition and condensed juxtaposition. The sleight-of-hand man teaches us how to watch carefully; he lures us into learning his codes until we feel we are members of an elite—players of a charming game whose rules are amusingly fluid but not invisible.

4. DEPENDABILITY AND GENEROSITY

Stevens can be counted on to return to the same problems again and again. The reader comes to trust that the basic issue of the imagination's response to reality will be at the heart of every poem; moreover, this issue will often be not merely a broadly implicit concern (the way we might say that mutability and mortality are always present as concerns throughout the work of a given poet) but an explicitly examined problem, picked up each time from a slightly new angle but always by means of the poet's increasingly familiar panoply of terms and associations.[13] At the same time, within this recognized framework Stevens is cornucopic, finding new (or apparently new) angles of approach with amazing virtuosity. This abundance seems to result partly from a generous patience, a desire to win the reader's involvement in the poetry's concerns through a gradual courtship comprised of hundreds of similar offerings. Our poet may repeatedly puzzle us, but we feel he is not going to disturb us with deeply discordant or risky or unforeseeable undertakings. Exceptions, including perhaps such poems of death as "The Owl in the Sarcophagus" and "Madame La Fleurie," may be precious in their specialness, but this specialness doesn't interfere with the larger pleasure—a pleasure verging on complacency—that readers derive from Stevens' abundant dependability.

5. Moodiness

Stevens is, for the reader who has caught on, a frankly moody poet. Because he is also a poet who nearly always addresses the same concerns and always wants to affirm certain attitudes, many readers have worn themselves out trying to convince themselves that he always feels the same way about his materials. But he does not, and realizing this is a great step forward in the initiation of anyone learning to read Stevens. Stevens is committed to the kind of honesty that is interested in, and candid about, the fluctuations of one's moods. Indeed, his ability to crystallize a range of moods in relation to recurring situations and issues—depression, grumpiness, self-disgust, weariness, anxiety, modest hope, yearning, relief, satisfaction—is a major reason why an oeuvre so consistently devoted to a specific group of concerns for the most part manages to avoid tedium. Putting this more positively, I say that his moodiness, together with his interest in moods, is among the special delights of Stevens' work; and I will suggest that the self-revealing candor involved seems friendly—unlike, say, the obsessive self-exposure of Robert Lowell in his autobiographical poems, whose factual candor may feel exciting, challenging, even frightening, but not friendly—partly because the moodiness of Stevens has to overcome his austerity to reach us, and partly because a person willing to show us his moods so extensively seems ready to acknowledge and respect our own moodiness.

6. Encouragement

Stevens assures us many times that our lives can be good. He returns to this assurance sometimes with a tone of strained anxiety and sometimes with a more or less convincing tone of hale and hearty confidence. Either way, providing us with encouragement is central to Stevens' project. He is not a neutral cataloger of the relations between imagination and reality; he quite openly yearns to describe, and to evoke a palpable sense of, certain such relations, those in which

> It seems as if the honey of common summer
> Might be enough, as if the golden combs
> Were part of a sustenance itself enough,
>
> As if hell, so modified, had disappeared,
> As if pain, no longer satanic mimicry,
> Could be borne, as if we were sure to find our way.   (*CP* 316)

Stevens wants this seeming to be a truthful seeming, and he exerts himself assiduously to convince himself and us that it may be so. His unusualness in this regard is not only that his affirmations of possible contentment are so explicit, but that indeed contentment, satisfaction, happiness is at stake. In other great poets, happiness is often conceived as not just elusive and ephemeral but decidedly inferior in importance to something else, such as understanding or spiritual improvement or contact with the divine, and thus to be a dangerous distraction or even a corrupting or delusive condition. Stevens repeatedly implies that we *can* and *should* find our way to happiness—as our most appealing (though perhaps not our most challenging) friends imply also.

7. HOLIDAY FROM RESPONSIBILITY
Stevens detaches urgency from action. Urgency animates many of the poems, but what we are urged to do is only to improve, or reconceive, our way of looking at the world. We must somehow face reality; in particular we must abandon religion, along with any other decayed and/or delusory myths. Stevens stressfully reiterates this demand as if he suspects us of a constant propensity to backslide into religion.[14] However, once we have dealt with this demand—which is remarkably comfortable for most of us in American academia in the second half of the twentieth century, because we are not seriously religious—we come to see that Stevens will never ask us to *do* anything else. Apparently he is not worried about what we might do, whether in the realms of love, work, or citizenship, so long as we have relinquished myth; either he is confident that we will do good things, or he doesn't care, or he thinks this is none of his business. We are released from responsibility. Life becomes an open-ended vacation, an endless sailing after lunch. There will be times of depression and nostalgia and vague yearning and sexual desire and even fear—as on any vacation—but we will never be challenged to alter our behavior in any way, because the unhappy moments are inevitable and should merely be sensitively en-

dured, indeed in a way savored. To the extent that we accept Stevens as our central poet, we free ourselves from all pangs of conscience about *actions*, omitted or committed.

I deliberately state this idea in provocatively simple form, because the matter has been mostly ignored by Stevens' critics. Examining my own conscience makes me suspect that this invitation to ignore or abandon responsibility is a crucial element in Stevens' appeal and in my own sense of having been befriended by Stevens. There is, I fear, a trace of moral corruption in my attraction to this poet who makes all my *choices* seem irrelevant or equally valid. Since Stevens criticism has mostly dodged this matter, and since it pertains troublingly to this book's focus on Stevens' troubled relation to the problem of interpersonal relations, I will say more (in the last part of this chapter) about Holiday from Responsibility than about any of the other six items on my list of Stevens' avuncular gambits; and I will then try to illuminate his irresponsibility by means of an extended comparison with the more drastic irresponsibility in the poetry of John Ashbery.

My reader has perhaps been wondering whether the seven features above will not be found, in varying degrees, in any poet's work. I suppose that all seven can be located *somewhere* within the oeuvre of any poet you wish to name, though in some cases the evidence would be scanty. Yeats may be seen as a game-player, but not much of an encourager, and he registers very few moods between visionary exaltation and bitter dejection. Eliot's humor, before *Four Quartets*, hardly feels friendly, and he is not at all cornucopic in his poetic output. Hardy shows generous dependability and moodiness, and some humor, indeed, in poems like "The Ruined Maid," but he does not send us away from responsibility. My claim about Stevens depends on the aggregate effect of all seven features together, and I propose that this aggregate effect distinguishes him from other poets.

What about Robert Frost? Does Frost exhibit all seven features? He is, I think, more like Stevens in his relation to the reader than any of their important contemporaries. There is the dry, even-toned humor that assumes the reader's alertness, as when his poem honoring New Hampshire ends, "At present I am living in Vermont." There is some game-playing, at least in a tendency toward quietly ambiguous syntax and riddling phrases, manifesting his sense that "Heaven gives its glimpses only to those / Not in position to look too close."[15] But in Frost there is nothing comparable to Stevens' quasi-systematic, copious deployment of symbolic imagery (colors, seasons, weather, etc.) and symbolic personages identifiable with forces or attitudes. Frost is certainly moody, but not candidly so; his defensive bristling irony is never absent for more than a few lines, and it serves to protect his stance of hard-won equanimity. This equanimity or poise (epitomized in the line about the oven bird who "knows in singing not to sing"), as of a poker player who can bluff all night, is so precious to Frost that no temptation toward candor (about depression or fear or self-criticism) is allowed to capsize it. Even a poem like "Storm Fear," though wonderfully expressive of a fearful mood, seems to assert a coolly proud resistance to fear by its deft rhyming and arch phrasing. There is a sense in which Frost strives always to be in the same mood, a spirit of guarded alertness, with something always held in reserve. When we feel that this striving arises from the fear of really radical fluctuations of mood (as in manic-depressive psychosis) we can be moved by it, but this does not, I suggest, involve a feeling that Frost is trusting us and befriending us. He maintains a distance cooler than Stevens' distance—partly because Stevens' worries about self-exposure, though strong and continuous, do not tap into fears and angers so ferocious as those fended off by Frost's poised poems.

The feature of dependability and generosity probably characterizes Frost just as much as Stevens, except that readers of Frost, while they may feel that the poems are abundantly adding up to something, feel much less confidence in stating what this something is than Stevensians feel. Stevens' critics typically sparkle with a happy readiness to reveal how splendidly coherent the poet's work is. A Frost critic cannot help being more wary.

Does Frost give his readers encouragement? He does, but such a tentative, hedging, unexalted encouragement. Poems such as "The Onset" and "On a Bird Singing in its Sleep" and "Our Hold on the Planet" suggest that we will probably survive, for a while. "Directive" notoriously invites us to a place "beyond confusion," but only by way of an imaginary journey which we will never (the poem implies) be able to make in reality. Frost promises nothing comparable to the utter fulfillment Stevens forecasts in passages like the following:

> there is an hour
> Filled with expressible bliss, in which I have
>
> No need, am happy, forget need's golden hand,
> Am satisfied without solacing majesty,
> And if there is an hour there is a day,
>
> There is a month, a year, there is a time
> In which majesty is a mirror of the self:
> I have not but I am and as I am, I am.   (*CP* 404–405)

The hypothetical status of this epoch of bliss does not undo Stevens' earnest affirmation of happiness as a real possibility.

Frost does use the pronoun *we* fairly often to imply that he is speaking sagely for all of us (not just for himself and a few neighbors); he uses it, for example, in such poems as "The Flood," "The White-Tailed Hornet," "Sitting By a Bush in Broad Sunlight," "Riders," and "On Looking Up By Chance at the Constellations." But the deeper Frost is the one who bristles with consciousness of his difference from others, the drumlin woodchuck who is thorough about his crevice and burrow; he is the man who is acquainted with the night, the man who wants a triple bronze barrier "Between too much and me," the man who knows he must mend the wall between himself and his neighbor, the man who says to a moth in winter, and by implication to pitiable human beings, "I cannot touch your life, much less can save, / Who am tasked to save my own a little while." In other words, Frost takes on the subject of the self's isolation, both as inevitable solitude and as chosen solitude, and makes this subject an explicitly central and personal and troubling concern; whereas Stevens, for whom it is also a crucial subject, as we have seen, strives to accommodate it within his overarching encouragement, by emphasizing the unvarying inevitability of solitude and by avoiding any dramatization of the separation between the self and specific others. The paradox in Stevens is that, though separate, we are all united as instances of The Imagining Self, interchangeable at the level of his philosophical concerns and thus easily representable by the words *we* and *one*.

Finally, what about Frost and the question of responsibility? Does he send us on holiday? There is an attractiveness in Frost that resembles Stevens' in this regard, though as usual Frost's relation to the question is more elusive and unsettling. He will not tell us simply that action is irrelevant. Stevens says, "Piece the world together, boys, but not with your hands" (*CP* 192). The mental work recommended here will never produce visible physical effects. Frost, who writes often about manual labor, implies that it matters how and why the work is done:

> The blows that a life of self-control
> Spares to strike for the common good
> That day, giving a loose to my soul,
> I spent on the unimportant wood.

He is on a kind of vacation in this poem ("Two Tramps in Mud Time"), but he knows it, and he knows that others are not:

> My right might be love but theirs was need.
> And where the two exist in twain
> Theirs was the better right—agreed.

Frost allows the possibility that one's action might be wrong—wrong morally, or wrong from the point of view of sustaining one's own health. In another poem he realizes, "I had to drop the armful in the road / And try to stack them in a better load." This effort may not involve responsibility to others, but it already distinguishes Frost from Stevens by presenting the image of an action whose practical consequences have to be described and evaluated. Frost loves the individual's (and humanity's) plucky stubborn resourcefulness in making life at least endurable; "The Investment" is a fine poem on this theme. In honoring such resourcefulness, Frost focuses often not on choices made but on the power to make choices. In "Riders" he imagines the earth as a headless horse on which humanity is uneasily mounted:

> But though it runs unbridled off its course,
> And all our blandishments would seem defied,
> We have ideas yet that we haven't tried.

This poem is so unprescriptive about how to ride that it may be felt to participate in a pervasive spirit of Yankee individualism in Frost whereby we are left free to try our own ideas. "Do whatever you have to do," Frost seems to tell his reader. But there is still a problem of *doing*, not just perceiving. In Frost's world, one must not only have ideas but *try* them. Some tries will succeed much better than others. "The Road Not Taken" is a poem about choice, about a choice that has mattered for the speaker. He admits that his choice was all but arbitrary, but it has had lasting and serious consequences:

> Two roads diverged in a wood, and I—
> I took the one less traveled by,
> And that has made all the difference.

It is true that these lines can be given an ironic interpretation: we may suspect that the choice has in fact made less difference than the speaker wants to believe. Nevertheless the poem addresses the fact that one does have to make choices in life and that these choices at least seem to have poignant and lasting effects. When Stevens recalls, in "The Poem That Took the Place of a Mountain," "how he had needed / A place to go to in his own direction" (*CP* 512), the sense of a road taken is remarkably unhaunted by any sense of other choices expensively discarded.

There is, then, much more acknowledgment of choice, of action and its cost, in Frost than in Stevens.[16] At the same time, though, there is in Frost a deep current of resistance to choice. A Frostian protagonist will not be pushed into action:

> I felt my standpoint shaken
> In the universal crisis.

> But with one step backward taken
> I saved myself from going.

Here he evokes a kind of anti-action, a movement made to avoid major movement ("going"). In "Time Out" Frost honors

> the obstinately gentle air
> That may be clamored at by cause and sect
> But it will have its moment to reflect.

And a line from another poem, about whether or not there is life after death, is quintessentially Frostian: "the strong are saying nothing until they see." Frost cherishes the strength required to refuse certain kinds of action, including speech. The cumulative impact of this current in Frost may be to endorse a kind of stoical, quizzical stillness, but it is not a relaxed or complacent stance. Frost's "time out" is not a holiday but a strategic withdrawal during an endless dangerous struggle that calls for strength.

If Frost were your uncle, such a view of life might be bracing and in a way invigorating—but rather chilly too. It is not comforting. Stevens as uncle, I have suggested, tries hard to make his nephews and nieces feel that life can become very warmly satisfactory, without any warfare of choices adopted or refused; we need not *do* anything, we need only *look* at the world through our uncle's lucid monocle—or rather, with eyes clarified by the attitude he recommends. Frost and Stevens share an aversion to the clamorous demands of interpersonal relations, but Frost knows, and is willing to reveal his knowledge, that such demands cannot be ignored or escaped for long; his great narrative poems, such as "Home Burial" and "The Death of the Hired Man," powerfully manifest this knowledge. Imagine Frost reading Stevens' "World Without Peculiarity"; he would see there Stevens trying to wish out of existence the kinds of pain and disturbance that need instead to be held off, nimbly deflected, barricaded away from the inmost heart again and again, because these demands from other people *will* continue to besiege the heart.[17]

Before expanding on each of the seven features of Stevens' poetry that I have singled out, let me push my avuncular metaphor so far as to consider, in a quick impressionistic spirit, how some other great modern poets might be figured as uncles.

HARDY: "Nephew has no choice but to come and bide in this world, and with luck we may be able to minimize his pain."

YEATS: "I don't recall what Nephew looks like, but in another life his soul may have been very great."

ELIOT: "Nephew is only human and must be kept under very strict control."

POUND: "Nephew is too sleepy, he must be galvanized! Send him to me in London, and before he arrives he must read these books!"

LAWRENCE: "Is Nephew really *alive*? Has he faced the animal in his blood?"

The comparably reductive sketch of Stevens might sound like this: "Nephew and I are going for a walk. We shall imagine the park. We are sure to find our way." One would want more than this from a father,[18] but if we are to choose a favorite uncle among the moderns, Stevens is our happiest choice.

1. SPEAKING FOR US: EXAMPLES AND FURTHER REMARKS

"Our happiest choice." But who are we? We are all the readers included by Stevens' generalizations, such as

> Death is the mother of beauty, mystical,
> Within whose burning bosom we devise
> Our earthly mothers waiting, sleeplessly.   (*CP* 69)

Or:

> We think, then, as the sun shines or does not.
> We think as wind skitters on a pond in a field
>
> Or we put mantles on our words because
> The same wind, rising and rising, makes a sound
> Like the last muting of winter as it ends.   (*CP* 518–19)

In his first-person-plural pronouncements, Stevens purports to speak at the level of universality, characterizing experiences and conditions so basic to humanity as to be shared by all persons. (He implies that all persons are at least potential readers of his pronouncements.) Presuming that we are all similar at this universal level, Stevens presumes that all of his readers must be thus similar to him, and he undertakes to speak for all of us. He would not assert that he speaks *instead* of us, quite, but he certainly has a strong sense of the poet's special empowerment as a representative: "The poet represents the mind in the act of defending us against itself" (*OP* 174). "The poet is the intermediary between people and the world in which they live and also, between people as between themselves" (*OP* 162). There is an implication here that people, however similar, may be rescued from the interpersonal embarrassment of speaking "between themselves" by the intercession of the poet's less personal speech. Though Stevens loves to suggest that in one sense every imagining person is a poet, still he is very interested in the literal sense in which the poet offers other people something they don't have. Out of the similarity we all share, he, the poet, creates "a present perfecting, a satisfaction in the irremediable poverty of life" (*OP* 167).

Obviously any writer must presume some similarity between himself and the reader; language itself rests on the faith that we are not utterly different from one another. My contention about Stevens is that he exhibits extraordinary confidence in his power to declare what "we" all feel, that he produces such declarations more often and more openly and more assuredly than other great poets,[19] and that this habit evokes in the reader a pleased sense of closeness with Stevens, a sense of being linked rather comfortably with his admired mind. To the extent that we find him brilliant in his thinking and lofty in his concerns, we can feel flattered by his belief that we are like him:

Natives of poverty, children of malheur,
The gaiety of language is our seigneur.   (*CP* 322)

We do not feel depressed or alarmed by this description of our condition, despite the ostensibly regrettable "poverty" and the ostensibly unhappy "malheur"; we feel we are being taught the motto of a spiffy club and that the poet has proclaimed our membership in this club. One of the club's enjoyable practices is the use of French words in unexpected, funny contexts. Paradoxically, though Stevens is ostensibly describing the condition of all human beings, we get a feeling that the club is exclusive to some degree: its true members are those of us who resemble our witty, wry poet in knowing about the gaiety of language and who can savor the ironically religious connotation of the word *seigneur*. There is something classy about having a "seigneur," even if it is only an imaginative process.

The comfortableness, for both poet and reader, of Stevens' first-person-plural statements can be recognized by way of a comparison with Eliot. In the following passage from "East Coker," Eliot may be said to presume that he and the reader are similar, but the reader is unlikely to feel flattered or gratified by the association since Eliot's basic emphasis is on our common inadequacy:

There is, it seems to us,
At best, only a limited value
In the knowledge derived from experience.
The knowledge imposes a pattern, and falsifies,
For the pattern is new in every moment

And every moment is a new and shocking
Valuation of all we have been. We are only undeceived
Of that which, deceiving, could no longer harm.
In the middle, not only in the middle of the way
But all the way, in a dark wood, in a bramble,
On the edge of a grimpen, where is no secure foothold,
And menaced by monsters, fancy lights,
Risking enchantment. Do not let me hear
Of the wisdom of old men, but rather of their folly,
Their fear of fear and frenzy, their fear of possession,
Of belonging to another, or to others, or to God.
The only wisdom we can hope to acquire
Is the wisdom of humility: humility is endless.[20]

We will never be humble enough for Eliot; even the word *enough*, so
crucial for Stevens, is for Eliot a gateway to spiritual failure.[21] Thus his
perception of constant change, which sounded Stevensian for a moment ("the pattern is new in every moment"), cannot melt into the
celebrations of lavish mutability that Stevens offers, as at the end of
"Esthétique du Mal":

So many selves, so many sensuous worlds,
As if the air, the mid-day air, was swarming
With the metaphysical changes that occur,
Merely in living as and where we live.   (*CP* 326)

Eliot does not want to hear of the wisdom of old men, not even of such
a subtle old man as the author of "Questions Are Remarks" (*CP* 462),
who happily attributes more wisdom to his grandson Peter than to old
men who approach reality with "antique acceptances." With Eliot, despite the spiritual firmness provided by such antique acceptances as
Anglicanism, we will always be wrong. Membership in his "we" will be
an awfully somber affair.

Much more appealing—unless you judge the description to be too
sentimental—is the life "we" share in one of Stevens' wistful secular
hymns:

The lover sighs as for accessible bliss,
Which he can take within him on his breath,
Possess in his heart, conceal and nothing known.

For easy passion and ever-ready love
Are of our earthy birth and here and now
And where we live and everywhere we live,

As in the top-cloud of a May night-evening,
As in the courage of the ignorant man,
Who chants by book, in the heat of the scholar, who writes

The book, hot for another accessible bliss:
The fluctuations of certainty, the change
Of degrees of perception in the scholar's dark.   (CP 395)

Here the happiness of a lover is assimilated to the happiness of a scholar (and anyone who reads "Notes Toward a Supreme Fiction," not to mention an essay quoting the poem, can feel pleasantly included by the word "scholar"), and we are allowed to feel good about being either or both.

Of course Stevens has his grimnesses and dark moods, but they seldom threaten the comfortableness, for us, of inclusion within his "we." When he says "We must endure our thoughts all night, until / The bright obvious stands motionless in cold" (CP 351), we feel the chill of the ironic connection between desirable certainty and deathly stasis, but the main force of the sentence is to credit us with admirable endurance. To be what we are is not fun at every moment, but it is all right. (This points to the theme of Holiday from Responsibility, which will be discussed again below.) It is to be like Stevens, and he is all right with us and we are all right with him.

Meanwhile, what we are is not very exactly or extensively recorded in Stevens, as the preceding chapters repeatedly observed. The blankness of Stevens' "we" must find its justification in the way abstraction and lack of vivid particularity are always justified, whether in poetry of the singular protagonist or of our collective experience. As it is justified here, for example, by Helen Vendler:

> In *Local Objects*, as in so many other poems, Stevens experiments with writing what might be called an algebraic statement into which each reader can substitute his own values for x and y . . . This sort of poetry was written before Stevens (notably by Dickinson) and has been written after him (especially by Ashbery). Stevens, and other such poets, presume that the experience under scrutiny is broad enough to be known to any reader . . . Stevens presumes, then, that his deprivations and his desires are ours.[22]

The suggestion is that Stevens, in a given poem, provides a carefully delineated outline or shape for a kind of emotional experience which each of us undergoes. The outline as provided by the poet has been purified of all merely personal oddities, and each of us can supply his or her own peculiar, colorful substance to fill it in. As we have seen in several contexts, Stevens loved the idea that there is a level at which

difference between persons becomes irrelevant while true and important things can still be said about us. (In chapter 3 we saw an unusually
forthright statement of this idea in "Things of August" VIII.) But
what if one of us—you, or I, or someone next door or in a poorer
neighborhood—has peculiarities which do not vanish so smoothly? In
other words, are we *all* among the "us" of Stevens' first-person-plural
sentences? Vendler's reference to Stevens' deprivations should make
us bat an eye: "His deprivations and his desires are ours." For it is
possible to imagine deprivations not compatible with being a wealthy
white male executive in Connecticut. From Stevens' vantage point, the
deprivations that might be attached to the condition of having skin
that is not white, for example, are merely peculiar deprivations, not
seriously interesting to him. (See note 29 below.) A person whose peculiar circumstances are quite different from Stevens' may feel that
the poet's inventory of significant deprivations is awfully limited, notwithstanding Vendler's confidence that each of us can plug our own
special disappointments and renunciations into Stevens' abstractions,
filling them with meaning via a "personal calibration."[23]

So the word *we* in Stevens has reawakened us—those of "us" who do
not sleep too soundly—to the issue of Stevens' elitism, which emerged
as a consideration in my first chapter. What I want to emphasize is that
the suspicious pleasantness of Stevens' "we," the palatability of the inclusion it offers us, should force us to consider the question of its implicit exclusions. The problem will arise again in relation to Stevens'
humor, and elsewhere. Stevens' typical reader, though, is someone
whose awareness of the poet's elitism (and other moral failings) has
not vitiated the special satisfactions of reading the poetry.

Let me put the proposition in empirical terms. If there are, let us
say, twenty thousand Americans today who have read more than fifty
of Stevens' poems and read them repeatedly (the criterion is meant to
leave out the casual or novice reader), I suppose that at least nineteen
thousand of them partake happily of the mixture of feelings I am
exploring, including feelings of being admired, comforted, performed for, and encouraged by the avuncular poet; and that this
happy response is much less ambivalent than the feelings engendered
in readers of Eliot, Frost, Pound, Yeats, and many another poet before
and after the moderns. But I have not taken a poll. If in fact there are
many more ambivalent and morally critical readers of Stevens than I
suppose, they are not well represented by the several hundred who
have written books and articles about Stevens. This elite group is by
and large hummingly unperturbed by the issues I want to pull into the
light. (Let the lamp affix its beam.)

Stevens' use of *one* has an effect akin to the effect of his *we*.[24] The

Stevensian reader feels included in this "one" and gladly so; "one" has been admitted to a fellowship in which life is very secular and earthy, yet somehow noble at the same time. "One's grand flights, one's Sunday baths, / One's tootings at the weddings of the soul / Occur as they occur" (*CP* 222). The statement's brio suggests that one's main work is to find lively phrasing for one's inevitably terrestrial and unsanctioned experience. One may have trouble adjusting to reality—"One feels a malady" (*CP* 63); "One might. One might. But time will not relent"*CP* 96)—but one's pain will be moderated by the pleasure of calling oneself "one" side by side with one's favorite uncle, savoring the faintly British aristocratic flavor of the pronoun while at the same time conscious of one's ironic American perspective on such pretension.[25] On the dump of American modernity, where traditional images have been discarded, one persists with a comical nobility, assisted by one's comical-noble diction:

> One sits and beats an old tin can, lard pail.
> One beats and beats for that which one believes.
> That's what one wants to get near. Could it after all
> Be merely oneself, as superior as the war
> To a crow's voice.   (*CP* 202–203)

It is true that an itchy kind of pain is expressed in "The Man on the Dump," but it is also true that a kind of solace is held out by the suggestion that what one wants to get near is after all merely oneself; and if so, then oneself cannot be so bad.

Marie Borroff hears Stevens' use of *one* as lofty and austere in a manner that sets the reader at a distance. She suggests that Stevens' speaker is "an austere personage who keeps his distance from us and confides nothing, seeming to dismiss as trivial all personal griefs and joys, if not all personal relationships whatsoever. A symptom of his loftiness of tone is his preference for the impersonal pronoun *one* over a possible *I* or *you*."[26] One of the passages Borroff then quotes as evidence of lofty tone is the end of "The Glass of Water." But I think she misses the ingratiating humor of the passage, which to my ear provides further evidence that the one "personal relationship" (if indeed it is in a sense personal) not disdained by Stevens is the relationship between poet and reader:

> In a village of the indigenes,
> One would have still to discover. Among the dogs and dung,
> One would continue to contend with one's ideas.   (*CP* 198)

Stevens surely knows this is funny, funny because of the juxtaposition of lofty pronoun with utterly unlofty environment. He says that you

and I, noble tourists like him even if comically mislocated among igno-
ble savages, would still carry on important imaginative life; and he
offers to share with us a smile at the incongruity involved.

At the same time, we know that he is happier in more genteel sur-
roundings, where he can more comfortably contend with his ideas.
But not entirely alone: he invites us along by making us feel included
in his pronouns. "Forces, the Will & the Weather," one of Stevens'
funniest good-mood poems, expresses his sense of imaginative at-
homeness on a lovely spring evening, and concludes with a charming
simile:

> The weather was like a waiter with a tray.
> One had come early to a crisp café.   (*CP* 229)

Stevens conveys his confidence that we, as members of his spiffy club,
know how it feels to sit at a crisp café (early, before the crowds of
nonmembers arrive, perhaps). Along with him we select a pastry from
the tray and continue to contend with our ideas; it is good to belong to
the Natives of Poverty Club on such a crisp spring evening. The café
simile is charmingly sociable in this way—unless we are somehow per-
verse enough to identify not with the imaginative customer but with
that waiter, whose perspective on such pleasures would be rather different. The simile subtly enforces our sense that Stevens' *we* and *one*
do include us but don't include everybody. A line in "Waving Adieu,
Adieu, Adieu" (*CP* 127) creates the same effect more purposefully.
The poem expresses the idea that in our mortal lives, "In a world without heaven to follow," all experience is a series of relinquishments, and
so we—we who see this—need to accustom ourselves to loss: "One
likes to practice the thing. They practice, / Enough, for heaven." The
word "they" should be heard with a stress that emphasizes the gap
between religious believers and us—we who have wisely said goodbye
to the idea of God. "They" are over *there*, while we are assumed to
belong with Stevens in an in-crowd of the undeluded, ready to feel
"jubilant" in merely natural sunny weather.

2. HUMOR: EXAMPLES AND FURTHER REMARKS

It is, of course, even less possible to "prove" that something is funny
than to prove that it induces pity and fear, or that it is paradoxical
rather than contradictory. Humor spurns explanation. Many critics
have credited Stevens with humor without laboring to prove the claim.
When Harold Bloom declares that "Mrs. Alfred Uruguay" is "a comic
masterpiece" and that the title character is "sublimely funny as a re-
ductionist,"[27] he says nothing to convince me that I should laugh or
smile along with him, because he feels the humor is plainly there for
the right reader to see. Stevens has made Bloom feel like the right

reader of Stevens: like most Stevens critics, Bloom feels fully initiated when he reads Stevens, as ready as anyone can be to catch the jokes, to distinguish solemnity from levity. The comedy Bloom sees in Mrs. Alfred Uruguay comes from the gap between her reality (velvet elegance though mounted on a donkey) and her aspiration ("the real" to be reached by rejections of myths and "moonlight"). Some such ironic gap is involved whenever we find something comic. For me the funnier part of the poem (a poem which on the whole strikes me as too noticeably contrived, a work of invention rather than discovery) is its opening, especially its first line:

> So what said the others and the sun went down
> And, in the brown blues of evening, the lady said,
> In the donkey's ear, "I fear that elegance
> Must struggle like the rest."   (*CP* 248–49)

The poem's opening collapses what could have been a lengthy narrative about certain "others" and their denial of the significance of something (the truth sought by Mrs. U.?) into a quick minimal account whose brevity is emphasized by the time-acceleration of "and the sun went down" and which is presumably at odds with the gravity the protoganist attaches to her mission. We are made conscious of a gap between a conventional narrative pace and the pace tolerable for our comic fabulist, who is impatient with ordinary storytelling and indeed with story itself as a mode of meaning. (He is impatient also, I suspect, with the melancholy vanity of Yeats and his lovely female companions in "Adam's Curse," who regret that "we must labour to be beautiful.") We may recall, as an alternate comic antinarrative strategy, the fanatically arch rhetoric which both stretches out and obscures (in the manner of Browning at his worst) the plot of "The Comedian as the Letter C."

Stevens' feeling that the quotidian facts of people's lives lack meaning unless transformed by imagination shows up in many poems, including "O Florida, Venereal Soil," "Depression Before Spring," "Frogs Eat Butterflies . . .," "Life is Motion," "The Man on the Dump," "Loneliness in Jersey City," and "Chaos in Motion and Not in Motion," all poems in which he tries to give images of mundane, fleshly life. Depression or disgust may underlie such poems but humor often helps the poet endure his bad mood.

> Mrs. Anderson's Swedish baby
> Might well have been German or Spanish,
> Yet that things go round and again go round
> Has rather a classical sound.   (*CP* 150)

If this closing stanza of "The Pleasures of Merely Circulating" is funny, the humor involves the extreme compression of two juxtaposed feelings: meaninglessness (nationality is an empty formality, individuals are interchangeable) versus the order created by perception and description (even merely observing a teleologically blank cyclical motion gives the observer a sense of order, a sense of being a connoisseur of chaos). The Swedish mother's pride is mocked with startlingly plain effrontery, but the simpleminded flavor of both supercompressed remarks serves to suggest the connoisseur's self-mockery at the same time. We are amused by the quick evenhandedness of this double disparaging, and by the fact that our poet, so concerned with the question of cosmic order or disorder, cannot escape acknowledging the naive immediacy of Mrs. Anderson and her untheoretical baby.

As I have no doubt just demonstrated, the attempt to analyze funniness tends to deaden rather than awaken our sense of it. Fortunately my business here is not to catalog Stevens' various ways of amusing us. I only need to indicate how his humor aims at his initiated reader, who feels entrusted with it. The humorous tone of the four lines quoted from "The Pleasures of Merely Circulating" is perhaps audible to any reader, but I here testify (or confess) that I have at least the illusion that I have heard the humor more precisely because Stevens has gradually taught me how to hear it. All right, one feels something like this about any difficult poet one has read over and over. But Stevens' humor, emerging at odd moments and in odd conjunction with challenging philosophical maneuvers, and thus calling for and anticipating our alertness, may nevertheless be one component of an unusual relation to the reader, which is on the whole a friendly, avuncular relation. "The moon follows the sun like a French / Translation of a Russian poet" (*CP* 234). Here Stevens gives us credit for familiarity with both earnest Russian writers and dapper French translators, with Slavic intensity and French delicacy. We feel flattered by the joke: Stevens has expected us to recall his many references to Frenchness and its "suitable amours" (*CP* 398), as well as his reference to a fanatical Russian named Konstantinov as "the lunatic of one idea" (*CP* 325). Stevens trusts us to be on his wavelength, and so we can feel included in a cordial relation of shared amusement.

Once in a while Stevens breaches his impressive decorum with an outburst, or a pretended outburst:

Say this to Pravda, tell the damned rag
That the peaches are slowly ripening.
Say that the American moon comes up
Cleansed clean of lousy Byzantium.   (*OP* 89)

In other words, pfui to Lenin, pfui to Yeats. It is as if our Uncle Wallace had drunk a bit more wine than usual.[28] We are delighted insofar
as we know enough to measure the gap between this outburst or
pseudo-outburst and his usual studied calm. Moreover, the cheeky
American rudeness is part of an insistence on being American which
we can feel as Stevens' affirmation of affiliation with us[29] as distinct
from "the hard hidalgo" in mountainous Spain (CP 345) or "Danes in
Denmark" (CP 419) or Englishmen in Ceylon (CP 215) or an Argen-
tine writer freezing in Paris (CP 457) or "a woman of Lhassa" (CP 52)
or "dark Brazilians in their cafés" (CP 38). Stevens' many references to
foreignness are all tinted with the red-blooded American's indelible
feeling that anyone living "over there" in countries to be imagined but
not visited is amusingly exotic (even if very much at home from their
own theoretically acknowledged points of view). Stevens is the kind of
uncle who comically purports to know much more about foreign
places than he knows from experience—he has his pet associations
with Paris and Ceylon and Guatemala—and if we are not offended by
this arrogance (a possibility I must allow, particularly as regards racism, though the present chapter assumes readers who have found
Stevens' voice seductive despite any moral misgivings such as those that
fueled my previous chapters), we can be entertained by it and feel that
Stevens is on our side, or at least that he thinks we are on his side.

Stevens writes a bleak poem about spiritual deprivation and calls it
"No Possum, No Sop, No Taters" (CP 293). This juxtaposing of title
and poem seems charmingly funny to me. I hear in it the affirmation
of Americanness I have just been noting, though the American dialect
chosen for the title is that of impoverished blacks whose experience,
from the vantage point of Asylum Avenue in Hartford, is at least as
foreign as that of Danes or Argentines. Stevens appropriates the blunt
expression of simple physical need as a metaphor for subtler spiritual
need. Is this funny? The maneuver resembles a maneuver I objected
to in "Idiom of the Hero" in chapter 1. Perhaps if I were black, the title
of "No Possum, No Sop, No Taters" would amuse me less. The humor
of it depends on the reader's sharing with Stevens a sense of being
American enough to be at home with the phrase, yet also safely distanced from the rude kind of physical poverty it evokes. Stevens presumes that we are not, after all, the black crow in the bleak landscape:
"One joins him there for company, / But at a distance, in another tree."

Having bumped into the issue of racist elitism in these notes on
Stevens' humor, I am reminded of a few passages alluded to in my
chapter on heterosexual love that might seem much less comic to a
feminist than to a male reader sharing Stevens' attitude toward femininity; the problem of an elitist complicity between writer and reader
as different from someone else becomes more bluntly manifest in rela-

tion to humor than in relation to other features of Stevens' poetry. I am inclined to describe the early poem "Peter Parasol" (*OP* 20) as humorously bleak in its lament that all women are not equipped with beauty as elephants are equipped with tusks; but if I were describing the poem thus to a female reader, particularly a woman with a low estimation of her own physical attractiveness, my sense of the poem's humor would wobble, and I would want to emphasize the way in which its title suggests an ironic view of the speaker's aestheticist melancholy. Similarly, to imagine a female reader of section XLV of "Like Decorations in a Nigger Cemetery," is to realize that a humorous barb aimed at simpleminded hedonism is spoiled by its own simpleminded sexism:

> *Encore un instant de bonheur.* The words
> Are a woman's words, unlikely to satisfy
> The taste of even a country connoisseur.   (*CP* 157)

The Shakespearean pun in "country" turns sour when we focus on the cheap maneuver whereby the phrase "a woman" is so confidently made to stand for a certain kind of foolish person.

Humor, as a quality constitutive of amiable relation between poet and reader, turns out to be an ethically volatile matter—reminding us that humor (including racist and sexist jokes) often achieves its pleasurable effect by suddenly jostling the listener's ethical pretensions, in a way that the listener may or may not pause to examine critically.

3. GAME-PLAYING: EXAMPLES AND FURTHER REMARKS

One night in 1967 I was summoned by Nick Sander after midnight to Paul Phillips' room in our freshman dormitory, to help in an emergency: Paul had to turn in a paper on "The Man With the Blue Guitar" next morning, and he could not understand the poem. (Paul was a musician, and I suspect he had agreed to write about the poem because of its attractive title.) I had read only a few short poems by Wallace Stevens, but Nick thought my general interest in poetry might make me useful. Paul stood in the middle of his room reading aloud the first section of the poem and muttering "What the fuck is this?" I looked at the poem, and my freshman arrogance wavered. However, taking our cue from Nick—"It's all about imagination and reality, and the guitarist symbolizes the poet"—we set to work. Nick and I walked in circles on the carpet, reading lines aloud and suggesting paraphrases for them, while Paul sat scribbling notes. "Yeah, yeah, that's great," he'd say, "but what about these mechanical beetles?" Nick and I were terrifically confused by the poem, but we refused to give up— partly because Paul threatened to plunge into theatrical despair if we did, but also because the challenge of producing plausible paraphrases became exhilarating. I have no doubt that most of what we offered Paul was mistaken (though I am glad that I am not asking myself today to paraphrase "The Man With the Blue Guitar," because some of it is still not clear to me, and I lack the energy I had in 1967); but I also have no doubt that what we said that night did pass through sudden rightnesses. What I remember feeling, as we hacked our way along, section by section, was: *We can play this game.* I realized happily that as long as each improvised paraphrase involved the idea that an imaginative recreation of reality is never quite true, never the same as the reality, and that this difference can be painful but also can be beautiful—as long as I hung on to this basic theme, my paraphrases would approach some sort of plausibility. The game was tricky and mysterious, but it was a game: take each section and rope it to the basic theme. It was a game which could promise a feeling of winning, a game in which victory (right interpretation), though uncertain and unstable, would be distinguishable from losing.

At 2:00 A.M. we were perhaps halfway through the poem, and Paul howled in frustration when he realized how far we had to go. I did feel a flash of fear when I turned the pages and saw that the poem ran to thirty-three sections; at the same time, though, Stevens' proliferation of sections, once recognized as a deliberately prodigal proliferation, made each section seem less important and hence less intimidating. When we reached section XX Paul announced that he would conclude his paper by saying that the last thirteen sections merely give variations on themes already explored. Nick and I went off to our rooms to sleep or to worry about hoped-for exterior paramours (Gayle Rogers in my case) while Paul went to his typewriter, a shearsman of sorts.

Since that night I have never liked "The Man With the Blue Guitar," but I did turn out to be a Stevens critic, of sorts, and the pleasure I felt that night with Nick and Paul must have been one germ of what eventually became my absorption in Stevens' poetry. The pleasure involved a sense of learning a high-class game. Many critics have learned to play the game and have enjoyed playing it and getting paid for playing it. Countless illustrations of their enjoyment are available from the critical literature, and here is one. Listen to Daniel Schneider's pleasure as he explains why the title "Like Decorations in a Nigger Cemetery" "may be roughly translated 'Imaginings in Reality'":

If such an interpretation seems forced, one has only to consider the many titles in Stevens' work which follow a similar pattern: "Hymn From a Watermelon Pavilion": a creation of the imagination issuing from a world of juicy vegetation—reality. "A Postcard from the Volcano": an imaginative creation, a poem, issuing from reality, a realm of violence and death. "The Dove in the Belly": the dulcet imagination in the grinding peristalsis of reality. "The Owl in the Sarcophagus": the owlish poet or imagination in the realm of death. "A Golden Woman in a Silver Mirror": the female, sunny earth reflected in the glass of the imagination. "Academic Discourse at Havana": an imaginative discourse in the lush physical world. "The Revolutionists Stop for Orangeade": poets in revolt, imaginative beings, stop for a drink from the juicy South, a drink of reality. "Nudity at the Capital": the absence of the imagination in the habitat of the imagination. "Angel Surrounded by Paysans": the imagination surrounded by reality. And so on![30]

The best critics of Stevens are naturally embarrassed by this game-playing aspect of the poet and the sort of criticism—assign each item either to column A (imagination) or to column B (reality)—that results. The best critics may complain that such criticism is reductive, but they cannot deny that it is inspired by actual qualities of the poetry; and if they are honest, I think they will admit that this quasi- (delight-fully quasi-) systematic aspect of Stevens, more and more recognizable as one reads more and more of the poems, was partly what first lured them into Stevens' palace of mirrors. Vendler is a bit smug in her sternness when she reviews the decoding of Stevens by game-oriented critics:

> This decoding produced some commentary of extraordinary banality, in which poem after poem was said to be "about" the encounter between "the imagination" and "reality." Commentary which impoverishes poems is a disservice to them. . . . To see the rich nature of these poems, one must not monotonously refer them to some single external theme, whether physical or metaphysical; rather one must reveal their depth and breadth of internal reference—a reference so full in the last poems as to make them readable only in the light of the earlier poetic illusions to which they allude. . . . Stevens' commitment to the secrecy of intertextual symbols like the dove, as well as to the secrecies of an impersonal presentation and a resolutely elliptical discourse, makes him a poet knowable in the instance only when he is known in the whole.[31]

In other words, the oeuvre of Stevens is a special game in its own ball-park, and rookies have to learn its special rules from Coach Stevens himself (and from assistant coaches like Vendler). A dove in Stevens means things (and means them in a quasi-systematic way, as Vendler has very helpfully shown)[32] that a newcomer to Stevens cannot see, even if the newcomer is clever enough to associate the dove with Venus and therefore with erotic desire. Familiarity with actual doves will not help the newcomer; familiarity with Greek mythology will only just barely help. Vendler may protest the unsubtle game-playing of some critics, but she cannot escape the fact that Stevens' poetry offers, like baseball, the pleasures of a self-sufficient, separate universe of interrelated signals and meanings; indeed this is what Vendler celebrates in the passage quoted above. As I sensed in my freshman dorm, reading Stevens is not like reading *The Waste Land* with Eliot's explanatory notes. Eliot's notes, while certainly necessary (any critic who says the notes were not called for is disingenuous), do not alleviate but rather intensify the new reader's sense of being egregiously, even hopelessly, ignorant of both Western and Eastern civilization; the freshman reader sees that for Mr. Eliot's course there are countless prerequisites. Mr. Stevens, though, runs his own separate college, or club. He may mention Nietzsche or Freud or Whitman; he may allude slyly to Shelley and Keats and Emerson; but the ephebe who has not studied these giants still feels quite welcome as a novice Stevensian.[33] The only necessary explanatory notes for a Stevens poem, one suspects, are Stevens' other poems. This is not only attractive but *inviting*, and it is inviting not only to freshmen but to seniors wearied by the paralyses of erudition.[34]

I may have given the impression that by Stevens' game-playing I mean only his use of symbolism. But symbolism is only the stylistic maneuver most easily pointed out and summarized. Another important gamelike feature is his play with syntax, including the use of rhetorical questions; the suspension of syntax through long series of phrases ostensibly offered as synonyms; the approbation implied by adjectival superlatives; and the implied affirmation of hypotheses achieved by manipulating verb tenses and hyperextending *as if* constructions. Reading such passages well is, again, very much a matter of having gotten used to Stevens. (The feature of Dependability, next on my list, is implicit here.) His syntactical trickery has been well analyzed by Vendler and others.[35] Rather than add to their observations, I will say more about how Stevens' gamesmanship makes a reader feel.

Now, I know that every reader is not inevitably beguiled; some readers on some days might even be nauseated by the feature I am discussing. ("If he says 'blue' one more time I will scream.") But I claim that on the whole, for the willing reader, the reader with enough affinity for Stevens to keep reading him, Stevens' game-playing quality is not only an initial attraction (as for freshmen) but also an ongoing cause of the feeling I have described as befriendedness, the feeling that Stevens' attitude toward the reader is a benevolent, warm (not torrid), avuncular caring. To support my (openly impressionistic) claim, I resort again to the Favorite Uncle metaphor. One way the man tries to please his nephew or niece is by teasing, a sort of verbal tickling. He dares us to figure out his coded messages, lacing them with just enough of his habitual clues (except when there are not enough; a few Stevens poems fall short in this regard)[36] to hold our interest and pull us along. "The poem must resist the intelligence / Almost successfully" (*CP* 350). This attitude toward the reader is a teasing one, a tickling one, indeed a rather sexy attitude in a way—playing a game of come-hither / take-your-paws-off-me, while intending not to lose the reader altogether.[37] Our uncle hands us tough nuts to crack (I vary my metaphors with an insouciance learned partly from him), but he also hands us his monogrammed nutcracker and drops hints on how to operate it. Even when we find this procedure annoying, we sense that he is interested in interesting us and not losing us; the poem must only be *almost* successful in resisting the intelligence.

The Stevensian ball game is (as I have suggested by way of contrast with Eliot) open to all comers, but because the game is tricky and requires immersion in the oeuvre, it also makes available to us the feeling (emphasized earlier in connection with the pronouns *we* and *one*) that we who have learned to play the game are rather special individuals and that we are deemed so by the poet. In "The Noble Rider and the Sound of Words," Stevens considers what a poet offers to readers:

> I think that his [the poet's] function is to make his imagination theirs [the readers'] and that he fulfills himself only as he sees his imagination become the light in the minds of others. His role, in short, is to help people to live their lives. Time and time again it has been said that he may not address himself to an élite. I think he may. There is not a poet whom we prize living today that does not address himself to an élite. The poet will continue to do this . . . for all poets address themselves to someone and it is of the essence of that instinct, and it seems to amount to an instinct, that it should be to an élite, not to a drab but to a woman with the hair of a pythoness, not to a chamber of commerce but to a gallery of one's own, if there are enough of one's own to fill a gallery.[38]

"Enough of one's own"—there is a flavor of intimacy in the phrase; if we are Stevens' preferred readers, those who can be helped by him, then we belong to him in a familial way. Yet, as the outlandish jungle-woman metaphor suggests, this bond is not boringly domestic. As receivers of his poems we are invited to consider ourselves as vital and exciting as "a woman with the hair of a pythoness," a sensation not undone but enhanced by our awareness that Stevens is being comical; in this sudden snaky metaphor, our uncle is pretending to rip his tie off. He likes us! He counts on us to know that fictive things wink when they will.

Of course it is always also true that the poet writes for himself, and that Stevens' elaborate gamesmanship is his way of creating an order for himself, a *mundo* to live in. Certainly, but this truth should never be divorced from the truth that a poet writes for readers, as Stevens affirms in the prose passage just quoted. This is true of Eliot (see note 4), and it is true of Yeats, who is in some respects (especially if *A Vision* is taken into account) a more insistent game-player, codemonger and system-builder than Stevens, providing fanciful patterns of meaning because he knows that if his ideas are not compelling to readers they will not be lastingly useful to him. In the last four lines of "A Prayer For My Daughter," Yeats explicitly turns toward us to help us understand his images:

> How but in custom and in ceremony
> Are innocence and beauty born?
> Ceremony's a name for the rich horn,
> And custom for the spreading laurel tree.[39]

But in neither Eliot nor Yeats do we sense the humorous interest in, and ingratiating solicitude toward, the reader that I have been attributing to Stevens.

4. DEPENDABILITY AND GENEROSITY: EXAMPLES AND FURTHER REMARKS
There may be little to say under this heading that has not been implied in the pages about Stevens' game-playing. My emphasis here is on Stevens' consistency and abundance. No doubt this point could be overstated; Stevens does achieve some variety (otherwise, intelligent critics would not have written so many books about him), and "The Comedian as the Letter C" is a long way from "The Plain Sense of Things." It is, and it isn't. Crispin, after all, in one of his phases sought the plain sense of things:

> He inhaled the rancid rosin, burly smells
> Of dampened lumber, emanations blown
> From warehouse doors, the gustiness of ropes,
> Decays of sacks, and all the arrant stinks
> That helped him round his rude aesthetic out.
> He savored rankness like a sensualist.
> He marked the marshy ground around the dock,
> The crawling railroad spur, the rotten fence,
> Curriculum for the marvelous sophomore.   (*CP* 36)

In "The Plain Sense of Things" (*CP* 502), the tone is different and the mood is different: the enthusiasm of a marvelous sophomore is so absent from the old poet's spirit that there is no need to satirize it, and the rankness of a decayed world, "The great pond and its waste of the lilies," is not a perception sought by the old poet but one inevitably imposed on him. Also his nose is less sensitive than Crispin's. Still, the basic concern has not changed: in what sense can we see things as they are, and how does it feel to attempt this? The reader who understands Crispin's project can, across more than 450 intervening pages and thirty years of Stevens' career, quickly grow comfortable with, and talk about, "The Plain Sense of Things."

Every poet has his or her temperamental continuity, but in some— Wordsworth, Tennyson, Yeats, Eliot, Auden, Lowell—the jumps from one phase to another are (however explainable in retrospect) much more jarring. (Later I will discuss an extreme case of unstartling continuity, in John Ashbery.) The persistence of Stevens' attention to his chosen problems is acknowledged by every critic, though some critics are eager to defend Stevens against the charge of mechanical self-echoing. I have no wish to challenge the admirable studies that show important movements in Stevens' style and attitude from *Harmonium* to *The Rock*; my own first chapter emphasized the distinctive concerns of *Ideas of Order*. But there is a quality of dependability in Stevens that I must try to bring out more clearly. It is mainly *not* a matter of boring repetitiousness. Though our uncle visits every weekend for years and years, he is almost always interesting. He comes wearing different hats, different ties, he affects different accents; he puzzles us with his endless variations on his old games—but he is always recognizably and comfortingly Uncle Wallace.[40] A visit from him is a fresh stimulus within certain very reliable limits, a routinely special occasion. He trusts us to figure out how this week's version of "the finding of a satisfaction" (*CP* 240) is interestingly though subtly different from last week's. Within his dependable devotion to that basic problem, he is tirelessly bountiful; each of his remarks calls to mind a dozen of his other remarks, each one just different enough.

This quality is especially endearing to those readers who become critics, because the critic always finds his or her hands full of apposite quotations; our cup runneth over. I think it could be proven that Stevens' critics quote lines and phrases more often from more poems than do critics of any other poet; the typical essay about Stevens is peppered with quotations from various parts of his oeuvre. In this book I have not always resisted the juicy handiness of the extra quotation. Stevens is a great Santa Claus of quotability; two critics could easily build long accounts of his ideas, each using many quotations, without ever quoting the same passage.

For the persistent reader of Stevens there is a basic experience that occurs over and over: a given passage stumps you or remains drily opaque to you, until one day you approach it from the right angle (catching on to a trick of syntax, perhaps) and it blossoms into meaning—familiar meaning. You feel the pleasure of decoding, together with the pleasure of a revived contact with friendly, comfortable ideas; you exclaim, *He's saying it again!* Part of the pleasure (for you, the willing reader, the addicted or at least charmed Stevensian) is in the comic juxtaposition of new language with old ideas. You share with Stevens a delight in his power to say his usual things in a fresh (and *almost* successfully puzzling) way. You smile with relief at the reconfirmation of your understanding. "The old boy had me buffaloed for a minute there, but then . . ." (I recall having this experience in 1985 with section IX of "Esthétique due Mal," one of so many passages in Stevens that can serve well, maybe too well, as a précis of his thought.) If the passage at hand varies by some nuance from your previous grasp of his ideas, this only makes your delight more piquant. Meanwhile, Stevens seems not to insist that we labor obsessively at grasping any one passage, though it may indeed be difficult. As I felt in Paul Phillips' room in 1967, Stevens can be counted upon to give us another chance. This generosity seems to flow from his awareness that, like him, we are endlessly subject to the dissolution of our solutions. As he says delightfully at the end of "Montrachet-le-Jardin,"

> And yet what good were yesterday's devotions?
> I affirm and then at midnight the great cat
> Leaps quickly from the fireside and is gone.   (*CP* 264)

There he goes saying *that* well again too.

One way to notice the feature I describe is to look at any extended commentary on "Notes Toward a Supreme Fiction." There are shifts of emotion and focus in the poem but even the most ingenious commentator will, if he or she addresses most of the thirty-two sections, say virtually the same thing about imagination (its power and its dependence on the real) over and over again. In the penultimate section of "It Must Give Pleasure," Stevens faced this aspect of his work and tried to contend that in a secular world repetition can be not only necessary but joyous:

>   the merely going round,
> Until merely going round is a final good,
> The way wine comes at a table in a wood.   (*CP* 405)

Rightly imagined, every hour can be happy hour; and the poet can keep saying so.

In the last stage of writing this essay I come upon a poem in *Opus Posthumous* called "Artificial Populations" (*OP* 112), and it is as if I had never read it before. It must have seemed inert and trivial to me before, but today it seems alive and significant, it seems to have been patiently "awaiting espousal to the sound / / Of right joining" (*CP* 464–

65). I can see how I could have used the poem in my chapter on solitude, since it rather touchingly expresses Stevens' desire for a community, a social life, though it also stubbornly (or helplessly) asserts that
the fellow citizens he will meet when life is good will be creations of his
mind, confections; and by the end of the poem these artificial people
have become no more than a pleasant experience comparable to sleep
or music (or the images generated by sleep or music). His people are

> The rosy men and the women of the rose,
> Astute in being what they are made to be.
>
> This artificial population is like
> A healing-point in the sickness of the mind:
> Like angels resting on a rustic steeple
> Or a confect of leafy faces in a tree—
>
> A health—and the faces in a summer night.
> So, too, of the races of appropriate people
> Of the wind, of the wind as it deepens, and late sleep,
> And music that lasts long and lives the more.   (*OP* 112–13)

The poem renews my sense that I was on target in my chapter on
solitude, and that I can trust Stevens to keep on being Stevens for me.

5. MOODINESS: EXAMPLES AND FURTHER REMARKS

A reader who has not yet realized that Stevens is a poet of many
moods, and a poet dedicated to the truth of moods, is blocked from a
full sense of Stevens' dependability—since Stevens is dependably
moody—and blocked also from the pleasures of seeing how vividly he
can embody moods. A mood is a way of seeing, an imaginative condition, a phase of one's continuous imaginative negotiation with the
world. Each mood has its own veracity; depression, for instance, taints
the world so that the world is filled with regrettable and ugly things.
Stevens always wants to claim greater truth for happy moods (as we
will observe in connection with Encouragement), but he knows that his
work of showing the imagination's life calls for the registering of many
different moods.[41] Thus we get the bleak wistfulness of "Debris of Life
and Mind," the wry disappointment of "Depression Before Spring,"
the sour sense of pointlessness in "Mandolin and Liqueurs" and "Gubbinal," the relinquishing of hope and energy in "Farewell Without a
Guitar" and "Lebensweisheitspielerei" and "Vacancy in the Park," the
misanthropic sarcastic alienation of "Loneliness in Jersey City" and
"The Drum Majors in the Labor Day Parade," the dejected self-deni-
gration of "The Dwarf," the grim self-criticism of "The Man Whose
Pharynx was Bad," the chilly self-counseling of "Secret Man" and

"Farewell to Florida"; as well as the puffed postprandial complacency of "A Rabbit as King of the Ghosts" and the unconflicted early-morning lucidity of "The Latest Freed Man" and the chipper self-delight of "Forces, the Will & the Weather." Stevens achieves an array of nuances in these mood poems more variously shaded than any comparable achievement by another poet, or so I wish to suggest.[42]

Helen Vendler may feel that "moodiness" is a term too mild and normalizing to encompass the poems of bitterness and frustration that Stevens writes with what she has persuasively called "brutality"; her analysis of such poems as "Chaos in Motion and Not in Motion," "The Motive for Metaphor," and "The Dove in Spring" is extraordinarily valuable on this point.[43] However, Stevens' moods never run wild; there is always an urbanity at hand to rein them in. Even when Stevens is very unhappy, his voice remains steady. As Vendler herself observes:

> Stevens' poems are often second-order reflections on the stormings of first-order sensation. They are distillations. . . . It is only after Stevens' fierceness of desire has finished its initial storming into despair that its essence is expressed in the poems.[44]

Thus in Stevens there is a pervasive sense of the speaker being quite able to survive his dejection or bitterness, whether by wry humor or stoic persistence or both (and this is why "despair" doesn't quite ring true in characterizing such poems); we hear, indeed, that the speaker has already outlived the worst of the mood. Admittedly some such statement can logically be made about nearly all poetry ("emotion recollected in tranquillity"), but reading Stevens is not like reading Hardy's "During Wind and Rain" or Eliot's "Preludes" or Ginsberg's "Howl" or Lowell's "Eye and Tooth" or Plath's "Lady Lazarus" or Jarrell's "90 North" or Adrienne Rich's "Rape"—a diverse handful of poems, in each of which we feel the poet gripped by the demon of a mood that may not let go. Such poems are frightening in a way that Stevens, candidly moody, is not. We are never afraid of him, nor afraid for him. He never seems suicidal, never desperate like the Hopkins of "No worst, there is none . . ." Once in a while ("The Dwarf," "Lebensweisheitspielerei") he sounds very curt and chilly, but only briefly. There is always with Stevens the sense that the mood will pass—thanks partly to the nearness and the candor of many poems of other moods.[45] This sense is also reinforced by Stevens' habitual association of mood with season, suggesting reliable cyclical change.

Stevens' late poetry is distinguished by several poignant expressions of a mood in which old age has brought loss of meaning. However, in these last years he was sometimes unwilling to let a bad mood remain intact on the page; instead of trusting that another poem would answer, he tried to build an answer to unhappiness into the same poem with the unhappiness. This is probably a reflection of the aging poet's impulse to show a balanced wholeness in each action, since each action could turn out to be his last. Instances include "Long and Sluggish Lines," the first section of "The Rock," "World Without Peculiarity," and "Puella Parvula." In each of these, Stevens' belief in the power of imagination urgently and forcibly generates a willed recuperation from the bitter mood of the poem's opening stanzas. The rescue is performed most unsubtly and fiercely in "Puella Parvula," when, in response to images of destruction, he proclaims:

> Over all these the mighty imagination triumphs
> Like a trumpet and says, in this season of memory,
> When the leaves fall like things mournful of the past,
>
> Keep quiet in the heart, O wild bitch. O mind
> Gone wild, be what he tells you to be: *Puella*.
> Write *pax* across the window pane. And then
>
> Be still.   (*CP* 456)

The demon in the heart is sternly disciplined. But even here Stevens does not shout, though "wild bitch" is enough to open our eyes wider. He is calm enough to avail himself of Latin, language of empire and scholarship. We see him asserting his power to manage his moods, and as he achieves this by means of "the mighty imagination" which he has taught us to identify with our humanity, the poem encourages us to feel that we can manage our moods too.

The overall effect of Stevens' poetry of mood is to suggest that emotional vicissitudes are colorful and interesting and not to be denied, but need never be disastrous or even lastingly painful. We can know that some aspects of real life are omitted by this suggestion, while at the same time taking comfort from it.

6. ENCOURAGEMENT: EXAMPLES AND FURTHER REMARKS

We can and should find our way to happiness—not merely to fortitude or peace or wisdom or vision or righteousness, but to happiness! What other great poet has told us this? Whitman, sometimes. Lawrence, occasionally. Not Frost, not Eliot, not Yeats, not Hardy, not Crane, not Larkin, not Lowell . . . It is an extraordinary view for a serious poet to take, and all the true things said about Stevens' fears and miseries and regrets in the poetry should not blind us to his specialness on this score. Critics concerned with protecting Stevens from an unfair perception of him as a hedonistic dandy have often gone too far in the direction of portraying him as essentially stern and bleak. Some of the critics' emphasis on Stevens' brave facing-up to the absence of God— which is, after all, old news inherited from Tennyson, Arnold, and Hardy (not to mention the ferocious Nietzsche)—seems to me a response to embarrassment about how pleasantly undisturbing Stevens really is. Harold Bloom is refreshingly frank when he admits that Stevens makes him feel good:

> His True Subject appears to be his own sense of glory, and his true value for his readers appears to be that he reminds us of our own moments of solipsistic bliss, or at least of our aspirations for such moments.[46]

Consider this passage (quoted in part earlier) from one of the last sections of "Notes Toward a Supreme Fiction," in which Stevens has imagined an angel of reality content with no more than reality:

> Is it he or is it I that experience this?
> Is it I then that keep saying there is an hour
> Filled with expressible bliss, in which I have
>
> No need, am happy, forget need's golden hand,
> Am satisfied without solacing majesty,
> And if there is an hour there is a day,
>
> There is a month, a year, there is a time
> In which majesty is a mirror of the self:
> I have not but I am and as I am, I am.
>
> These external regions, what do we fill them with
> Except reflections, the escapades of death,
> Cinderella fulfilling herself beneath the roof?   (CP 404–405)

The passage begins and ends with reminders of the worry that our happy projections are *only* projections, but the main force of the passage is in its earnest wishing for that time of majesty and bliss, and the passage's main effect, I think, is to affirm that such bliss can be reached. The "Woman Looking at a Vase of Flowers" reaches it, and Stevens tells us that in her terrestrial epiphany

>   the inhuman colors fell
> Into place beside her, where she was,
> Like human conciliations, more like
> A profounder reconciling, an act,
> An affirmation free from doubt.
> The crude and jealous formlessness
> Became the form and the fragrance of things
> Without clairvoyance, close to her.   (CP 247)

There she is, a beautifully happy person—and all she is doing is looking. Students of literature, including readers of Stevens, are people who do a lot of careful looking. Stevens affirms that observation, if it is alert to the richness of reality (this alertness can involve more or less stress on the observer's imaginative power, depending on Stevens' mood), is a mode of happiness: not just a road to happiness, but a form of it. This is a lovely theme for us, we who are devoted to our perceptions (notwithstanding the difference between looking at a vase of flowers, or ducks in a park, and looking at poetry). Moreover, Stevens encourages us to believe not only in our possible bliss but in our possible majesty; that is, he repeatedly suggests that our imaginative, sensory life, in conjunction with our endurance in a world divested of God and other supernatural myths, is rather noble, indeed in a way heroic (connecting us, after all, to his "central man" and to "the hero," figures that sum up our power to believe in humanity and not in the divine). This point emerged in the preceding chapter, and in this chapter's section on Speaking for Us, and it will have to return yet again in the section on Holiday from Responsibility. A Stevens reader who believes all that Stevens taught and strove to believe is licensed not only to feel good (happy) but to feel proud and to feel proud of feeling good, and all this will flow from the "profounder reconciling" of unreligious, undeluded observation:

> The burgher's breast,
> And not a delicate ether star-impaled,
> Must be the place for prodigy, unless
> Prodigious things are tricks.   (*CP* 143–44)

We infer that our prodigious kinsman thinks that we are or may be prodigious. And how noble we seem to be in "Evening Without Angels" on the earth that is bare

> Except for our own houses, huddled low
> Beneath the arches and their spangled air,
> Beneath the rhapsodies of fire and fire,
> Where the voice that is in us makes a true response,
> Where the voice that is great within us rises up,
> As we stand gazing at the rounded moon.   (*CP* 138)

We are great—and all we have to do is look and appreciate.

7. HOLIDAY FROM RESPONSIBILITY: EXAMPLES AND FURTHER REMARKS

All we have to do is look and appreciate—like tourists on a cruise. There is in Stevens a general lack of interest in, and sometimes an edgy aversion to, *any* kind of action other than perceiving: "Piece the world together, boys, but not with your hands" (*CP* 192). Anyone with a project that involves physical alteration of the world or active engagement with the world (including other human bodies) is either ignored or glancingly satirized in Stevens' poetry. During the early seventies, already worrying about the ethics of my favorite poet, I repeatedly turned to his poem "How to Live. What to Do" and repeatedly felt frustrated, until I realized that the poem's title is a deliberate tease. No doubt the title holds a serious (all too serious) meaning for Stevens, but at the same time it is a satirical jab at anyone who turns to poetry for a simple set of instructions and, more importantly, at anyone who assumes that the problem of how to live is a matter of what to *do*. What is to be done? In Stevens' poem the only present action is "standing still to rest," along with the perceiving being done by "The man and his companion":

How to Live. What to Do

Last evening the moon rose above this rock
Impure upon a world unpurged.
The man and his companion stopped
To rest before the heroic height.

Coldly the wind fell upon them
In many majesties of sound:
They that had left the flame-freaked sun
To seek a sun of fuller fire.

Instead there was this tufted rock
Massively rising high and bare
Beyond all trees, the ridges thrown
Like giant arms among the clouds.

There was neither voice nor crested image,
No chorister, nor priest. There was
Only the great height of the rock
And the two of them standing still to rest.

There was the cold wind and the sound
It made, away from the muck of the land
That they had left, heroic sound
Joyous and jubilant and sure.   (*CP* 125–26)

The two perceivers in the poem (are they two persons?—we cannot trust the word "companion" to mean a separate person in Stevens) have climbed "away from the muck of the land," though the poem does not deign to describe the actual climbing. They experience an epiphany of essential earthly reality ("this tufted rock") divested of myth, and they seem to have thus attained a kind of heroism, though Stevens evasively attaches the word "heroic" not to them but to the mountain and the sound of the wind. The two perceivers have achieved Stevensian fulfillment, Stevensian transcendence—they have made it! Do they interact? Do they nudge each other, do they converse? Why bother? For Stevens they have already done all there is to do. Indeed the presence of the "companion" in the poem is a disingenuous maneuver by Stevens, because if the companion is a friend or lover (and not merely the man's imagination or some aspect of it), then the poem ought to have something to say about how the companion's presence matters to the man. Stevens allows himself an ambience of interpersonal sentiment without taking any responsibility for the significance of the fact that the great epiphany has occurred when the protagonist is (apparently) not alone.

The epiphany has been achieved "away from the muck of the land"—but what is wrong with the land? After all, this poet is our poet of "bare earth" (*CP* 137) and "the immense dew of Florida" (*CP* 95) and "Bottles, pots, shoes and grass" (*CP* 203)—yet he yearns for a separation between himself and "the common life" (*CP* 221). Down there in the muck of the land there is too much confusion, partly because too many people are challengingly present with their different views, and also because they are *doing* things. The muck of the land is the world of action, the world of work, the world of consequences. In "How to Live. What to Do" and in his work as a whole (poetry being the only kind of *work* that interests him in his poetry, regardless of how much he enjoyed the insurance business), Stevens invites us on a vacation from that world, from the world of action and the choices that produce action. My contention is that this summoning to vacation is a crucial element in the reader's sense of being befriended by Stevens, perhaps even more crucial than the element of Encouragement to which it is closely related.

To accompany Stevens in his poetry is to go on an outing or expedition which certainly has its difficulties on the level of interpretation but which is astonishingly free from implications about difficulties of other kinds. Stevens carries us into a realm where no question of right or wrong—the sort of question that continually troubles "The evilly compounded, vital I" (*CP* 193) down in the muck of the land, or so one would have supposed—can arise.[47] Assuming we have agreed to jettison Christianity and any other religion, Stevens will be a marvelously undemanding host: we feel we will not be judged. As I have said before, we might well want more than this from a parent, but as a favor-

ite uncle Stevens is charming. His niece Jane MacFarland Wilson recalled in an interview a delightful outing with him in 1945:

> He took me to lunch at the Waldorf-Astoria and then to see *Bloomer Girl*. He
> loved it; I loved it. Ours was a very light thing; we never got into the deep
> things. This was probably relaxation for him, and he knew I enjoyed it. And
> he did, too, wholeheartedly.[48]

In one sense, of course, we readers of Stevens do get "into the deep
things," the complexities pondered by thousands of pages of criticism;
but the deep mysteries of how to live and what to *do* cannot be
plumbed in a realm divorced from action. It is one thing to recommend a cessation of action, as Eliot sometimes does, and another thing
to say that action does not matter and even to speak as if actions never
really occur. As I hope I have sufficiently admitted, Stevens is wonderfully good at making us feel that we are plumbing with him the significant mysteries of life; but when we step back a pace, we can see that
his repudiation of action, along with his repudiation of the interpersonal (these two dimensions of life overlap but are not identical),
causes a monstrous constriction of his portrayal of life. This is why G.
S. Fraser was not just being stuffily British in 1955 when he asked
about Stevens' oeuvre, "What is it that one misses?" and answered:

> the urgency of ordinary human passion, the sense of commitment and the
> moment of final concentration. In one crude human sense, Mr. Stevens'
> enormous talents are being exploited a little frivolously; in all one's continu-
> ing pleasure and admiration while reading him, there is a sense all the time
> of a lack of the highest tension.[49]

Fraser might have learned to see more human passion in Stevens if he
could have read Vendler's *Wallace Stevens: Words Chosen Out of Desire*
(1984), but his sense of the lack of "the highest tension" in Stevens
remains valid. The fact can in part be ascribed to Stevens' practice of
giving what Vendler calls (in a phrase I quoted earlier) "second-order
reflections on the stormings of first-order sensation," but the more
important reason why Stevens' poetry lacks tension is that nothing is
ever at stake except an adjustment of vision and attitude.[50] (I trust my
reader to recall important flickering exceptions to this generalization
in a few poems such as "Arrival at the Waldorf" and "Mozart, 1935.")

There are times, though, when we don't want tension, and especially not the highest tension. We want a holiday from the hurly-burly
of work and from the demands that others make on us and from the
demands that we make on ourselves (sometimes as a result of reading
literature). Stevens is unembarrassed by the idea that his poetry is *like*

a holiday (but he needs the stress on "like"; see the discussion of "Table Talk" below). The relevance of the metaphor and his consciousness of this relevance are reflected by his taste for the words *park* and *café* [51] and *hotel* and the scenes of relaxed, if not passive, recreation these words call to mind (unless the hotel is hosting the MLA convention). In section II of "The Pure Good of Theory," a "platonic person" convalesces at a Brazilian hotel, needing to get back in touch with sensual reality:

> Green glade and holiday hotel and world
> Of the future, in which the memory had gone
> From everything, flying the flag of the nude,
>
> The flag of the nude above the holiday hotel.
> But there was one invalid in that green glade
> And beneath that handkerchief drapeau, severe,
>
> Signal, a character out of solitude,
> Who was what people had been and still were,
> Who lay in bed on the west wall of the sea,
>
> Ill of a question like a malady,
> Ill of a constant question in his thought,
> Unhappy about the sense of happiness.   (*CP* 330–31)

In this particular instance of Stevens' always internal drama, emphasis falls on the unappeasability of the questioning mind. The invalid— "He was a Jew from Europe or might have been"—cannot relax and accept the nourishing relief of hot, fleshy Brazil. His doubts keep him ill. The suggestion that he is a Jew, and the references to memory and the past, might encourage us to think that the sick man's problem involves his awareness of the world of action, of cause and effect, of history—the world of the Holocaust; a world in which much is at stake (the poem was written in 1945). However, the poem does not allow this meaning, which would have complicated the definition of mental health in a way that Stevens would not enjoy. Instead, what the "platonic person" worries about is kept abstract enough ("the sense of happiness," "a soul in the world") so that issues of history and action and responsibility cannot come into focus.

We must notice the oddity (in light of the avoidance of such issues) of the phrase by which Stevens introduces this protagonist: "a character out of solitude." That is, the phrase would seem odd to us if we were not Stevensians, if Stevens had not trained us to accept the word *solitude* as a vaguely awesome reminder that the aloneness of modern humanity is an isolation from any god and a more remediable isolation from nourishing nature (Brazil). These are the good old Stevensian meanings of *solitude* which Stevens invites here, so that the poem will not turn on questions of the relation between its unhappy protagonist and other people. If the emaciated thinker were to grow healthy, his cure would have nothing to do with meeting other guests at the holiday hotel, apparently, and even less to do with the peasants whose labor brings food to the hotel restaurant or with any decision in response to the fate of Jews in Europe. Health will not come from *doing* anything, it will come only from some negotiation between the man's spirit and nature, the green glade, whereby somehow the spirit can satisfy "the final need / Of final access to its element" (*CP* 333). While watching for that imaginative access, the guest at the holiday hotel can quite properly, for Stevens, sit all day on the terrace sipping Meursault or Brazilian coffee.

At a holiday hotel, if the guests read anything at all it is likely to be what is called escapist literature. Surely Stevens writes a kind of literature more serious than that? Stevens bristles impressively in "The Noble Rider and the Sound of Words" when he introduces the word *escapism*:

> The poetic process is psychologically an escapist process. The chatter about escapism is, to my way of thinking, merely common cant. My own remarks about resisting or evading the pressure of reality mean escapism, if analyzed. Escapism has a pejorative sense, which it cannot be supposed that I include in the sense in which I use the word. The pejorative sense applies where the poet is not attached to reality, where the imagination does not adhere to reality, which, for my part, I regard as fundamental.[52]

This is bluster designed to frighten objectors into silence. The crucial issue, the entire problem of morality, which would be the main impetus for anyone to "chatter" about escapism, is buried by Stevens in the phrase "attached to reality." When the poet is attached to reality, does he respond differently to questions of social responsibility and interpersonal relationship than when he is detached from reality? If so, how? How does his attachment to reality manifest itself in his poetry's treatment of (or at least cognizance of) the wide range of social relations? If escapism is artful evasion of those aspects of reality most troubling to a writer, and if we have seen in preceding chapters that the interpersonal troubled Stevens much more than the various vicissitudes of his imaginative experience of nature, then nearly all of his poetry is escapist in a way he fails to dispose of by generally affirming his attachment to reality.[53]

I have spoken of the poetry's avoidance both of the subject of action and of the subject of interpersonal relations. These two vast subjects are distinguishable (distinguishable not only in the sense that some actions don't involve other people, but also in the sense that looking at someone, receiving service or homage from someone, and even caring about someone passively could be considered nonactive interpersonal relations), but they have in common the array of interpersonal relations that entail demands for action. It is of course the abandonment of this realm of responsibility that my previous chapters have examined from several angles, and the aspect of Stevens' vacation spirit most pointedly relevant to my project is the implicit invitation to abandon interpersonal responsibility. In the context built up by Stevens' poetry, any idea of striving in relation to others, whether as a problem of competition or of cooperation, is a bizarrely foreign idea. Stevens may be said to have fought for the independence and prestige of the poet, but his poetry cannot imagine anything else worth fighting for. This is why "The Men That Are Falling" (*CP* 187–88) is such a bad poem: Stevens feels an impulse to praise the republicans in the Spanish Civil War, but his entire sensibility resists the moral implications that would follow from such praise. "This man loved earth, not heaven, enough to die"—the notion of heroic self-sacrifice is wildly out of place in Stevens' oeuvre, and the poet's awareness of this is reflected by the way the republicans' political cause is dissolved safely into the gentle, undemanding word "earth." Vendler comments helpfully on Stevens' use of metaphor to escape from the social reality of the subject he has wandered into:

> Stevens thinks to turn his attention here to those moral "words" of heroic action "that are life's voluble utterance," insisting that right action alone is the arena for the resolution of inner pain. But by turning the acts of soldiers into a form of utterance, he suggests that his own "immaculate syllables" spring as well from a form of death, symbolized by the absence of the inamorata on the pillow.[54]

Stevens needs to retreat into the sense that the soldier's political and military struggle is ultimately not different from his own struggle with loneliness in his Connecticut bedroom. To achieve this melding he needs to convert action in battle into a kind of speech; if combat is only speech (from a perspective like the perspective from which a young woman named Susanna exposed to sexual assault is only a conception of beauty), then heroism in combat is no rebuke to the noble poet who stays at home and only speaks.

"Imago" is a lovely poem about how a people imagines its nation:

> Making this heavy rock a place,
> Which is not of our lives composed . . .

Lightly and lightly, O my land,
Move lightly through the air again.   (*CP* 439)

Reading this we can actually feel a stirring of patriotism; but we must realize that this is a do-nothing patriotism. For Stevens, the imaginative citizen's love of country entails no physical motion; acts like voting and military service don't seem to have crossed the poet's mind. Indeed, even the imaginative love of country is not presented as a duty or a task or a disposition to be carefully maintained; it is merely a mood that happens to come along occasionally among "the imagination's mercies"—in February, perhaps. Stevens is telling us that a national culture thrives only by means of such imagining, but what he won't acknowledge is that such imagining, while necessary, is not sufficient. The first two lines of "Imago" ask "Who can pick up the weight of Britain, / Who can move the German load"; we should see how absurd it is to imply that moving "the German load" is purely a business of imagining, a sort of collective levitation. Choices and actions in schools and legislatures and factories and military bases will be required. And what if Germans decide to move the German load against one's own culture? Nothing in Stevens' poetry ponders the problems involved in picking up the weight of Britain, or America, to meet such an onslaught.

Perhaps the argument here has come to sound like an apology for the Pentagon budget. That is far from my intention. But I am conscious of an insidious comfortableness that "Imago" has often induced in me. Ah, to be an imaginer, to spend one's life above the bustle of actual load-moving, discriminating sensitively among "ghostlier demarcations, keener sounds" (*CP* 130), and to be able to see oneself as a good American in the bargain! 'Tis a career devoutly to be wished, a vacation not only perpetual but noble. Stevens has thus bestowed a calming kind of hope and pride and self-esteem upon me and thousands of other English professors and future English professors. Moral problems can be so bothersome, and some authors make them more vividly so (Fielding, Austen, Dickens, Gaskell, George Eliot, Gissing, James, Conrad, Forster, Faulkner, Orwell . . . and poets too, as I suggested in the early pages of chapter 1). Stevens brings relief! What could be less bothersome—if you accept it—than the diaphanous meaning of *morality* in Stevens? "The morality of the poet's radiant and productive atmosphere is the morality of the right sensation."[55] The word "right" here can mean nothing more than "apt," and "morality" must mean something like "charm."

What I have left out of account, in the last several pages, is of course the one kind of interpersonal relationship that for Stevens does entail responsibility, as we recognized earlier in surveying the friendly features of his work: his relationship with the reader. He is always telling us (or implying) that life involves no responsibilities, yet we see that in his treatment of us, just us, he is, as far as his mercurial, sensitive temperament allows, quite carefully responsible. This naturally makes us feel specially preferred; in a world where no choices are ever obligatory, particularly choices in relation to other persons, he nevertheless seems to have chosen us to amuse and guide and encourage.[56] He happens to like us, and despite his own rejections of responsibility and his acceptance of moodiness, there is a consistency in the befriending that follows from his liking us.

He happens to like us, yes, and we are glad; but the bond seems awfully fragile with no developed principle of responsibility to reinforce it. In a life where morality is only a question of "the right sensation," who can be trusted? All human connections are as flimsy as chains of dew, and people are free to treat each other as nothing more than diverting spectacles; like single men and women in a crowded dance hall, free to make and break connections with only noncommittal glances. (Or to spurn the dance hall and sit alone on a mountain.) When one is unable, due to some drooping of mood, to muster the exhilaration of feeling that one's sensations are "right" (as in "Forces, the Will & the Weather"), one notices the fearful flimsiness of the life in which everything is a matter of taste. Stevens' poem "Table Talk" catches this with remarkable clarity. We should hear it as an antidote to the mesmeric exaltation of poems like "Imago."

TABLE TALK

Granted, we die for good.
Life, then, is largely a thing
Of happens to like, not should.

And that, too, granted, why
Do I happen to like red bush,
Gray grass and green-gray sky?

What else remains? But red,
Gray, green, why those of all?
That is not what I said:

Not those of all. But those.
One likes what one happens to like.
One likes the way red grows.

It cannot matter at all.
Happens to like is one
Of the ways things happen to fall.

(*OP* 40)

Here the realization of our irredeemable mortality leads straight to the shedding of all moral standards. The speaker does not apply this view to any specific moral issue. He doesn't seem interested in doing so, and by his lights there is no reason why he "should"; but if he did, he would presumably have to say that murder and rape are not wrong but merely unpleasant (and unpleasant only for now: tomorrow they might have more appeal). Moreover, he has lost not only all moral standards but all standards of affective preference: "Not those of all. But those." He sees no basis for liking one thing more than another. Language, including poetry, is not exempt: all speech, including this poem, is merely table talk.

Stevens is, obviously, in the kind of mood Vendler calls brutal, deliberately pushing toward a grim extreme; but to acknowledge this is not to remove the fact that this voice of dead-end amorality, a voice soberly authoritative (rather than ironized) in its poem, is one of the real voices in Stevens' head. The poem sheds light on Stevens' long war with religion: if a man feels that the loss of Christianity can lead straight to *this* sense of life (instead of to a noble rising of "the voice that is great within us" as in "Evening Without Angels"), then he may very understandably be obsessed with Christianity and yearn ultimately less to reject it than to replace it.

> It cannot matter at all.
> Happens to like is one
> Of the ways things happen to fall.

The verse has a dying fall, dying into the silence of enervation in a life that cannot be conceived as "fallen" because there are no hierarchical heights from which to fall. "Table Talk" is a poem of the vacation that has become a life sentence in the prison of mere pleasure, the vacation so vacant of work and of any principles for choice and action ("What else remains?" Nothing, except colorful objects to look at) that pleasure has lost all meaning. A day of pleasure no longer feels holy or special in relation to other days. The pleasure of a holiday is defined by its difference from the life of effort that surrounds it. Hence nobody wisely wants a perpetual vacation; it will eventually decay into ennui and disgust.[57] Someone who invites us on such a vacation is friendly in a dangerous way.

We have observed that Stevens encourages us to adopt the holiday metaphor for imaginative experiences in his poems. (See *OP* 107 for another instance.) Implicit in the holiday metaphor, as we noted a moment ago, is the idea of a life of effort surrounding the special time of relief. But I have been arguing that in Stevens' poetry there is no significant recognition of any life of effort or responsibility. There is instead the persistent implication that the pleasurable delicacies of imaginative adjustment are all that matters in life. Happy imaginative moments—"Ecstatic identities / Between one's self and the weather and the things / Of the weather" (*CP* 258)—stand out only against a backdrop of inferior sensations. (Comparison with another poet will soon force me to qualify this statement by allowing, once again, for the effect of Stevens' unspoken or underspoken, but still palpable, tensions and fears.) Thus Stevens' relation to the holiday metaphor must be skittish: he likes the holiday idea as metaphor for his favorite moments or phases of experience, but he can't accept the idea that such moments *are* a holiday from the life of work, choice, and obligation— because that would be to admit that his poetry, which is devoted to the examination of sensations and which he regards as either analogous to, or the embodiment of, life's best (richest, deepest, truest) sensations, leaves out the main part of life (fifty weeks of the year, as it were). This is a suspicion he cannot tolerate.

> I wonder, have I lived a skeleton's life,
> As a disbeliever in reality,
>
> A countryman of all the bones in the world?   (*OP* 117)

"As You Leave the Room" is a project in repressing this suspicion and resuscitating his claim to have encompassed "major reality" in his poetry. His suggestion that the poetry has made available to him a reality that he can "touch every way" is self-consoling bravado; to think of all the ways of touching that are involved in all the interpersonal relations of love and work is to hear a sweet pathos of sorely needed illusion in Stevens' phrase.

Meanwhile, we—we who are not permanently beguiled by our adorable sleight-of-hand man—know that there is more to life than adjustments of vision and emotional responses to sensation. For us, the dismissal of all responsibility in Stevens' poetry makes the experience of reading it (though there is effort involved, as there is in good games) a vacation—not just *like* a vacation—from the large part of life in which conscience gives pangs. Stevens' oeuvre is a resort with a holiday atmosphere so absorbing (partly because its pleasures are more subtle than banal Disneyland fun) that we can forget, for a while, much of what painfully and profoundly matters to us. We know that our uncle's visits (in my other metaphor) are only visits, and that adults have problems he never mentions, yet his charms and skills and virtues can make his visits seem infinite, and infinitely sufficient as epitomes of how to live—unless we listen closely to his "Table Talk."

"One likes what one happens to like." There is a contemporary poet for whom this line provides a sort of modus operandi, a poet for whom the idea that life is only a flux of impressions pervades his poetry, *including* his relationship to the reader, so thoroughly as to make Wallace Stevens seem by comparison a hero of responsibility. Considering the poetry of John Ashbery in connection with the idea of Holiday from Responsibility will help us recognize ways in which this idea does not entirely suffice in characterizing Stevens' attitudes toward action-in-the-world, and toward the reader.

First, the comparison helps us recall that the hedonism in Stevens is effortful;[58] its approaches to joy and to "belief" are always palpably achieved against some resistance, against what Stevens called "the pressure of reality,"[59] which includes the pressure of conceivable responsibility to "the community and other people"[60]—even though explicit acknowledgment of such threatening pressure is, as we have observed again and again, *almost* consistently avoided throughout his poetry. Ashbery presents the amazing (but tiresomely amazing) spectacle of an intelligent poet for whom the affirmation and evocation and poetic embodiment of irresponsibility seem effortless.

The performance flows on and on in book after book, fueled by an energy difficult to understand (but arguably narcissistic)[61] since the poet's attitude toward all kinds of exertion seems mildly disdainful or mildly satirical. Most Ashbery poems seem to be demarcated as separate entities only for the sake of amusement—in Ashbery's ever-renewed parody of conventional shapeliness and closure—or for the sake of convenient publication. Phrases and lines and stanzas often seem interchangeable; we feel they could be transferred into different Ashbery poems without any impediment at all. The poems seem only arbitrary chunks of the infinite strudel of Ashbery's imitation of mental experience just prior to the crystallization of an idea.

This phase of mental experience—the confusion of tantalizing fragments which one feels floating through one's mind before selection and ordering and assertion have been performed—is Ashbery's congenital topic. It is a real topic; but it is his only full-scale topic, the only subject to which his poetry applies in any sustained way. His long-sustained commitment to this topic, moreover, conveys an implicit valuing of the getting-nowhere mental condition which he depicts, an implicit approbation of the status of being not-yet-coherent, not-yet-decided, hence not-yet-active. Sometimes this valuing becomes explicit; Ashbery does approvingly summarize his subject in many fragments of his poetry. (I will return to this crucial point about Ashbery's didacticism.) But his main approach to the subject is not to discuss it but to imitate it, to make the poetry *resemble* a mind in which ideas have not yet formed (though they are often maddeningly imminent). This imitative approach is no doubt the means whereby Ashbery attains his undeniable and celebrated originality (although, at the same time, it is in fact very imitable), but it is also the reason why his poetry must seem so effortless and indeed ought to *be* effortless: because to strive is to have a goal or purpose and to have a goal or purpose is to have a formed idea of need or value. Any such formed idea is forbidden by Ashbery's topic. If such an idea enters a poem (and one of the small pleasures of reading Ashbery is to watch the way coherent thoughts repeatedly creep in like lobbyists at an anarchists' convention), it must be quickly shredded. Can this shredding itself be an effortful process for the poet? A few images or phrases unrelated to the incipient idea, plus perhaps a mild syntactical discontinuity (within the smooth rhythm of ostensible continuity that has prevailed in Ashbery's recent books) will do the trick. Like most tricks, comically easy once learned.[62] It is difficult to imagine Ashbery working very hard on his poems. There are exceptions, yes: there is the much-praised "Self-Portrait in a Convex Mirror"; there is a funny meditation on old-photograph nostalgia called "Mixed Feelings"; there are seriously interesting passages of ten or even twenty lines in perhaps two dozen poems; there is a lovely thoughtful prose poem about cinematic reality called "The Lonedale Operator."—But these are exceptions, because at any given juncture "An inexhaustible wardrobe has been placed at the disposal / Of each new occurrence."[63] There are millions of phrases that would not be wrong (they would be wrong only if they made too much sense or sounded trite rather than mock-trite), and there is no standard by which any one phrase would be uniquely right. "One likes what one happens to like." Ineffable intuition holds uncontested sway.

Writing about Ashbery will always tend to have a seamless quality; it will always tend to resemble the poetry in this way. "He has nothing to say and he says it endlessly." This reductive sentence, which has been unfairly uttered about Stevens, can be less unfairly uttered about Ashbery *and* about his critics. (No doubt a sentence quite close to it appears somewhere in Ashbery's extremely self-conscious oeuvre.) With Ashbery, once you're in the mood, there is a heady sense of everything being relevant at once; thus to write a paragraph on Ashbery (or to write an Ashbery poem) is less like building a barn than it is like trying to let fifty cows nuzzle their way into the barn at more or less the same time. What I've been saying and will say about Ashbery has been mostly said before—of course it has, since there is so little else to say about him—yet one can fall into a mood in which one wants to say this Ashbery thing at great length. The desire is interesting: I think it involves an envy of Ashbery's monumental undisturbability, a desire to share in the safety that Ashbery has apparently attained by abjuring all topics except his one ubiquitous topic.[64] This desire is comparable to a desire manifested by critics of Stevens, which we noted under the

heading of Dependability and Generosity: the desire to adduce innu-
merable quotations from Stevens while stating and restating and restating his view of the dance of imagination with reality. Stevens in his
poetry seems (to the ready reader) to have found the ingredients, the
recipe for a happy peaceful life, though (as we have observed) his
happy peace is often a threatened potentiality rather than a fait ac-
compli. If one is in a Stevensian mood, one wants to live in his space,
on his mountain, abide with him in "a dwelling in the evening air" (*CP*
524), "if only in sense, / And in that enormous sense, merely enjoy" (*CP*
430). A way to share this life with him, one feels, is to borrow phrases
from him and patch them together as if they were one's own, as I have
just done.

So Ashbery and Stevens have in common a power to make the
reader/commentator wish to participate in the spirit of the poetry by
imitating it. And this power is related to the quality of continuity in
each poet, the quality that gives rise to the feeling that all the poems by
each man are essentially pieces of the same huge poem, The Ashbery
Poem, The Whole of Harmonium. But there are crucial differences!
Stevens' poetry is not seamless in the way Ashbery's poetry is. Even if
some Stevens poems are so similar as to have passages which look interchangeable, still we feel that each Stevens poem builds a statement
or performs an action. At the end of a Stevens poem (with arguable
small, early exceptions such as "Colloquy With a Polish Aunt" or "In-
dian River"), we feel that something has been completed. Thoughts
and images cohere into some statement or inquiry or mininarrative.
We feel we can paraphrase the poem or at least that a paraphrase can
be promisingly attempted (even if we shrink fastidiously from such
plebeian behavior). Ashbery's poems, meanwhile, fend off paraphrase, because they don't want to be statements, they want to be imi-
tations of what comes before statement.[65] Hence the only "paraphrase" for an entire Ashbery poem would be another Ashbery
poem—but to say this is to bleed the meaning out of *paraphrase*. To say
that an author does not want us to be able to paraphrase his poem—I
take for granted the fact that a paraphrase is always imperfect and
probably inferior to the poem, but this fact should not become a dis-
abling piety—is to say that he doesn't want us to be able to *do* anything
with it. We are invited merely to appreciate its tone and mood, and to
accept the absence of usable meaning.

> And already the sky is getting to be less salmon-colored,
> The black clouds more meaningless (otter-shaped at first;
> Now, as they retreat into incertitude, mere fins)
> And perhaps it's too late for anything like the overhaul

That seemed called for, earlier, but whose initiative
Was it after all? I mean I don't mind staying here
A little longer, sitting quietly under a tree, if all this
Is going to clear up by itself anyway.

There is no indication this will happen,
But I don't mind. I feel at peace with the parts of myself
That questioned this other, easygoing side, chafed it
To a knotted rope of guesswork looming out of storms
And darkness and proceeding on its way into nowhere
Barely muttering. Always, a few errands
Summon us periodically from the room of our forethought
And that is a good thing.[66]

This passage comes near the end of "A Wave," though it could ride almost anywhere else on the Ashbery surf. It is one of the relatively coherent, paraphrasable fragments in Ashbery that can be taken as a summary or metaphorical epitome of his approach to poetry throughout his oeuvre. Such passages appear remarkably often, though perhaps this is natural in a body of work that has only one obsessive subject. In Stevens too there are many passages which offer in capsule form what we might be tempted to call the essential Stevens. This tendency to resummarize one's own constant project suggests a kinship between Stevens and Ashbery, and Ashbery is most like Stevens when he is doing this. But Stevens wants his self-summaries to support and illuminate each other, while Ashbery requires himself to undermine each of his by surrounding it with unconnectable stuff and by letting it be infiltrated at least slightly by discontinuity. Hence in the passage above we are deflected by the surreal references to a rope "looming out of storms" and muttering and by the inappropriateness of the verb "chafed" in "chafed it / To a knotted rope." Even when focused briefly on the pleasantness of his own outlook and procedure, Ashbery wants his poem to resist the intelligence successfully.

The passage expresses contentment: "I don't mind staying here," "I feel at peace," "that is a good thing." Though the speaker says he has done some questioning, the contentment is essentially passive ("sitting quietly under a tree" or being summoned by "a few errands"), and it is a response to meaninglessness, incertitude, lack of clarity in life. At the end of the passage Ashbery's pronoun shifts from "I" to "we" ("us," "our"), and "we" is the pronoun in much of "A Wave," but (*I* think) we feel unable to trust that Ashbery's "we" means us in this context of no definable context, where incertitude is accepted not so much stoically as complacently. Ashbery saying, "a few errands / Summon us periodically from the room of our forethought / And that is a

good thing" is different from Stevens saying, "We must endure our
thoughts all night, until / The bright obvious stands motionless in cold"
(*CP* 351). The difference is not only a matter of the thing being said
but also a matter of the relation between the speaker and us. Stevens,
we feel, speaks to us and for us impelled by a kind of urgency, though
an urgency he can manage with an outwardly calm, suave demeanor.
He is working to express for us the difficulty of living imaginatively in
uncertainty, and while the poem "Man Carrying Thing" is aware of
the fascinations of confusion, it is also aware of our need (which we
share with Stevens) for emergences of clarity and belief. Stevens recognizes and respects our need to be able to make something definite
out of what we see, the temporary peace of "a thing affirmed" (*CP*
247), and he takes care to make sure that we will be able to make something of a poem like "Man Carrying Thing," though he also tries to
prevent us from doing so too easily, lest we forfeit the play of imagination that gives life its interest and nobility.

Ashbery, meanwhile, spurns the idea of helping us to *make* anything. Each imaginative making, insofar as it achieves a condition of
meaning "for a moment final" (*CP* 168), is unwelcome in Ashbery's
vision, and this reflects his being even more radically estranged from
action-in-the-world than Stevens is.[67] The poem below has a title more
unremittingly sardonic than Stevens' "How to Live. What to Do":

BUT WHAT IS THE READER TO MAKE OF THIS?

A lake of pain, an absence
Leading to a flowering sea? Give it a quarter-turn
And watch the centuries begin to collapse
Through each other, like floors in a burning building,
Until we get to this afternoon:

Those delicious few words spread around like jam
Don't matter, nor does the shadow.
We have lived blasphemously in history
And nothing has hurt us or can.
But beware of the monstrous tenderness, for out of it
The same blunt archives loom. Facts seize hold of the web
And leave it ash. Still, it is the personal,
Interior life that gives us something to think about.
The rest is only drama.

Meanwhile the combinations of every extendable circumstance
In our lives continue to blow against it like new leaves
At the edge of a forest a battle rages in and out of
For a whole day. It's not the background, we're the background,

On the outside looking out. The surprises history has
For us are nothing compared to the shock we get
From each other, though time still wears
The colors of meanness and melancholy, and the general life
Is still many sizes too big, yet
Has style, woven of things that never happened
With those that did, so that a mood survives
Where life and death never could. Make it sweet again![68]

For reasons I have already indicated a critic is bound to take a pratfall if he or she tries to paraphrase an Ashbery poem; thus Ashbery criticism will always consist mainly of countless repetitions of reasons why the poems can't be paraphrased.[69] However, Ashbery has said in interviews that his poems begin with distinguishable promptings (distinguishable for him), and though "My poetry doesn't have subjects," still "I do have a very general idea which it would be very difficult to tell anybody about before I had written the poem . . . I guess I feel that subject matter is, might well be, some tributary part of a poem."[70] With this wobbly encouragement I hazard the suggestion that "But What is the Reader to Make of This?" is, despite its title, one of those Ashbery poems whose seed-theme or Ur-subject has not quite vanished. It is, to that extent, a poem about history and the individual's relation to history, hence about how the individual is to respond to the mildly distracting tumult of social reality, the movement of society through time, "the general life." Moreover it is, I think, despite the essential Ashberian aversion to made meanings expressed in the title, a didactic poem, one in which Ashbery recommends an attitude. The attitude recommended is such that the recommender cannot be felt to care whether we adopt the attitude or not. He warns us against the "monstrous tenderness" that is associated with "archives" and "facts" and whose realm is apparently to be recognized as "only drama," by contrast with "the personal, / Interior life," which is much more interesting. The "monstrous tenderness" is compassion for people caught up in history; it is what pressed Stevens in "Mozart, 1935" to tell his protagonist "Be thou, be thou / The voice of angry fear, / The voice of this besieging pain" (CP 132). Ashbery recommends an endless modesty, which turns out to be indistinguishable from complacency, in response to the battle of circumstance (history): we are to see that we are only the background, but also that the foregrounded battle is unimportant except as a colorful entertainment, producing nothing of interest to us except a mood ("a mood survives / Where life and death never could"). Presumably, if we are to obey the closing injunction to make this mood sweet again, we will manage this by the passive response of turning away from ashen fact toward "the personal, / Interior life." Or perhaps the "it" which we are invited to resweeten is this poem against making, and caring about, historical sense; perhaps in the experience of taking in the poem without shriveling its spirit by reducing it to argument (as I have sourly done), we may be said to have replenished the honey of happy indeterminacy. We should notice that this is very different from the Stevensian honey that comes from a fulfillment of meditation in "The Rock"—

> so that the year is known,

> As if its understanding was brown skin,
> The honey in its pulp, the final found,
> The plenty of the year and of the world.   (*CP* 527)

While recommending the personal instead of the historical, does Ashbery recommend the interpersonal? "The surprises history has / For us are nothing compared to the shock we get / From each other . . ." Here for a second we glimpse a great subject, the one Stevens is at such pains to escape. As we have noted, comparable glimpses of the reality of the interpersonal are afforded us in Stevens' poetry, for example in the last line of "Prologues to What is Possible" and the last stanza of "Yellow Afternoon" and the last two lines of section XII of "Esthétique du Mal" and the second stanza of "Re-statement of Romance." But Ashbery is not at pains to escape the subject of "the shock we get / From each other." He is the poet of supreme insulation, the Teflon poet; all subjects wash away from him in a jiffy. Since his poetry never undertakes to examine the shocks of the interpersonal (despite many references to love), we must suppose that interpersonal relations are like all other "circumstance" for Ashbery, more colorful shiftings of the kaleidoscope, which we should passively watch, safe from being shocked.[71]

In the last line of "Rain Moving In" there is another glimpse of interpersonal experience, but since nothing is really interesting except the flow of one's consciousness, other persons are valuable only as a rather bland stimulation, the minimal stimulation of being politely asked, "Where are you from?" Interaction cannot but be small talk, table talk.

RAIN MOVING IN

The blackboard is erased in the attic
And the wind turns up the light of the stars,
Sinewy now. Someone will find out, someone will know.
And if somewhere on this great planet

> The truth is discovered, a patch of it, dried, glazed by the sun
> It will just hang on, in its own infamy, humility. No one
> Will be better for it, but things can't get any worse.
> Just keep playing, mastering as you do the step
> Into disorder this one meant. Don't you see
> It's all we can do? Meanwhile, great fires
> Arise, as of haystacks aflame. The dial has been set
> And that's ominous, but all your graciousness in living
> Conspires with it, now that this is our home:
> A place to be from, and have people ask about.[72]

This short poem seems insidious to me. A sense of impending disaster—suggested by the rain, the wind, the fires; "The dial has been set / And that's ominous"—dominates the poem, or would dominate it if anything in Ashbery could supersede his pleasure in not letting any idea hold sway in his mind. (Can an idea hold our attention and belief without oppressing us? No one doubts it more than Ashbery; he is *sure* that the yearning for final clarity that Stevens feels in "The Man Whose Pharynx Was Bad" and "This Solitude of Cataracts" is sheerly a mistake. That is the ultimate irony of Ashbery: he is very clear and final in his rejection of clarity and finality.) "Rain Moving In" could be considered a miniature version of "The Auroras of Autumn" with all the intensity subtracted, both the intensity of fear and the answering intensity of the affirmation of life's tender innocence (in sections VIII and IX). "Rain Moving In" is one among a few poems in Ashbery's most recent work that seem unable to ignore death, but even here the living is awfully easy, characterized by "graciousness" that can't be deemed courage, because there is no special pressure upon it. If a truth is found somewhere, the discovery will be inconsequential, so we are advised not to seek truth—about nuclear weapons, for instance, or the erosion of the earth's ozone layer, or the greenhouse effect, or the pollution of the oceans—at all: "Just keep playing, mastering as you do the step / Into disorder this one meant. Don't you see / It's all we can do?" In another poet, the metaphor of mastering a dance step could entail some responsibility to other people (dance partners) or society or at least one's own career or life story; but in Ashbery no such meaning is summoned to fill the metaphor. He says to us: Why worry? What's the point? Spare me from ideas of order! He lacks the tension and ambivalence that Stevens brought to the different but related subjects of truth-seeking and social responsibility; by comparison with Stevens, Ashbery is decisive and even aggressive, despite all undercutting, in repudiating the truth-seeking that must accompany social responsibility. (Meanwhile, social responsibility is constituted by more than truth-seeking alone, as Stevens grimly suspected when he wrote such poems as "Sad Strains of a Gay Waltz" and "Mr. Burnshaw and the Statue.")

Quoting Ashbery's didactic fragments—which, though numerous, are really un-Ashberian paraphrasable impurities in his output—edges us away from the big fact of his poetry's cultivation of discontinuity. I return to this fact to emphasize that this, rather than his overt propositions, is the deeper way in which his poetry both manifests and fosters irresponsibility in relation to others, including the reader. He is more willing than Stevens to include references to action, work, and relationship in his poetry,[73] but the references are weightless because the flow of the poem always dissolves them. This dissolution implies, of course, that they are not important; only the flavor of the poem is important. "The words had a sort of bloom on them / But were weightless, carrying past what was being said."[74] The verb "carrying past" seems to express an approval for a kind of significance beyond the denotative—the kind of significance, indeed, that we like to call poetic. But such significance gives words weight, so that they, and the things in life they signify, are then less easily dissolved in the flow of time and discourse. Ashbery, by contrast, travels with a suitcase made of air, carrying only items alchemized down to no pounds and no ounces. Ashbery's manipulation of semantic logic and syntax helps create a kind of speech (or apparent speech) whose tone usually sounds earnest but which avoids the encumbered quality of the speech of someone trying to communicate with another person. It is more like the speech of someone devoted to what the American government calls "disinformation," someone trying to give the appearance of candor while actually covering up a truth and throwing truth-seekers off the scent.[75]

An Ashbery defender would say that I reveal pre-postmodernist naiveté about the nature of truth (which is so amazingly plural and polysemic and evanescent). I grant that Ashbery concerns himself with truths (of how the mind encounters the flux of emergent experience) less determinable than those pursued by, say, a Senate subcommittee investigating fraud; but by imitating confusion so thoroughly in an ostensible effort to illuminate or appreciate or evince modest respect for that confusion, Ashbery behaves in a way barely different from the way he would behave if his purpose were merely to splash around in confusion or indeed to increase it. Thus it is as if his task were to protect confusion, as if he felt that oppressive clarifications and codifications of experience were threatening our freedom from all sides, brandishing an imminent totalitarianism of certainty; as if he trembled twenty-four hours a day in fear of the apocalyptic black-and-white simplification of reality envisioned by Hopkins in "Spelt From Sibyl's Leaves." (America in the nineties is vastly in trouble, but not that kind of trouble. The repellent absolutism of Jesse Helms is much less powerful than the plutocratic insincerity of George Bush.) Along these lines, a few of Ashbery's admirers have tried to cast him as a political hero of pluralism. However, quite apart from the misreading of American political culture implicit in this evaluation, it is a defense of Ashbery that ignores the blasé spirit throughout Ashbery's poetry, which I have pointed out and which can hardly be plainer than he has made it.[76] There is no emergency in Ashbery, only ubiquitous emergence; no threat, no sweat. There may be countless references to mortality, but the poetry takes these in stride with everything else, absorbing them into the endless flow of highly articulate confusion.[77] The confusion of consciousness is, as he reminds us over and over, ineluctable; it needs no protection. He does not suggest that American government or American bourgeois culture or American departments of English threaten to force his thinking into prescribed channels: no such forces impress him.

Stevens, meanwhile, also resorts to evasive syntax and odd semantic combinations, and sometimes more blatantly than Ashbery, for Ashbery since *The Double Dream of Spring* (1976), has maintained a lulling smoothness whereby his sentences, short or long, lure the reader with the rhythm of sense. Apparently Ashbery wants to avoid alarming the reader with immediately visible oddities; his strangeness comes less in flare-ups than in a constant oozing. Stevens sometimes disorients the reader more bumpily than recent Ashbery:

> To grasp the hero, the eccentric
> On a horse, in a plane, at the piano—
> At the piano, scales, arpeggios
> And chords, the morning exercises,
> The afternoon's reading, the night's reflection,
> That's how to produce a virtuoso.
> The drill of a submarine. The voyage
> Beyond the oyster-beds, indigo
> Shadow, up the great sea and downward
> And darkly beside the vulcanic
> Sea-tower, sea-pinnacles, sea-mountain.
> The signal . . . The sea-tower, shaken,
> Sways slightly and the pinnacles frisson.
> The mountain collapses. Chopiniana.   (*CP* 274–75)

The disjunctive hop from piano-playing to submarine voyage in this section (IV) of "Examination of the Hero in a Time of War" can be glossed[78]: the undersea adventure exemplifies a kind of cartoon version of heroic humanity (really heroic masculinity) resulting from an uninspired, learned-by-labor type of creativity, and Stevens rejects this approach by equating it with the minor music-making of a Chopin (as opposed to a Beethoven?). Nevertheless, the passage is initially baffling in its movement, and if it were typed in longer and less even lines it would be at home in an Ashbery poem as one of the poem's more peculiar passages. There, though, it would mean much less. The reason why a Stevens critic can interpret this passage and then hurry along to find better things in the poem is because Stevens has assembled a context that fosters interpretation and because he does finally want the section to be interpretable. The passage's disjunctiveness does not reflect an Ashberian laissez-faire, anything-goes openness to the flotsam of consciousness; it reflects, rather, Stevens' tension and embarrassment about his subject. (Many passages of "Owl's Clover" are obscure for the same reason.) There is something in Stevens that is attracted to the images of heroism that flow from preadolescent and/ or fascistic machismo: "the man-like body / Of a primitive. He walks with a defter / And lither stride. His arms are heavy / And his breast is greatness" (CP 277). (And, we might add, he goes on amazing submarine voyages . . .) But Stevens sees the silliness of such notions of heroism, and he works in an edgy, agitated spirit throughout "Examination" to find more tenable evocations. Something is at stake for him: he feels that he could get it wrong, and that we could get it wrong, and to get it wrong would matter.

That is tantamount to saying that Stevens feels a responsibility not only to his subject (or, to his own need to get at the truth of his subject) but also to his reader. When we read a puzzling passage in Stevens like "Examination" IV we sense that its strangeness is controlled by these responsibilities. His way of being responsible to us has generated consistent features of his work (as I have argued), and our awareness of these features fortifies us as we set about to make sense of the puzzling passage. In doing so we feel we are doing what Stevens meant us to do. But the reader of Ashbery does not seem to have Ashbery's blessing for the attempt to make sense of a puzzling passage, and Ashbery is original enough to make this apparent. This is why my readings of "But What is the Reader to Make of This?" and "Rain Moving In" felt a little fishy, and this is why Helen Vendler's efforts to normalize Ashbery into a Keatsian lyrical lamenter are also off-target.[79] Ashbery's poetry submits to that analysis only to the extent that it lapses from being Ashberian. If he is responsible to his reader, the reader is not Vendler: he is not responsible in the sense she proposes when she says (after a fairly convincing but extremely broad interpretation of Ashbery's "Landscapeople" as a declaration of human futility and mortality, an interpretation achieved through selective quotation): "I have been extracting chiefly the more accessible parts of Ashbery, but it is possible to explain his 'hard' parts, too, given time, patience, and an acquaintance with his manner."[80] When Vendler hears Ashbery telling her that our lives become futile and then we die, she hears him telling her just what she specializes in hearing. If Ashbery abides by any responsibility to the reader, it must be the kind indicated by this statement in his *New York Quarterly* interview: "My intention is to communicate and my feeling is that a poem that communicates something that's already known by the reader is not really communicating anything to him and in fact shows a lack of respect for him."[81] Does Ashbery respect us in a way that Stevens (like other paraphrasable poets) does not? Does Ashbery respectfully refrain from the avuncular condescension of Stevens who bestows wisdom on us (however delicately)? I think Ashbery offers here the right strategic defense for his style, and we need not doubt that it is heartfelt.[82]

But the problem is that so little gets communicated as a result of Ashbery's radical respect for us. It is as if he thinks we know so much that only the inexpressible can be added to our store of knowledge; the only thing he can "tell" us that we haven't heard is what can't quite be said. What comes across? There is on every page the Big Blur theme, in which all is tolerable flux of impressions and graceful confusion in response to tolerable flux. And there are the many embedded paraphrasable fragments, including the intimations of loss and mortality which make Vendler shiver, but these violate the task (better say the antitask) Ashbery has set for himself. The satisfactions of more communicative poetry are withheld from Ashbery's readers, so that after reading him they (we) are unlikely to feel that his poetry "Took on color, took on shape and the size of things as they are / And spoke the feeling for them, which was what they had lacked" (*CP* 424).

Have we concluded, then, that Ashbery's responsibility to his subject (the Big Blur of consciousness just prior to, or just after the collapse of, definite ideas) is so loyal as to prevent valuable responsibility to the reader? Perhaps. But is Ashbery responsible to his subject? How do we know? For evidence we have the earnestness in his interviews, his frequent production of serious fragments that describe his own approach, and his sheer persistence—nearly a thousand pages in a style that one might have expected would exhaust itself much sooner. And yet: isn't there something seemingly mechanical in Ashbery's disjunc-

tiveness, which puts a strain on our trust? How do we know that his
jumps and skips are not artificially invented rather than discovered by
him in monitoring his own consciousness? Consider this poem:

PASTE

Just because a thing is immortal
Is that any reason to worship it?
Sometimes disappearing into valleys, but always on the way,
No farther than those first few steps
In the suddenly mild open air,
Between these extremes the others muddle through
Like us, uncertain but wearing artlessly
A randomness, a darkness of one's own.
Then later it's forget-me-not time, and rapturous
Clouds appear above the lawn,
The theatre is filled with flying birds, wild wedges,
A web in a corridor or massive portico.
Was it for this you led your sisters back from sleep
To the extreme point of legibility?
As we advance, it retreats; we see
We are now far into a cave
As we pick up a lemon-colored light horizontally
Projected into the night
And rain on the bristly wool of your topcoat.
It's a hard thing, a milestone of sorts in some way,
An overflowing cesspool
Among the memoirs of court life,
Not like a great victory that tirelessly sweeps over
Mankind again if it is going to be perpetually five o'clock
A few seconds after the bus pulled out.
We get lost in life, but life knows where we are.
Like pools that soon become part of the tide
It seeps unrecognizably into the familiar structures
That must be stirred before disappointment can begin,
Like a vast and diaphanous though indestructible framework
Between our slightest steps and the notes taken on them.
It's fun to scratch around and maybe come up with something—
Summer, the ball of pine needles, the loose fates
Serving our acts, and a sign: "Van Camp's Pork and Beans."
If only the curtain-raiser would end, but it is interminable.
You might as well linger on verandas, enjoying life,
The complications of our planet, its climate, its sonatinas

And the criticism is thrown down
Like trash into a dim, dusty courtyard,
A path decorated with our comings and goings.
How will it end?
The mailman, or a butler enters with a letter on a tray.
The dog barks, the caravan passes on.

Do we believe that this poem comprises, or imitates, one wave or phase of consciousness? I have no doubt that Vendler could, if she chose, explicate this poem as a meditation on our experience of time and our inability to find a supreme fiction and our ability to "muddle through," "enjoying life" without a supreme fiction. Ashbery pretends to wish that "the curtain-raiser would end," but the casual flow of his poetry abundantly shows that he doesn't need the big event or main drama that would follow the interminable preliminary experience in which we can just "scratch around." He seems to be able to live twenty-four hours a day (minus a few anxious minutes perhaps) in the undemanding condition that Stevens' Latest Freed Man can inhabit only at 6:00 A.M.: "To be without a description of to be" (*CP* 205). Except that in Ashbery's case it is to be without anything *but* a description of to be, a description so imperturbably constant and imperturbably incomplete that it is very much like not describing.[83] A poem like "Paste" can be paraphrased and summarized if you are willing to skate over the potholes of disjunction, but if you take them all into account, your sense of the poem's value depends, I suppose, on your trust in Ashbery's fidelity to the motions of his own mind. Undoubtedly some Ashbery poems earn this trust somewhat more than "Paste" does, since I constructed "Paste" by lifting phrases and sentences from more than twenty Ashbery poems.[84] My liftings were not random, but they were not especially ingenious either; the composition took me forty minutes, and I feel sure that by taking a little more time I could, repeatedly, construct more convincing Ashberian composites.

The point of my insolence should be clear: I don't say that Ashbery fakes his poems, but that a kind of poetry so easily faked can hardly inspire our confidence that it is devotedly pursuing fresh truths about consciousness. Most good poets are manifestly conscientious; Ashbery requires us to take his conscientiousness on faith.

All seven of the features that together, I have suggested, generate the friendliness of Stevens' poetry, are echoed in some way by Ashbery but with different effect—because in an existence so freed from responsibility to other persons including even the reader, befriending would make no sense. Or rather, it would make too much *sense*: to befriend someone is to choose to be good to that person instead of doing something else; it is a choice and an action whose consequences will have to be dealt with. The holiday metaphor that I needed for Stevens is inadequate for describing Ashbery because a holiday is *from* something, as noted earlier. I argued that Stevens' poetry includes no significant recognition of any life of effort or responsibility (apart from his relation to the reader), but I have also argued, in all four of my chapters, that in Stevens we feel at certain points the pressure of what is being omitted, especially the challenges of interpersonal relations. This is why the experience of reading him is a kind of vacation for us. Though he likes to use the holiday metaphor without addressing the question of the working life on either side of the holiday, he proposes, in effect, an endless vacation, and we take up his poetry as a temporary one. With Ashbery the holiday metaphor collapses because he conveys no awareness that he has denied the importance of a great portion of life. In Ashbery, whatever you might do with your colleague, your compatriot, your client, your landlord, your friend or your lover is morally and spiritually indistinguishable from hang-gliding or floating in a hot tub. Interpersonal relations are not omitted from his omnivorous poetry; they are instead sterilized or reduced to harmlessness in the endless stew of inconsequentiality—no need to omit them, since they don't finally matter. With such a view of life Ashbery (the Ashbery in the poetry) cannot figure as anyone's friend, or guide, or Favorite Uncle.

And yet: there remains the pleasure of reading Ashbery. It is a kind of pleasure one doesn't want every day—pistachio ice cream—but a kind that can bring on a binge. It is like a drug that stimulates you (if you love to manipulate language) while also essentially tranquilizing you:

> Just keep playing, mastering as you do the step
> Into disorder this one meant. Don't you see
> It's all we can do?

Ashbery's oeuvre does not so much include game-playing as a useful enticement as it becomes the image of one all-inclusive all-day game indistinguishable from any other experience, so easy to play, so relaxing.[85] What would constitute a failure to master the steps? Only a stubborn determination to mean something definite and to imply that some steps are morally necessary. Ashbery is not like a man on vacation but like the prince of a kingdom with no foreign policy and no laws, only a humorously uncodified decorum. To immerse oneself in his poetry is to feel princely—suavely above all obligations—until the drug wears off. Despite my long-winded skepticism, the drug has been in my veins throughout the last twenty pages, making me want to linger in a lotos-land where it seems always afternoon (in Tennyson's phrase) or always (as for Stevens' Freed Man) a morning of "color and mist, / Which is enough" (*CP* 204).

Ashbery is wily. As I've said, he seems to anticipate whatever can be said about him. Having reached nearly this point in writing my critique, I came upon an amazing stanza in his poem "Sighs and Inhibitions" which sounds almost as if it were written to preempt my critique:

> I remember in the schoolyard throwing a small rock
> At some kid I hated, and then, when the blood began
> To ooze definitively, trying to hug the teacher,
> The boy, the world, into ignoring what I'd done,
> To lie and thus escape through a simple
> Canceling, not a confession, to wipe the slate clean
> So as to inhabit another world in which
> I bore no responsibility for my acts: life
> As a clear, living dream.[86]

For a moment it is as if we have heard him renounce the safe irresponsibility of his entire oeuvre, under pressure from a Wordsworthian epiphany-via-memory. There is a flash of brave honesty here which at first seems even more impressive than the one we saw in Stevens' "Arrival at the Waldorf." However—and I confess that it is with a kind of relief that I say this—the next and last stanza of "Sighs and Inhibitions" steps in (like a White House spokesman expert in "damage control") to undo what was startlingly done:

> And I have not been spared this
> Dreadful state of affairs, no one has, so that
> When we think we think, or turn over in our sleep,
> Someone else's business is boldly attached to this,
> And there is no time for a reckoning.
> The carpet never stretches quite far enough,
> There is always a footfall on the stair.

If all of us all the time inhabit the "state of affairs" that is "a clear, living dream"—Ashbery's neutral kingdom—then calling it "dreadful" doesn't change the implication that we bear no responsibility for our acts because we never quite know what's happening, "And there is no time for a reckoning." Is it possible to interpret the stanza in the opposite way, as if it began with "But" rather than "And," so that the "Dreadful state of affairs" would be precisely the responsible condition of having an impact on others, on "Someone else's business"?

Such an un-Ashberian meaning doesn't fit with the examples of "acts" which affect others: "When we think we think, or turn over in our sleep"—both examples imply the impossibility of clear conscious control over our acts. In any case the ambiguity of the stanza effectively defuses the moral force of the previous stanza; and the poem leaves the bleeding classmate in the dust. So Ashbery is still dependably Ashberian here, on the whole; and I admit that I enjoy this dependability, but with such a limited and thin kind of pleasure. Ashbery appeals to something in me that wants, like a dreamy schoolboy, to forget about everything really difficult.

That appeal is more obviously dependent on a false account of what life involves than Stevens' invitation to an endless and possibly majestic vacation, and therefore less morally dangerous. Both poets are deliciously tempting in their ways of discarding responsibility, but I think a reader who would advocate Ashbery as our central poet would have to be someone already deeply alienated from responsibility, someone whose relation to the moral realities of choice, work, citizenship, and love was already very tenuous. Stevens is deliciously tempting even to a less alienated reader because some things do matter to him: his devotion to demythologized vision as a source of health and peace, and his responsible relation to the reader. The reader sees a seriousness in these fidelities, and as a result the reader is more susceptible to Stevens' charisma, more prepared to think that this poet may have the whole story on what counts in life. Vigilance against the essential frivolity of Ashbery *should* not be very necessary (though in fact he is being called great by many critics); vigilance is more necessary with Stevens because he has a better chance of convincing an adult reader that a life lived by his poetry would be sufficiently serious and effectual and indeed noble. We feel summoned to sit up straight and be soberly proud when Stevens says, at the beginning of "Asides on the Oboe,"

> The prologues are over. It is a question, now,
> Of final belief. So, say that final belief
> Must be in a fiction. It is time to choose.   (*CP* 250)

It sounds as if our bravery will be greatly tested if we go with Stevens, and the pleasure in this sense of our own heroism tempts us to forget that the choice Stevens calls for has almost no bearing on the choices we must make every day in relationships with other people. To remember this casts new light on the easiness, from some perspectives, of the life Stevens urges with his talk about "final belief" or about "A daily majesty of meditation" (*CP* 518). We can then (seeing this) knowingly go with Stevens on a spiritual search for a secular supreme fiction, a search which may be wondrously difficult in some ways but is also a holiday from responsibility. Or we can succumb more fully to temptation and repress or excuse Stevens' repression of the interpersonal—extend the holiday till we nearly forget that it *is* a vacation.

Vigilance! In section VI of "Things of August," Stevens writes about how the world precedes a man's imagining of it. There is an admirable anti-Hoon humility in the passage, but then Stevens adds one more example (like a senator attaching a devious rider to a bill) of how a man is not the originator of his experience:

> The woman is chosen but not by him,
> Among the endlessly emerging accords.   (*CP* 493)

I think we must reply, "No! That is not the truth about human love relationships." No matter how symphonic the endless Ashberian emergence in which we exist, that wave does not choose our lovers for us. Despite all that can be said about the forces that have prepared them for each other, the woman a man loves is chosen by him, in a series of many choices; and the choices matter; and some of them are hard.

This chapter's proposal was that Stevens' relation to the reader, including his holiday invitation (which can feel friendly even if it is as dangerous as I've argued), comes across as a kind of benevolent caring. I have called this a befriending, while acknowledging distance between the reader and Stevens. The Favorite Uncle metaphor itself implies a gap, a difference of levels, helping us recall that Stevens is willing to befriend us only in the indirect kind of encounter poetry allows. Thus it is not surprising that I have not gone so far as to say that we feel *loved* by Stevens.

Or do we? Can we feel, for a moment at least, that *we* (not Henry Church, and not the supreme fiction) are being addressed in the first line of "Notes"? "And for what, except for you, do I feel love?" Perhaps we *can* feel loved at moments while reading Stevens, moments when we are so far under his spell as to feel the kind of union between reader and poem and poet that we saw, early in this chapter, Stevens adumbrating as an ideal in "The House Was Quiet and the World Was Calm." If so, then we can credit Stevens with a kind of interactive power beyond (but I do not intend "beyond" here to mean "morally superior to") the capacity for interpersonal caring whose effects I have described in this essay. We can thus acknowledge that there seem to be moments in reading Stevens when "difference disappears" (*CP* 454) and indeed *we* become the interior paramour:

Out of this same light, out of the central mind,
We make a dwelling in the evening air,
In which being there together is enough.   (*CP* 524)

Perhaps so. However, even if we could feel sure that Stevens would tolerate our notion that we are so intimate with him, moments are only moments. An ethical life cannot be built only of marvelous moments, nor can a healthy life. It is important to notice that Stevens mostly cannot escape the word *moment* when describing a possible happy relation to the world (see *CP* 168, 184, 202, 204, 227, 248, 265, 298, 302, 303, 333, 378, 380, 386, 398, 427, 472, 496, 497, 513, 516, and *OP* 37, 51, 107, 112), while the passage about "an hour / Filled with expressible bliss" (*CP* 404–405) palpably strains away from the word *moment*. A person who lives only for moments, even if the moments bring spiritual oneness with another person, will be a rather useless person most of the time, if not indeed a harmful person. The cult of the sublime moment is in some ways like devotion to the kind of high provided by amphetamines. The moment becomes a heaven, the heaven possible on earth:

          It would be enough
If we were ever, just once, at the middle, fixed
In This Beautiful World Of Ours . . .   (*CP* 430)

But such a fix usually cannot be found, while other people continue to swirl around us. Most of our dealings with other persons on earth do not even come close to union. They are negotiated across gaps—the width of a desk or conference table, the width of a subway car, the width of a bed. The interpersonal is a realm in which we may sometimes be similar, but never the same. I have tried to make the case that Stevens' relation to the reader—setting aside sublime moments—comprises a modeling of one good, though limited, kind of interpersonal relation: a nonpassionate, avuncular sort of caring. I don't know if I have convinced *you*, my stubbornly separate reader, about this. Whether I have or not, I trust we can agree that while we need Stevens, we also need acquaintances, colleagues, friends, and poets whose relation to the work of interpersonal relations is warmer, closer and stronger.

NOTES

INTRODUCTION

1. George Herbert, "Affliction (I)," *The Works of George Herbert*, ed. F. E. Hutchinson (London: Oxford University Press, 1941), p. 47.

2. On the constriction of Keats' conception of poetry see John Barnard's useful discussion in *John Keats* (Cambridge: Cambridge University Press, 1987), pp. 141–46.

3. Emily Dickinson, "Much Madness is divinest Sense," poem 435 in *The Complete Poems of Emily Dickinson*, ed. Thomas H. Johnson (Boston: Little, Brown, 1960), p. 209.

4. Dickinson, "On a Columnar Self," poem 789 in Dickinson, p. 384.

5. *Secretaries of the Moon: The Letters of Wallace Stevens and José Rodríguez Feo*, ed. Beverly Coyle and Alan Filreis (Durham: Duke University Press, 1986), p. 2.

6. Thus I think Denis Donoghue is wishfully wrong when he claims that Stevens turns toward "other lives" in his last poems and that in *The Rock*, "for the first time Stevens has written a book which says *Thou*." Even if Donoghue were right in finding more references to "other lives" in *The Rock*, this would not constitute a new attention to interpersonal *relations*. See Denis Donoghue, *The Ordinary Universe* (New York: Ecco Press, 1987; originally published 1968), pp. 236–38.

CHAPTER ONE

1. Summarizing Stevens' work in an essay entitled "Poetry: After Modernism," Daniel Hoffman writes: "This enterprise is noble, yet his repudiations, whether conscious or temperamental, are a measure of the desolation that his work must fill. In that work there are no relationships between the poetic speaker and other persons, no passions, neither human love nor hatred, no sense of the self as a member of any society save the select company of abstract characters the poet has imagined." Daniel Hoffman, "Poetry: After Modernism," in *Harvard Guide to Contemporary American Writing*, ed. Daniel Hoffman (Cambridge, Mass.: Harvard University Press, 1979), p. 443.

2. Wallace Stevens, *The Collected Poems of Wallace Stevens* (New York: Alfred A. Knopf, 1954), p. 240. Subsequent page references will be given in my text, identified with the abbreviation *CP*.

3. One of the poem's beauties is the wonderfully delicate line break in "a woman / Combing." The voice pauses, as if taking great care to *see* precisely what ordinary human action this woman is performing, an action different from dancing (and poignantly different also, we may feel, from kissing—from the loving which the observer might desire).

4. See Marjorie Perloff's comment on "Of Modern Poetry" in "Revolving in

Crystal: The Supreme Fiction and the Impasse of Modernist Lyric," in *Wallace Stevens: The Poetics of Modernism*, ed. Albert Gelpi (New York: Cambridge University Press, 1985), p. 62.

5. Walt Whitman, "Song of the Open Road," *Leaves of Grass*, Norton Critical Edition, ed. Sculley Bradley and Harold W. Blodgett (New York: W. W. Norton & Co., 1973), pp. 151–52.

6. Whitman, "Salut au Monde!" p. 147. Because of Whitman's tendency to declare his oneness with others he does sometimes seem to lack respect for their separate experience. This is why a critic like Thomas Byers can see Stevens rather than Whitman as the poet who shows real respect for persons. Comparing section IV of "It Must Change" (*CP* 392) with Whitman's "There Was a Child Went Forth," Byers makes Stevens' version of the self's relation to the world sound morally preferable: "The difference is between *partaking of* and *becoming* the other, and between taking character from the thing and dissolving it into the self. Whitman's love is founded on the transcendent identity of all things. Stevens's is founded on interdependence and sharing, but these, like a poem's mediations, are transactions between ourselves and others who remain irrevocably a reality not ourselves. I must love the world not because it is myself, but at least partly because it is not." Thomas B. Byers, *What I Cannot Say* (Urbana and Chicago: University of Illinois Press, 1989), p. 75. But my argument about Stevens arises precisely in response to the moral fudging (fostered by Stevens) which is reflected by the shift from "others" to "world" in Byers' account of Stevens' "love."

7. In his preface to the first edition of *Leaves of Grass* (1855), Whitman said of "the great poet," "He sees eternity in men and women . . . he does not see men and women as dreams or dots" Norton Critical Edition, p. 715. In lines like the following from section 37 of "Song of Myself," I hear an authentic empathy more than I hear the absurdity of Whitman's claim to constant universal empathy:

> Not a mutineer walks handcuff'd to jail but I am handcuff'd to him and
>   walk by his side,
> (I am less the jolly one there, and more the silent one with sweat on
>   my twitching lips.)
>
> Not a youngster is taken for larceny but I go up too, and am tried and
>   sentenced.
> Not a cholera patient lies at the last gasp but I also lie at the last gasp,
> My face is ash-color'd, my sinews gnarl, away from me people retreat.

> (pp. 71–72)

And I want particularly to mention "Come Up From the Fields Father" as a poem exemplifying Whitman's empathetic capacity.

8. William Wordsworth, "Preface to the Second Edition of *Lyrical Ballads* (1800)," in *Selected Poems and Prefaces by William Wordsworth*, ed. Jack Stillinger (Boston: Houghton Mifflin Co., 1965), pp. 449–50.

9. See Milton J. Bates, *Wallace Stevens: A Mythology of Self* (Berkeley: University of California Press, 1985), pp. 165–66.

10. In his essay "The Irrational Element in Poetry" (1936), Stevens acknowledged this problem as a matter of "the pressure of the contemporaneous" and the imagination's need for resistance to such pressure. *Opus Posthumous*, ed. Samuel French Morse (New York: Alfred A. Knopf, 1957), pp. 224–25. Subsequent page references will be given in my text, identified by the abbreviation *OP*.

11. See Justin Kaplan, *Walt Whitman: A Life* (New York: Simon and Schuster, 1980), pp. 264–66 and 276–85.

12. I omit discussion of "Owl's Clover" (1936), despite its complex, ambivalent response to the Depression and Marxism, because the poem seems to me so unrewardingly murky, and my points can be made more clearly with reference to shorter poems. The Old Woman of the first section of "Owl's Clover" is not an example of Stevens vividly conceiving the human reality of an individual sufferer. As Milton J. Bates says, "The woman is a sufficiently generalized symbol of the Depression as not to raise specific social and political questions" (p. 186). And Helen Vendler remarks of Stevens: "His contact with the individual poor is tenuous, not to say nonexistent, and it is only when one of them rises above the million-in-the-mass and becomes the Old Woman that he can grasp her. Even then, what he grasps in her is himself; she exists purely as a medium for the lyric voice." Helen Vendler, *On Extended Wings* (Cambridge, Mass.: Harvard University Press, 1969), p. 100.

13. See especially *The Necessary Angel* (New York: Alfred A. Knopf, 1951), pp. 28–29, and of *Letters of Wallace Stevens*, ed. Holly Stevens (New York: Alfred A. Knopf, 1966), pp. 289 and 340.

14. Milton J. Bates says that the pianist's new music "will still be Mozart" but with a changed "interpretation of the score" (pp. 169–70), but I think the line "We may return to Mozart" (the first line of the poem's last stanza) may be heard to mean, "We may some day return to Mozart if we ever get out of this trouble."

15. Gerald L. Bruns remarks appositely: "He is a poet troubled by the sort of poetry he is *not* writing and perhaps can't bring himself to think of *as* poetic—the poetry of the other, disturbing our monumental slumber." Gerald L. Bruns, "Stevens Without Epistemology," in *Wallace Stevens: The Poetics of Modernism*, ed. Albert Gelpi (New York: Cambridge University Press, 1985), p. 35.

16. Helen Vendler, writing about "Notes Toward a Supreme Fiction," is inclined to justify: "One signal claim relinquished by the poem is any overt social or human connection. The introduction . . . is addressed to the interior paramour, and signifies Stevens' final acceptance of his remorseless, if involuntary, isolation from the human world: 'And for what, if not for you, do I feel love?' The only alternative object of love proposed is 'the extremest book of the wisest man,' not any human being. In ceasing to attempt the poetry of human relation, Stevens becomes, paradoxically, most human." *On Extended Wings*, pp. 327–28.

17. *The Nation*, vol. 164, no. 14 (April 5, 1947), p. 400.

18. In "The Noble Rider and the Sound of Words" Stevens says of the nobility to be achieved by imagination: "It seems, in the last analysis, to have

something to do with our self-preservation; and that, no doubt, is why the expression of it, the sound of its words, helps us to live our lives." *The Necessary Angel*, p. 36.

19. Lucy Beckett, *Wallace Stevens* (Cambridge: Cambridge University Press, 1974), pp. 123–24.

20. *The Complete Poems of Thomas Hardy*, ed. James Gibson (New York: Macmillan Publishing Co., 1976), p. 737.

21. Hardy, p. 810.

22. In this essay I use the word *sympathy* not in the broad sense of sharing in *any* feeling of the other—which is how Robert Langbaum uses the word (apparently regarding it as a synonym for *empathy*) when he characterizes the effect of "the poetry of experience" in *The Poetry of Experience* (New York: W. W. Norton & Co., 1957), pp. 86, 93, 96, etc. I use the word *sympathy* in the more narrow colloquial sense of compassionate feeling for someone suffering. Compassion involves the wish that the suffering be alleviated.

23. Hardy, p. 774.

24. See my slightly longer comment on this passage in chapter 2, p. 57.

25. Helen Vendler, *Wallace Stevens: Words Chosen Out of Desire* (Knoxville: University of Tennessee Press, 1984), p. 52. Hereafter cited as *Words Chosen Out of Desire*.

26. John Keats, "The Fall of Hyperion," lines 148–149, in *The Poems of John Keats*, ed. Jack Stillinger (Cambridge, Mass.: Harvard University Press, Belknap Press, 1978), p. 481.

27. A. Walton Litz is one of the critics who have praised this action of Stevens' war poetry as unsentimental without addressing the problem of whether the poet has, in refusing sentimentality, refused compassion also: "By displacing and generalizing the subject, turning the soldier into a 'major man' and war into the destructive force which poetry both shares and controls, Stevens absorbed the experience of war into his poetic. Stated in this way the process sounds like the worst kind of hypocritical evasion, but the experience of reading Stevens' war poems is quite different. Such apparently diverse works as 'Man and Bottle,' 'Of Modern Poetry,' 'Asides on the Oboe,' [and others] form a chorus on the war which is unsentimental and immensely powerful." A. Walton Litz, *Introspective Voyager* (New York: Oxford University Press, 1972), p. 265.

28. *On Extended Wings*, p. 209.

29. Harold Bloom, *Wallace Stevens: The Poems of Our Climate* (Ithaca, N.Y.: Cornell University Press, 1977), pp. 232–33.

CHAPTER TWO

1. Peter Brazeau, *Parts of a World: Wallace Stevens Remembered* (New York: Random House, 1983), p. 248.

2. *The Necessary Angel*, p. 18.

3. Irvin Ehrenpreis, "Strange Relation: Stevens' Nonsense," in *Wallace Stevens: A Celebration*, ed. Frank Doggett and Robert Buttel (Princeton University Press, 1980), p. 230.

4. A reader who claims that the speaker of this poem is a woman may be comfortable with the first stanza but hard pressed to explain why the speaker's femininity is not elsewhere insinuated and why her suitor is associated with Florida, which is feminine in other poems, such as "Farewell to Florida."

5. Frank Doggett, *Stevens' Poetry of Thought* (Baltimore: Johns Hopkins University Press, 1966), pp. 45–46.

6. "Stevens' readers have liked nothing better than to bypass the personal and material levels of his writing, and in this late metapoetical reflection we appear to be given license by the poet himself who seems to tell us that his real subject (poetry itself) is and has been all along unencumbered." Frank Lentricchia, *Ariel and the Police* (Madison: University of Wisconsin Press, 1988), p. 217. A fleshy woman in one's ideal dwelling would be the ultimate encumbrance.

7. Eugene Paul Nassar, *Wallace Stevens: An Anatomy of Figuration* (Philadelphia: University of Pennsylvania Press, 1965), p. 134.

8. The early "Peter Parasol" (*OP* 20) may seem harmlessly ordinary in lamenting the fact that all women are not beautiful, but it participates in the feeling that women exist only for men and have no autonomous validity. See also the passage from "The Common Life" quoted near the end of this chapter.

9. "I do not mean to sentimentalize Stevens in insisting that his poems are meditations on emotions of love, idolatry, loss, self-loathing, and self-forgiveness. He is so chaste in self-revelation that his emotions are easily passed over." And again: "Stevens is a genuinely misunderstood poet, it seems to me, in the world at large; he is rarely called a passionate writer, or a poet of ecstatic or despairing moments—and yet that is what he is. He is often a despairing lover, blaming himself for the failure in love, blaming his wife as well, and finally, in *The Rock*, blaming only the biological necessity that brings men and women together." *Words Chosen Out of Desire*, pp. 27 and 32.

10. This resistance is reflected, I suspect, by Holly Stevens' feeling that she had to fight to be seen by her father as an independent person. See Brazeau, p. 283.

11. *Souvenirs and Prophecies: The Young Wallace Stevens*, ed. Holly Stevens (New York: Alfred A. Knopf, 1977), p. 175.

12. See Brazeau, pp. 234–35, 237–38, 245–53.

13. Brazeau, p. 244.

14. Though see also "Good Man, Bad Woman" (*OP* 33) in which the man's whole experience of life is in danger of being poisoned by the woman's spite, notwithstanding his claim to "rest intact in conscience and intact / In self."

15. Vendler, *Words Chosen Out of Desire*, p. 18.

16. Denis Donoghue, *Connoisseurs of Chaos: Ideas of Order in Modern American Poetry* (New York: Columbia University Press, 1984), p. 200.

17. As chapter 3 will show more fully, the point is not that Stevens *never* noticed in poetry the differences between persons but that his mind habitually strained away from this recognition. See, for example, the urgent momentum toward the conception of an admirable solitary figure capable of subduing or subsuming eccentricity in the last stanza of "A Primitive Like an Orb":

> That's it. The lover writes, the believer hears,
> The poet mumbles and the painter sees,
> Each one, his fated eccentricity,
> As a part, but part, but tenacious particle,
> Of the skeleton of the ether, the total
> Of letters, prophecies, perceptions, clods
> Of color, the giant of nothingness, each one
> And the giant ever changing, living in change. (*CP* 443)

18. "I am some hundreds of years behind other people, and it is going to be a long time before I let a commercialism like sex appeal get any farther than the front fence." *Letters of Wallace Stevens*, p. 251.

19. Lucy Beckett comments on this faintly pornographic scene: "The powerful sexual emotion is, as often in Stevens' work, no more than the only appropriate image for love and desire of another kind. The transposition is a natural one which, for not dissimilar reasons, was once common in Christian mystical writing" (p. 152). Like many critics, Beckett unconvincingly tries to excuse Stevens from any responsibility for having conceived of heterosexual relations in certain preferred ways. When Nanzia Nunzio strips, one of the things happening is that Stevens is writing about women and male desire for women in a way that he finds gratifying.

20. Is this merely something that can naturally be said of every male poet? I don't think so. Wordsworth's Poor Susan and Martha Ray, Tennyson's Mariana, Hardy's Chapel Organist, Frost's Hill Wife, Yeats's Woman Young and Old come to mind—they all seem more humanly individual than, say, Stevens' High-Toned Old Christian Woman, whose character is confined mainly to the title that names her, or than the ethereal singer at Key West. But the point is not simply to inventory the female characters created by male poets, but rather to notice the essential position offered to a female reader by a set of poems. In many oeuvres by male poets, a female reader need not often feel pushed away from the point of view of a given poem because it is proposed as essentially masculine.

21. *Letters of Wallace Stevens*, p. 250.

22. Frank Lentricchia, insisting on a solipsistic meaning for the poem, fails to register its main current of emotion, which defies, I think, the theme proposed by the title: "Her power, literally within the domestic dwelling place, is the power of lyric meditation, whose actual domestic site is a figure for a site and dwelling which she makes and which is impervious to male presence: it needs no real Ulysses to fill her desire, for there, in the dwelling she makes, she is the composer of selves, the single artificer of the world in which she dwells" (p. 241).

CHAPTER THREE

1. Harold Bloom also takes too much for granted when he declares why we, in our solitudes, need Stevens: "Stevens is uniquely the twentieth century poet of that solitary and inward glory we can none of us share with others. His value

is that he describes and even celebrates (occasionally) our selfhood-communings as no one else can or does. . . . He is the poet we always needed, who would speak for the solitude at our center." Harold Bloom, Introduction to *Wallace Stevens: Modern Critical Views* (New York: Chelsea House, 1985), p. 5. Apparently Stevens *has* shared some of his inward glory, or else what is Bloom responding to? I will argue that to accept Stevens' "self-joying solipsism" (as Bloom calls it) so unskeptically is to excuse Stevens from a great and interesting problem which Stevens himself could not entirely ignore.

In the same introduction, Bloom suggests that Stevens' self-devotion is quintessentially American, "exposing the essential solipsism of our Native Strain" (p. 12) as seen in Emerson, Whitman, Thoreau, Dickinson, and Frost. My project does not address this very broad issue—ultimately *the* issue of Americanist studies—but as my readings of Dickinson below will imply, I am inclined to see solipsism as one side of a dialectic, the other side of which, in each of our great writers, is a passionate interest in, and engagement with, the minds of other Americans.

2. This is a truth that Emerson, great Transcendentalist advocate of the self-reliant poetic soul, could deal with when his mood was not utterly exalted. In his essay "Manners," he recognizes that meeting another person can happen, does matter, and does involve contact between different selves. When he writes, "In all things I would have the island of a man inviolate," he speaks from a sense that men can have meaningful (and sometimes harmful) impact on one another. "We should meet each morning, as from foreign countries, and spending the day together, should depart at night, as into foreign countries." This may be austerely lonely but it is already different, in its engagement with the issue of how people *should* be together, from the characteristic attitude of Stevens who once referred to poetry as "The Switzerland Of The Mind" and aspired to a mountainous neutrality safe from others and from strong feelings about others. ("World Without Peculiarity" is a telling illustration of this.) Emerson has a fierceness about interpersonal contact that makes Stevens' caution seem anemic. Writing about being introduced to another man, Emerson says: "A gentleman never dodges: his eyes look straight forward, and he assures the other party, first of all, that he has been met. For what is it that we seek, in so many visits and hospitalities? Is it your draperies, pictures, and decorations? Or, do we not insatiably ask, Was a man in the house? I may easily go into a great household [like the Palaz of Hoon] where there is much substance, excellent provision for comfort, luxury, and taste, and yet not encounter there any Amphitryon, who shall subordinate these appendages. I may go into a cottage, and find a farmer who feels that he is the man I have come to see, and fronts me accordingly." *The Essays of Ralph Waldo Emerson*, ed. Alfred R. Ferguson and Jean Ferguson Carr (Cambridge, Mass.: Harvard University Press, Belknap Press, 1987), pp. 298, 297. The essay was originally published in 1844.

3. Lucy Beckett calls this a religious poem about "that love of which the human and sexual passion of the poem is only an image . . . The real subject of 'The World as Meditation' (and its title should help us to realise this) is not love seen, as it were, partially, from the point of view of the lover regarding the

object of his love. The poem's real subject is the complete relationship, the full ambiguity of the genitive in such a phrase as 'the love of God', which is in any case perhaps the most appropriate expression that can be used to paraphrase the extraordinary sense of spiritual strength which the poem creates" pp. 199–200. Beckett's reading would make Stevens writhe, I suspect, but the poem's ambiguous sublimating invites such trouble.

4. Among the relevant poems are "Yellow Afternoon," "The Hand as a Being," and "Bouquet of Belle Scavoir," discussed in chapter 2.

5. Bates, p. 209.

6. Stevens does not, however, produce any sustained argument for the value of solitude; to do so would require some sustained admission of the threatening or distracting qualities of others. There is nothing in Stevens comparable to Thoreau's chapter on solitude in *Walden* with its candidly polemical passages: "Men frequently say to me, 'I should think you would feel lonesome down there, and want to be nearer to folks, rainy and snowy days and nights especially.' I am tempted to reply to such,—This whole earth which we inhabit is but a point in space. How far apart, think you, dwell the two most distant inhabitants of yonder star, the breadth of whose disk cannot be appreciated by our instruments? Why should I feel lonely? is not our planet in the Milky Way? This which you put seems to me not to be the most important question. What sort of space is that which separates a man from his fellows and makes him solitary? I have found that no exertion of the legs can bring two minds much nearer to one another." Henry David Thoreau, *Walden*, ed. Owen Thomas, (New York: Norton Critical Edition, 1966), p. 89.

7. Frank Doggett proposes that the empty bed in "Gallant Château" represents "the nothingness of death" (pp. 128–29). Doggett flees from the idea that the empty bed might be literal the way Steven flees from the hair, eyes, and hands of women who are not in the bed.

8. "Most people stand by the aid of philosophy, religion and one thing or another, but a strong spirit (Anglais, etc.) stands by its own strength. . . . If men have nothing external to them on which to rely, then, in the event of a collapse of their own spirit, they must naturally turn to the spirit of others. I don't mean conventions: police." *Letters of Wallace Stevens*, p. 348.

9. See the opening stanza of "Credences of Summer" (*CP* 372). See also stanza VI of "A Primitive Like an Orb" (*CP* 441), where the self of summer is heard "denouncing separate selves." In the third stanza of "Credences," I suspect the fathers, mothers, and lovers do not alleviate but rather exemplify the "false disasters" which threaten the heart. Certainly the passage is ambiguous exactly where it ought to be unambiguous if Stevens intended an unusual (for him) affirmation of family ties and romantic love. Bloom tries cautiously for the affirmative reading: "Stevens seems ready enough to accept a second-best in the fulfillment of others, a pattern in which Coleridge excelled but which comes hard to any American poet whatsoever." *The Poems of Our Climate*, p. 245. Eugene Paul Nassar declares firmly what I also suspect: "The fathers, mothers and lovers represent all those personal longings, desires for permanence of the self and relation to the world, that the world is not constituted to

satisfy. (It is wrong, Stevens is saying, to sap the spirit by impossible yearnings for the continuation of things as they once were, or for values that are more than expressions of shifting feelings.)" (p. 19).

10. For Stevens' awareness of the idea in Nietzsche, see Bates, p. 203. Pater wrote that our experience "is ringed round for each one of us by that thick wall of personality through which no real voice has ever pierced on its way to us, or from us to that which we can only conjecture to be without. Every one of those impressions is the impression of the individual in his isolation, each mind keeping as a solitary prisoner its own dream of a world." Walter Pater, *The Renaissance* (London: Macmillan, 1900; originally published 1873), p. 235. In his notes to *The Waste Land*, T. S. Eliot quotes from F. H. Bradley's *Appearance and Reality*: "My external sensations are no less private to myself than are my thoughts or my feelings. In either case my experience falls within my own circle, a circle closed on the outside; and, with all its elements alike, every sphere is opaque to the others which surround it. . . . In brief, regarded as an existence which appears in a soul, the whole world for each is peculiar and private to that soul." T. S. Eliot, *The Complete Poems and Plays 1909–1950* (San Diego: Harcourt Brace Jovanovich, 1971), p. 54.

11. In chapter 1, I discussed the moral dangers in this idea of the representative and/or "central" man, in relation to other human beings who are in pain; see the pages on section VII of "Esthétique du Mal."

12. The phrase is from "Asides on the Oboe" (*CP* 250). See Bates, pp. 238–45 for a helpful account of this idea.

13. D. H. Lawrence, *Studies in Classic American Literature* (Harmondsworth, England: Penguin Books, 1971; originally published 1923), p. 174.

14. Lawrence, p. 185.

15. The assertion of solitude is too uncontested by Bloom who says of the section: "There is nothing communal here. Stevens celebrates an apprehension that has no social aspect whatsoever and that indeed appears resistant to any psychological reflections we might apply." Introduction to *Wallace Stevens: Modern Critical Views*, p. 6.

16. "I detest 'company' and do not fear any protest of selfishness for saying so," Stevens wrote in his journal in 1906. "People say one is selfish for not sharing one's good things—a naively selfish thing in them. The devil take all of that tribe. It is like being accused of egoism. Well, what if one be an egoist—one pays the penalty." *Souvenirs and Prophecies*, pp. 163–64.

17. *On Extended Wings*, p. 100. The quotation is from "Repetitions of a Young Captain" (*CP* 309).

18. *On Extended Wings*, pp. 327–28.

19. For an insightful discussion of these poems, see Christopher Benfey, *Emily Dickinson and the Problem of Others* (Amherst: University of Massachusetts Press, 1984), pp. 83–90.

20. Dickinson, p. 276.

21. Dickinson, p. 319. See also poem 1053.

22. See William H. Shurr, *The Marriage of Emily Dickinson* (Lexington: University Press of Kentucky, 1983), pp. 148–50.

23. Dickinson, pp. 329–30.

24. *Letters of Wallace Stevens*, p. 759.

25. In 1906 Stevens noted: "One sees the most painful people, wherever one goes. Human qualities, on an average, are fearful subjects for contemplation. Deceit—how inevitable! Pride, lack of sophistication, ignorance, egoism—what dreadful things!" *Souvenirs and Prophecies*, p. 158.

26. *The Necessary Angel*, pp. 122–23.

27. Stevens' radical discomfort with the problem of a social poetry is amusingly apparent in "A Note on 'Les Plus Belles Pages.'" See the dainty haste with which he sidesteps the possibility he has introduced: "The inter-relation between things is what makes them fecund. Interaction is the source of poetry. Sex is an illustration. But the principle is not confined to the illustration. . . . The principle finds its best illustration in the interaction of our faculties or of our thoughts and emotions" (*OP* 290–91).

28. *The Poems of Our Climate*, p. 231.

29. *On Extended Wings*, p. 208.

30. The poems appear in the following books: *Words For the Wind* by Theodore Roethke (New York: Doubleday, 1958); *Life Studies* by Robert Lowell (New York: Farrar, Straus & Giroux, 1959); *Golden State* by Frank Bidart (New York: Braziller, 1973); *The Sacrifice* by Frank Bidart (New York: Random House, 1983); *In a U-Haul North of Damascus* by David Bottoms (New York: William Morrow, 1983); *The Book of Fortune* by Daniel Mark Epstein (New York: Overlook Press, 1982); *God Hunger* by Michael Ryan (New York: Viking, 1989); *Palm Reading in Winter* by Ira Sadoff (Boston: Houghton Mifflin, 1978); *Happy Hour* by Alan Shapiro (Chicago: University of Chicago, 1987); *A Guide to Forgetting* by Jeffrey Skinner (St. Paul, Minn.: Graywolf Press, 1988); *Flesh and Blood* by C.K. Williams (New York: Farrar, Straus & Giroux, 1987).

31. *The Poems of Our Climate*, p. 235.

32. Donoghue, *Connoisseurs of Chaos*, p. 209.

33. The first five stanzas of section IX of "The Auroras of Autumn" (*CP* 419) seem to want to be an examination of intimacy, but I think the passage is too much in thrall to the argument in favor of "innocent earth," which leads Stevens to idealize family relations.

34. Ronald Sukenick, *Wallace Stevens: Musing the Obscure* (New York: New York University Press, 1967), p. 227.

35. My sense of what "Re-statement of Romance" does and doesn't accomplish is paralleled by what Robert Hass insightfully says about the limitedness of Rilke's view of love: "Mostly, people experience the possibility of union with the other in their bodies, with other people. But it would seem that for Rilke this was not so. He defined love once as two solitudes that protect and border and greet each other. And though it is a moving statement, it leaves out the fury of that greeting. It makes people sound as if they were soap bubbles bouncing off one another, whereas each of those two solitudes is a charged field of its own energy, and when they meet, they give off brilliant sparks." Robert Hass, *Twentieth Century Pleasures* (New York: Ecco Press, 1984), p. 255.

36. For an earnestly elaborated sense of what the poem doesn't wade into, we may wade into this paragraph from Martin Buber's essay "The Question to

the Single One" (I am amused to think of how Stevens might recoil from this passage, and not only because of its religious underpinnings):

> "That the men with whom I am bound up in the body politic and with whom I have directly or indirectly to do, are essentially other than myself, that this one or that one does not have merely a different mind, or way of thinking or feeling, or a different conviction or attitude, but has also a different perception of the world, a different recognition and order of meaning, a different touch from the regions of existence, a different faith, a different soil: to affirm all this, to affirm it in the way of a creature, in the midst of the hard situations of conflict, without relaxing their real seriousness, is the way by which we may officiate as helpers in this wide realm entrusted to us as well, and from which alone we are from time to time permitted to touch in our doubts, in humility and upright investigation, on the other's 'truth' or 'untruth,' 'justice' or 'injustice.' But to this we are led by marriage, if it is real, with a power for which there is scarcely a substitute, by its steady experiencing of the life-substance of the other as other, and still more by its crises and the overcoming of them which rises out of the organic depths, whenever the monster of otherness, which but now blew on us with its icy demons' breath and now is redeemed by our risen affirmation of the other, which knows and destroys all negation, is transformed into the mighty angel of union of which we dreamed in our mother's womb."

Martin Buber, *Between Man and Man*, trans. Ronald Gregor Smith (New York: Macmillan, 1965), pp. 61–62.

37. The first line of "This Solitude of Cataracts" (*CP* 424). And in "Notes Toward a Supreme Fiction," Stevens speaks of "the heat of the scholar, who writes / / The book, hot for another accessible bliss: / The fluctuations of certainty, the change / Of degrees of perception in the scholar's dark" (*CP* 395).

CHAPTER FOUR

1. See p. 120 below for a fuller speculation about these "many readers."

2. "One must be fond of people and trust them if one is not to make a mess of life, and it is therefore essential that they should not let one down. . . . I hate the idea of causes, and if I had to choose between betraying my country and betraying my friend, I hope I should have the guts to betray my country." E. M. Forster, *Two Cheers For Democracy* (New York: Harcourt, Brace & World, 1951), p. 68.

3. John Ashbery, in some of his poetry, apparently attempts to be a diarist of the preconscious mind. See my discussion of Ashbery near the end of this chapter.

4. I think T. S. Eliot is clinging much too stubbornly to a half-truth when he asserts the existence of a "poetry of the first voice" in which the poet "is not concerned with making other people understand anything. He is not concerned, at this stage, with other people at all: only with finding the right words or, anyhow, the least wrong words. He is not concerned whether anybody else will ever listen to them or not, or whether anybody else will ever understand

them if he does. He is oppressed by a burden which he must bring to birth in order to obtain relief." Eliot undercuts this presentation two pages later without registering the depth of the undercutting: "But if the poem were exclusively for the author, it would be a poem in a private and unknown language; and a poem which was a poem only for the author would not be a poem at all." T. S. Eliot, "The Three Voices of Poetry," in *On Poetry and Poets* (New York: Farrar, Straus & Giroux, 1956), pp. 107 and 109.

5. Alexander Pope and Frank O'Hara (an odd couple) have occurred to me as candidates, but of course the easier point is that most poets since the late eighteenth century—including Gray, Goldsmith, Crabbe, Wordsworth, Tennyson, Hardy, Hopkins, Frost, Masters, Eliot, Williams, Dylan Thomas, and Philip Levine—have written mostly about persons less literate than themselves and their readers.

6. Whitman, "Full of Life Now," *Leaves of Grass*, p. 136.

7. Vladimir Nabokov, *Lolita* (New York: G. P. Putnam, 1958), pp. 32–33.

8. Quoted in A. Walton Litz, "Particles of Order: The Unpublished Adagia," in *Wallace Stevens: A Celebration*, ed. Frank Doggett and Robert Buttel (Princeton: Princeton University Press, 1980), p. 68.

9. Wolfgang Iser, *The Implied Reader* (Baltimore: Johns Hopkins University Press, 1974), p. 293.

10. "In Stevens we are made aware of a deliberate impersonality, a refusal to use the poem as a vehicle for the direct outpouring of emotion. This impersonality impresses us not as the bloodlessness of a shallow temperament, but as restraint, the reserve of a man who will accept us as fellows in a communal intellectual enterprise but has no interest in making us his confidants." Marie Borroff, Introduction to *Wallace Stevens: Twentieth Century Views* (Englewood Cliffs, N.J.: Prentice-Hall, 1963), p. 7.

11. Stevens' sense of the comic opportunity in the title of a meditative poem is tantalizingly reflected by some of the titles he considered and recorded in a notebook but did not use: "Life Among Drones," "Man & Catsup Bottle," "Mythological Beast in a Bourgeois Town," "Kate the Contrast to Charley," "Naked and Playing the Harp," "Idyllist & Night Mare," "The Onions of Thirty Years Ago," "The Halo That Would Not Light," "A Jackass in His Own Clothes," "Don't You Love Yams?," "Really a Nun," "A Great Big Handsome Cow-boy," "Pretty Hot Weather For Dead Horses," "Preparing a Child To Eat Eclairs," "Emotion Complicated by the Viola," "Egotism & Beverages," "Why Flies Don't Fight," "Bad Money at the Six O'Clock Mass," "Lunch Without a Fork," "Still Life With Aspirin." See George S. Lensing, *Wallace Stevens: A Poet's Growth* (Baton Rouge: Louisiana State University Press, 1986), pp. 166–87.

12. See Vendler, *Words Chosen Out of Desire*, pp. 50–52.

13. Referring to the self-echoing in Stevens' oeuvre, biographer Joan Richardson goes so far as to say: "This kind of variation, formally adopted from music, gave a unity to the body of Stevens' work unparalleled since the Middle Ages." Joan Richardson, *Wallace Stevens: The Later Years, 1923–1955* (New York: William Morrow, 1988), p. 155.

14. The magnetic attractiveness of the idea of a transcendent creative spirit ("God") is recognized many times in the poetry, but the idea is always found to be fictive. This is why Joseph Carroll's exhaustive attempt in *Wallace Stevens' Supreme Fiction* (Baton Rouge: Louisiana State University Press, 1987) to place religious hope at the center of Stevens' work is ultimately wrongheaded, stubbornly inverting the poet's meanings.

15. Robert Frost, "A Passing Glimpse." The poems by Frost mentioned in my discussion appear in *The Poetry of Robert Frost*, ed. E. C. Lathem (New York: Holt, Rinehart & Winston, 1969) and are listed here with page numbers from that edition: "A Passing Glimpse," 248; "The Oven Bird," 119; "Storm Fear," 9; "The Onset," 226; "On a Bird Singing in its Sleep," 302; "Our Hold on the Planet," 349; "Directive," 377; "Acquainted With the Night," 255; "A Drumlin Woodchuck," 281; "Triple Bronze," 348; "Mending Wall," 33; "To a Moth Seen in Winter," 356; "Two Tramps in Mud Time," 275; "The Armful," 266; "The Investment," 263; "Riders," 267; "The Road Not Taken," 105; "One Step Backward Taken," 376; "Time Out," 355; "The Strong Are Saying Nothing," 299; "Home Burial," 51; "The Death of the Hired Man," 34.

16. Richard Poirier, commenting on Frost's commitment to subjects "common in experience" (and alluding to Frost's poem "The Investment") writes: "What is 'common in experience'? Obviously it could be said that one common experience is 'impoverishment,' as in a run-down house, and that another is the attempt at solace, as in painting the house. And it could also be said that these 'experiences' can be found as frequently in Stevens as in Frost. But the difference is that in Stevens they are not 'common'; it can be said without disparagement that they are instead literary and theoretical; they are states of poetic rather than of social consciousness; they call for actions of mind rather than actions of bodies." Richard Poirier, *Robert Frost: The Work of Knowing* (New York: Oxford University Press, 1977), p. 51.

17. The tone, at least, of Frost's likely response to "World Without Peculiarity" can be inferred from a portion of a 1948 letter to Lawrance Thompson, a deliberately elusive and ambiguously satirical passage about the religious impulse in general and specifically as manifested by Stevens' hero from his Harvard days, George Santayana: "Faith faith! What a thing it is. The last pop of poppycock was for Santaanna [Santayana] to say, 'true illusion and false illusion that is all there is to choose between.' True illusion would be the falsity then and false illusion the truth. Did it ever strike you that we owe it entirely to two or three Greeks that we arent all orphic (alias Christian) mystic fools crossing ourselves up with word tricks. Such as that the truth will set you free. My truth will bind you slave to me." *Selected Letters of Robert Frost*, ed. Lawrance Thompson (New York: Holt, Rinehart & Winston, 1964), p. 531.

18. This is why Theodore Roethke's "A Rouse for Stevens" has never quite rung true, with its exclamation, "Brother, he's our father!" *The Collected Poems of Theodore Roethke* (Garden City, N.Y.: Doubleday Anchor, 1975), p. 258.

19. Probably almost every poet offers at least a few such generalizations about "us." Wordsworth had the habit, as in sections 9 and 10 of the "Immortality" ode. Often Wordsworth's "we" is challenging to prospective members

in a way that Stevens' "we" is not. In "After-Thought" (p. 431), Wordsworth writes:

> Still glides the Stream, and shall for ever glide;
> The Form remains, the Function never dies;
> While we, the brave, the mighty, and the wise,
> We Men, who in our morn of youth defied
> The elements, must vanish;—be it so!
> Enough, if something from our hands have power
> To live, and act, and serve the future hour;
> And if, as toward the silent tomb we go,
> Through love, through hope, and faith's transcendent dower,
> We feel that we are greater than we know.

The first person plural here is sternly sobering because it proposes that we do something with our mortal lives; the demand on us is vague, but it is palpably a demand. We don't feel eased and relieved by affiliation with Wordsworth's "we."

20. Eliot, *The Complete Poems and Plays*, pp. 125–26.

21. I think it is no accident that the word *enough* never appears in *Four Quartets*. Elsewhere Eliot seems to instinctively eschew the word where we might have expected it. It is not, for example, allowed to complete the thought in "What the Thunder Said": "If there were the sound of water only . . ." The speaker in "Journey of the Magi" says grimly of the Nativity: "it was (you may say) satisfactory." Eliot, *The Complete Poems and Plays*, pp. 48, 69.

22. *Words Chosen Out of Desire*, p. 8.

23. *Words Chosen Out of Desire*, p. 8.

24. Notice especially the smooth shift from "one" to "our" and "us" in "The Poems of Our Climate," and the same shift in the final section of "Esthétique du Mal."

25. My very American friend Anne Carter once remarked, "As soon as one starts referring to oneself as 'one,' one knows one will end up an English professor."

26. Marie Borroff, "An Always Incipient Cosmos," in *Wallace Stevens: Modern Critical Views*, ed. Harold Bloom (New York: Chelsea House, 1985), p. 96.

27. Bloom, *The Poems of Our Climate*, p. 161.

28. Though it is not quite as if he were on a picnic drinking beer and singing Hi-li Hi-lo. See *Letters of Wallace Stevens*, p. 352. For another delightful comic poem whose tone is comparable to that of "Memorandum," see "Agenda" (*OP* 41).

29. It could be skeptically suggested that the real meaning of "us" here, and to some debatable extent at various other spots in my commentary on the reading of Stevens, is not simply "we Americans" but "we white male Americans." Stevens' elaborate sexism was examined in my second chapter. His lazy-minded racism is a clear subject for an essay that could be written, an essay which I imagine as rather short and rather grim, since I doubt that there are interesting variations in Stevens' racism. See *CP* 47, 50, 71, 102, 111, 126, 145, 148, 150, 195, 265, 270, 415, and *OP* 20, 59 (this is not an exhaustive list of

Stevens' references to black people). For a remarkably unveiled example of how a critic devoted to Stevens' array of ideas can remain blithely unconcerned about any political/moral significance in Stevens' allusions to social reality, see Daniel Schneider's tracing of Stevens' association of "Negro" with "opulent fleshiness" and "hot sensuality." Daniel Schneider, *Symbolism: The Manichean Vision* (Lincoln: University of Nebraska Press, 1975), pp. 162–66.

30. Schneider, p. 166.

31. *Words Chosen Out of Desire*, pp. 53, 54, 57.

32. *Words Chosen Out of Desire*, pp. 26–28 and 54–56.

33. "Stevens, in contrast to the Yeats of 'Sailing to Byzantium,' can find neither consolation nor enlightenment in 'studying / Monuments of [the soul's] own magnificence.' Indeed, the monuments, all that may be called the authorized version of cultural history, are an active threat to the mind seeking to relate itself to the world of the present." Borroff, Introduction to *Wallace Stevens: Twentieth Century Views*, p. 3.

34. Stevens, in his relation to the reader, thus resembles his Penelope in her relation to Ulysses: "She wanted nothing he could not bring her by coming alone. / She wanted no fetchings" (*CP* 521).

35. See especially Vendler, *On Extended Wings*, pp. 13–37 and 115–17, and *Words Chosen Out of Desire*, pp. 63–65 and 68–69.

36. Most critics dodge "The Owl in the Sarcophagus," for example, because its hieratic mysticism feels un-Stevensian. Only the overconfident critic will try to explicate all of "Like Decorations in a Nigger Cemetery."

37. Consider this lightly sexist and sexual remark with which Stevens concludes a paragraph about himself as poet: "We are all busy thinking things that nobody ever knows about. If a woman in her room is such an exciting subject of speculation, a man in his thoughts is equally exciting," *Letters of Wallace Stevens*, p. 306.

38. *The Necessary Angel*, p. 29.

39. William Butler Yeats, "A Prayer For My Daughter," *The Complete Poems of W. B. Yeats* (New York: Macmillan, 1956), p. 187. Admittedly Yeats is usually not so gently parental, or avuncular.

40. Again I will cite Daniel Schneider as one example of the many critics gleefully unbored by Stevens' recurrent meanings. When Stevens wrote "The Auroras of Autumn," "His virtuosity had become so great that he was able to express his Manichean vision of the admixture of reality and imagination whenever he wanted to. Almost every word springing to his pen had a place in the vast scheme, the vast poem, that he had been working out in his head for fifty years" (p. 202).

41. "Moment by moment, poem by poem, he committed himself to the 'mental state' of the occasion, doing his best to make it lucid if nothing else. If it occurred to him that these local commitments were contradictory, he was not distressed, because he trusted that the work would conform to the nature of the worker, and no other conformity was required." Donoghue, *The Ordinary Universe*, p. 225.

42. Rivals include Shakespeare in his Sonnets, Tennyson in *In Memoriam*, and Frank O'Hara.

43. See especially *Words Chosen Out of Desire*, pp. 10–15 and 23–28.

44. *Words Chosen Out of Desire*, p. 39.

45. "The poetry of Stevens . . . reflects those fluctuations of inner strength whereby the adversities that depress us at one time exhilarate us at another. But more importantly, it reflects the fact that, while the goal of the mind remains constant, our progress toward it takes different forms according to our inner state or the conditions of the external world." Borroff, Introduction to *Wallace Stevens: Twentieth Century Views*, p. 17.

46. Bloom, Introduction to *Wallace Stevens: Modern Critical Views*, p. 6.

47. In his 1906 journal, Stevens wrote: "It must be a satisfaction to be without conscience. Conscience, nowadays, invades one's smallest actions. Even in that cell where one sits brooding on the philosophy of life, half-decided on 'joyousness'—one observes one's black brother in a corner, and hears him whisper, 'The joyous man *may* not be right. If he dance, he *may* dance in other people's ashes.'" *Souvenirs and Prophecies*, p. 164.

48. Quoted in Brazeau, p. 269.

49. G. S. Fraser, quoted by Geoffrey Moore in "Wallace Stevens: A Hero of Our Time," in *The Achievement of Wallace Stevens*, ed. Ashley Brown and Robert S. Haller (Philadelphia: Lippincott, 1962), p. 250.

50. The problem—though not seen as a problem by Stevens and his leading critics—is strangely reminiscent of the malady Matthew Arnold (a less consolable thinker than Stevens) diagnosed in his own poetry in 1853: "What then are the situations, from the representation of which, though accurate, no poetical enjoyment can be derived? They are those in which the suffering finds no vent in action; in which a continuous state of mental distress is prolonged, unrelieved by incident, hope, or resistance; in which there is everything to be endured, nothing to be done. In such situations there is inevitably something morbid, in the description of them something monotonous." Arnold, "Preface of 1853," in *The Poems of Matthew Arnold*, 2d ed., ed. Miriam Allott (London and New York: Longman, 1979), pp. 665–56.

51. "A poem is a café. (Restoration.)" (*OP* 170). In other words, a place in which to rest and watch the world go by, after the departure of the Puritans.

52. *The Necessary Angel*, pp. 30–31.

53. Ashbery is even less troubled by the term than Stevens: "Since, as I said, I write mainly for escapist purposes, that's the kind of poetry that comes out. I am aware of the pejorative associations of the word 'escapist,' but I insist that we need all the escapism we can get and even that isn't going to be enough." Interview with John Ashbery by Sue Gangel in *American Poetry Observed*, ed. Joe David Bellamy (Urbana and Chicago: University of Illinois Press, 1984), pp. 13–14.

54. *Words Chosen Out of Desire*, p. 20.

55. *The Necessary Angel*, p. 58.

56. Of course in his prose Stevens sometimes directly affirms that the poet's responsibility—or at least, the poet's necessary task—is to help the reader and sometimes implies it. See especially *The Necessary Angel*, pp. 29–30 and 36. But I am trying to characterize the attitude implied by the poetry itself.

57. It may be argued that Stevens knows this very well and expresses it in poems of dissatisfaction with some heretofore pleasurable arrangement, such as "O Florida, Venereal Soil," "Two Figures in Dense Violet Night," and "The Poems of Our Climate." But these poems do not challenge the primacy of sensation. They express the need for adjustments of pleasure, not a need for another way of shaping one's life.

58. I remind my reader that hedonism is not the same as happiness: a man can be very unhappy, can have a "bad pharynx" or a "malady," and still identify some kind of pleasure as his highest value; he can search for a belief and still be a hedonist, if the belief is desired only because it will offer the comforts of a "douce campagna." I have not said at any point that Stevens is "only" a hedonist (even when the word is understood as I have just outlined), but hedonism is more deeply ingrained in him than some critics want to realize.

59. *The Necessary Angel*, pp. 22 and 36; and *OP* 224–25.

60. *The Necessary Angel*, p. 123.

61. See Paul Breslin, *The Psycho-Political Muse: American Poetry Since the Fifties* (Chicago: University of Chicago Press, 1987), pp. 218–19 and 224.

62. Consider this poem, "Good Pain":

GOOD PAIN

What is the question, someone said, toward which
every inadequate answer tends? Those folks over there

need to know and, like violins, they convey
enthusiasm that would be vulgar if not so classical;
entrances and exits that might as well not even be
detailed in the script they are so inevitable

have led the secretaries to feel sore misgivings
and it's not even 8:30 yet. The early hour
revives that gray sense of persistence being required,
dishing out small fishy problems as if merely brown bottles
every old customer holds in an outcropping of Utica,
resting till something else floats up to the level of signals

while what you fully intended has grown so mildewed
only your great-aunt can still even claim to believe. Yet
remnants of those shiny striated destinies can be heard
klaxoning on a distant autobahn, and the lone flute

through thin walls marks out a provisional positive view
over and over without a credit card, as if

desire were not wall-to-wall and all-weather, subtly checked,
on the floors of where you have to live recalling the south.

"Good Pain" is perhaps a shade too readable to be vintage Ashbery, but how many critics could show it lacks the master's touch? I drafted it in seventeen minutes in Au Bon Pain on Chestnut Street in Philadelphia on July 28, 1988, and revising it felt like buttering a croissant.

63. John Ashbery, *Selected Poems* (New York: Viking Penguin, 1985), p. 169.

64. Ashbery's pervasive sense of passive well-being, as well as the didacticism with which he proposes that we share his attitude, are more clearly and extensively visible in his prose poem "The System" than anywhere else. See especially the nakedly didactic, even evangelical passage on pp. 141–142 of *Selected Poems*, where he tells us that between formed ideas, "there is almost a moment of peace, of purity in which what we are meant to perceive could almost take shape in the empty air, if only there were time enough, and yet in the time it takes to perceive the dimness of its outline we can if we are quick enough seize the meaning of that assurance, before returning to the business at hand . . ."

65. As Paul Breslin has observed, and as I am about to demonstrate, "Paradoxically, this most antidiscursive of poets, by systematically destroying the sustained relationships of image and metaphor that might convey meaning indirectly, forces the reader to place all the more weight on the fragmentary assertions embedded within the poems" (p. 234).

66. John Ashbery, *A Wave* (New York: Viking Penguin, 1984), pp. 88–89.

67. For Ashbery an accumulation of facts into a story is felt to be dangerous, as in the following passage in "The System": "The resulting mountain of data threatens us; one can almost hear the beginning of the lyric crash in which everything will be lost and pulverized, changed back into atoms ready to resume new combinations and shapes again, new wilder tendencies, as foreign to what we have carefully put in and kept out as a new chart of elements or another planet—unimaginable, in a word. And would you believe that this word could possibly be our salvation?" *Selected Poems*, p. 159.

68. *A Wave*, p. 13.

69. Marjorie Perloff finds the indeterminacy in Ashbery exciting but she can only say so, over and over, as long as she avoids the folly of paraphrase. The dilemma can be seen in her comments on Ashbery's "Two Scenes": "The 'laughing cadets,' the 'water-pilot,' the 'tips of mountains'—these are arresting images of some mysterious truth half-glimpsed, but their signification is purposely left blurred and open. In the first dream scene, there are references to light, sparks, warmth, hair, water, and mountains; in the second, to rain, fumes, a canal, drought, poverty, and paint cans. How the second evolves out of the first is an 'absorbing puzzle.' One can invent a story about a 'train bringing joy,' possibly carrying a group of 'laughing cadets' into the mountains, possibly passing a canal where a 'water-pilot' waves to them. I am reminded of the train emerging from the flowering Russian steppes, so gorgeously filmed in *Dr. Zhivago*. But many other films or fictions come to mind." Marjorie Perloff, *The Poetics of Indeterminacy* (Princeton: Princeton University Press, 1981), pp. 267. Seldom has a critic floundered so helplessly. What is funny in the passage is Perloff's utter failure to present the poem as an absorbing puzzle. For another example of such helplessness, see her account of a portion of Ashbery's "The New Spirit" (p. 274).

70. Interview with Ashbery by Janet Bloom and Robert Losada in *The Craft of Poetry*, ed. William Packard (Garden City, N.Y.: Doubleday, 1974), p. 117.

71. The last verse-paragraph of "The Ongoing Story" presents a remark-

able quasi-exception to the point about Ashbery's lack of interest in relationships. But even here what is valued is consciousness rather than interaction: "A knowledge that people live close by is, / I think, enough." *A Wave*, p. 11.

72. *A Wave*, p. 2.

73. "Our daily quandary about food and the rent and bills to be paid"; "A corresponding deterioration of moral values, punctuated / By acts of corporate vandalism every five years"; "Let's go on and out, somewhere / Through the canyons of the garment center / To a small café and have a cup of coffee"; "a series of interludes / In furnished rooms (describe wallpaper) / Transient hotels (mention sink and cockroaches) / And spending the night with a beautiful married woman / Whose husband was away in Centerville on business." *Selected Poems*, pp. 87, 101, 182, 186–87.

74. *Selected Poems*, p. 173.

75. This can be seen even in a relatively focused poem like "Paradoxes and Oxymorons" (*Selected Poems*, p. 283), a poem all-too-ironically about nonconnection between writer and reader:

This poem is concerned with language on a very plain level.
Look at it talking to you. You look out a window
Or pretend to fidget. You have it but you don't have it.
You miss it, it misses you. You miss each other.

The poem is sad because it wants to be yours, and cannot be.
What's a plain level? It is that and other things,
Bringing a system of them into play. Play?
Well, actually, yes, but I consider play to be

A deeper outside thing, a dreamed role-pattern,
As in the division of grace these long August days
Without proof. Open-ended. And before you know it
It gets lost in the steam and chatter of typewriters.

It has been played once more. I think you exist only
To tease me into doing it, on your level, and then you aren't there
Or have adopted a different attitude. And the poem
Has set me softly down beside you. The poem is you.

76. Reviewing *April Galleons* in *The Gettysburg Review* (vol. 1, no. 2, Spring 1988), J. P. White describes Ashbery's unworried spirit cogently:

There is both a refusal to change the self and a refusal to believe that the truth, however it might be disclosed, would make a difference in this world of layered incompletions: "Will the truth leak out / And, if so, will there have been any advantage to proving / Over and over again that it wasn't worth doing / And we did it to please our neighbors and the little girl / With the hoop?" I suppose one might argue that this poem's urbane acceptance of the world's inequities and concealments is an all too frighteningly believable portrait of American society and that Ashbery's tone is cast in a parody of our cultural relativism. This view ignores, however, the absence of any adversarial tension or conflict that would signal a crisis in the speaker's consciousness. There is no quarrel in the poem, only a weightless complacency willing endlessly to invent new ways to adorn the questions of weather that haunt the soirée. If there is to be always a premium on perception and never one on action, then the poet need only be ready to observe the predetermined flux, as he does in "Never to Get It Really Right": "I have my notebook ready. / And the richly falling light will transform us / Then, into mute and privileged spectators. / I never do know how to end any season, / Do you?"

77. The spiritual limpness and anemic, complacent fatalism of this sense of life are both described and embodied in John Koethe's poem "A Sunny Day," which is less disjunctive than some Ashbery poems but purely Ashberian in attitude.

A Sunny Day

So this is the fruition
Of all our intense reflection about
The mechanisms of our lives: same kind of day,
Same smooth buds about to burst into bloom,
Same old junk on the lawn. Easy things these,
And maybe omens also of a kind of life that is best for us,
The most realistic kind of life for you and me.

Yet a while ago it was supposed to be different today,
With the sucked-out vacuum refilled by a vigorous new
Sense of attention to the small things around us,
Things meaning little or nothing in themselves, but which in chorus
Promised to spurt out a song of the whole world,
But whose relation to each one of them was to be transparent.

Working patiently and productively
This emotional farm yields, by the end of summer,
Merely a stack of artful impressions of a lapse of memory
Concerning the big things in our lives (whatever they were),
With the juice squeezed out, and the veins full of a thin fluid
Of the wrong kind of dreams, the kind we didn't know about
Until it was too late to do anything, after they had come true.
But this must have been what we were meant for
All along, and mistook for a poor and disappointing thing
In the half-light of a fantasy of living inside each moment
As it came over us for the first time, early in the morning
Just as the fog was turning bright and starting to lift.
We have lived here, in a dispositional sense, most of our lives—
Basically at home, occasionally out galavanting around somewhere—
Only now this thing we belong to is free finally
To admit us in our undisguised form, sweeping us along
In its stagnant motion, around and around.

In Koethe's poem the mind lays by its trouble (as Stevens puts it in "Credences of Summer") so easily that we can hardly believe there were any "big things" or any "intense reflection" to begin with. "A Sunny Day" is quoted from John Koethe, *The Late Wisconsin Spring* (Princeton: Princeton University Press, 1984), pp. 21–22.

78. See Vendler, *On Extended Wings*, p. 157, and Bates, p. 246.

79. Determined not to be nonplussed by Ashbery, Vendler tries to make him resemble her Stevens and her Keats, as far as themes go. In order to say that Ashbery's poems "are all 'about' something" she has to extract paraphrasable nuggets from each poem and ignore the rest of it. This happens in her explication of "Houseboat Days," though the poem does offer more chunks of available meaning than is typical of Ashbery. For instance, she sees "a meditation on the ubiquitous presence . . . of intractable pain" in the poem and supports this by quoting a segment as follows: "Do you see where it leads? To pain . . . / It . . . happens, like an explosion in the brain." But the passage actually goes like this (*Selected Poems*, p. 231):

> do you see where it leads? To pain,
> And the triumph over pain, still hidden
> In these low-lying hills which rob us
> Of all privacy, as though one were always about to meet
> One's double through the chain of cigar smoke
> And then it . . . happens, like an explosion in the brain,
> Only it's a catastrophe on another planet to which
> One has been invited . . .

To get lyrical sense from Ashbery, Vendler needs to rewrite him. In her reading his poems are a mix of nuggets and white noise, and except for obligatory nods to Ashbery's polyphonic drift, the white noise is to be ignored. Helen Vendler, *The Music of What Happens* (Cambridge: Harvard University Press, 1988), pp. 238, 228–30.

80. *The Music of What Happens*, p. 240. Notice the unintentional funniness of the next sentence: "It is possible also to characterize that manner—by turns so free-floating, allusive, arch, desultory, mild, genial, unassertive, accommodating, wistful, confiding, oscillatory, tactful, self-deprecatory, humorous, colloquial, despairing, witty, polite, nostalgic, elusive, entertaining." Vendler's adjectival heap is trying to tell her something.

81. Quoted in *The Craft of Poetry*, ed. William Packard (Garden City, N.Y.: Doubleday, 1974), p. 112.

82. Two stanzas of Ashbery's recent poem "Vaucanson" seem to catch his deep feeling that discursive clarity is undesirable, that meaning is demeaning:

> There had to be understanding to it.
> Why, though? That always happens anyway,
> And who gets the credit for it? Not what is understood,
> Presumably, and it diminishes us
> In our getting to know it
>
> As trees come to know a storm
> Until it passes and light falls anew
> Unevenly, on all the muttering kinship:

> Things with things, persons with objects,
> Ideas with people or ideas.

April Galleons (New York: Viking Penguin, 1987), p. 25.

83. As often happens with Ashbery, you choose a way to criticize him only to find that he has been there first. His commitment to the mind of 6:00 A.M. is expressed in this piece of "Grand Galop," along with a satirical echo of critics like me:

> And so from a day replete with rumors
> Of things being done on the other side of the mountains
> A nucleus remains, a still-perfect possibility
> That can be kept indefinitely. And yet
> The groans of labor pains are deafening; one must
> Get up, get out and be on with it. Morning is for sissies like you
> But the real trials, the ones that separate the men from the boys, come later.

Selected Poems, p. 176.

84. I have quoted *Selected Poems* (*SP*) and *A Wave* (*W*) as follows: *SP* 115, 116, 140, 170, 242, 242 again, 181, 182, 184, 73, 72; *W* 35, *W* 35 again; *SP* 341, 340, 307, 309; *W* 10, *W* 6; *SP* 40, 140, 69, 323, 90, 176, 271, 340, 273, 298, 227, 175, 173. The eleventh and twelfth lines of "Paste" come from Stevens' "The Auroras of Autumn" VI.

85. Though Ashbery has expressed admiration for Stevens, as well he might, a surprising outburst in "Self-Portrait in a Convex Mirror" could be aimed at the kind of poetic behavior I have called game-playing in Stevens. Ashbery dismisses clever players:

> those assholes
> Who would confuse everything with their mirror games
> Which seem to multiply stakes and possibilities, or
> At least confuse issues by means of an investing
> Aura that would corrode the architecture
> Of the whole in a haze of suppressed mockery,
> Are beside the point. They are out of the game,
> Which doesn't exist until they are out of it.

Selected Poems, p. 200. Little games are foolish interferences with the Total Game.

86. *April Galleons*, pp. 51–52.

INDEX OF WORKS BY WALLACE STEVENS

INDEX OF PERSONS